MICHELANGELO
DRAWINGS
PHAIDON PRESS

Cat. No. 129

MICHELANGELO DRAWINGS

BY LUDWIG GOLDSCHEIDER

PHAIDON PRESS · LONDON

FIRST EDITION 1951 · SECOND EDITION 1966
BOOK DESIGNED BY THE AUTHOR
MADE IN GREAT BRITAIN

INTRODUCTION · CATALOGUE AND PLATES REVISED

5 CROMWELL PLACE · LONDON · SW · 7
PLATES PRINTED BY CLARKE & SHERWELL LTD · NORTHAMPTON
TEXT PRINTED BY HUNT BARNARD & CO LTD · AYLESBURY · BUCKS

FOREWORD TO THE FIRST EDITION

The vulgar sort of infidell people which scarcely beleeve any hearbe but such they see in their owne Gardens, or any knowledge but such as is bred in their owne braines, or any birds which are not hatched in their owne Nests . . .

EDWARD TOPSELL, 1607

THIS VOLUME was conceived a long time ago on a much more problematic and less popular basis, namely, as a critical sifting of those drawings which in my opinion have been wrongly attributed to Michelangelo, and an attempt to define the work of his various imitators. Originally I intended to have separate chapters on Antonio Mini, Marcello Venusti, Raffaello da Montelupo, Bacchiacca, Battista Franco, Tribolo, Taddeo Zuccaro, etc., but in the course of my studies it soon became evident that so many genuine drawings of Michelangelo's had been rejected by more recent critics, that the generally accepted criteria of attribution seemed to have vanished and had first to be restored.

In addition to this, there is still no complete corpus of Michelangelo drawings, and the quality of the reproductions leaves much to be desired. Even the costly collotype plates in Frey's publication were severely criticized by Berenson (Catalogue, 1938, pp. 160–161): 'Among the less trustworthy are the reproductions in Frey's indispensable work on Michelangelo. . . . Considering that most students, particularly in Germany, will base their studies on Frey's reproductions, they must be seriously warned that they seldom do justice to the originals, and that conclusions regarding the originals should not be derived from them. . . .'

Apart from the question of quality, the volumes of reproductions hitherto published are none of them complete. On the other hand, an almost complete catalogue of all Michelangelo's drawings is available to the student, provided he is willing to combine the catalogues of Frey, Thode, Berenson and Wilde, to which must be added the drawings in the Archivio Buonarroti and the Codex Vaticanus published by Charles de Tolnay.

Having thus altered my conception of the task, I have tried to give, by means of a selection, an intrinsically complete idea of all the phases and forms of Michelangelo's art of drawing. As this involves the inclusion of as many as possible of those drawings by Michelangelo which have been wrongly rejected, I must expect a certain amount of opposition. The appearance of Wilde's Catalogue of the Michelangelo drawings at Windsor Castle makes my position less solitary than before, and in doubtful cases I have derived encouragement from Wilde's balanced and well-founded opinions.

I have reproduced only drawings of which I have seen the originals; but in a number of cases—e.g. the drawings at Haarlem—it is a long time since I saw them. Architectural drawings have been excluded, as these deserve, and need, a volume to themselves.

The drawings at Windsor Castle are reproduced by gracious permission of His Majesty the King. For kind help I am indebted to the Royal Librarian, Sir Owen Morshead.

In the course of my work I have also received cordial co-operation from the Directors of all the collections concerned, and I owe special thanks to Mr. A. E. Popham, who, despite difficult circumstances, placed all the Michelangelo drawings in the British Museum at my disposal. Dr. K. T. Parker, of the Ashmolean Museum, gave me most generous assistance and was also kind enough to read through my text; but the responsibility for any errors therein remains exclusively mine.

London, Spring 1951 L.G.

NOTE TO THE PRESENT EDITION

Since 1951 – the date of the first version of the present book – more books and articles on Michelangelo's drawings have been published than in all the years before that date.[1]

Now, at last, we possess critical and well-illustrated catalogues of the Michelangelo drawings in the British Museum (1953), in the Ashmolean Museum (1956), and in the three public collections of Florence (1962 & 1964).

Of Tolnay's 'Michelangelo' two more volumes have come out,[2] and his catalogue of the drawings is now complete.[3]

A posthumous edition of Berenson's 'Drawings of the Florentine Painters' was published in 1961 in Italian; and it contains a large number of revises, together with many reproductions not shown in the English edition of 1938.

Another complete – though sparingly illustrated – catalogue of Michelangelo drawings is the large and authoritative volume by Dussler (1959).[4]

During the past fourteen years I have taken another look at the drawings by Michelangelo and his followers, including those at Haarlem and the Casa Buonarroti. For the present edition I have reconsidered my chronology and – I hope – corrected it. On the other hand, I have found no persuasive reasons to take back any of the attributions proposed in the first edition. Nevertheless, the Plate Part appears here much altered. It is arranged in a different sequence, more in conformity to the revised chronology. Some of the less important drawings have been omitted, and drawings which – at least to my mind – are among Michelangelo's greatest achievements have replaced them. The Catalogue Part is made more concise, and references to recent literature are included. The former Introductory Essay has been exchanged for a new and simpler one.[5]

Special thanks are due to the Duke of Portland, for help in securing a photograph from which it was possible to prepare a adequate reproduction of the drawing, 'Madonna del Silenzio'; to the Earl of Leicester, who granted permission for a photographer to visit Holkham Hall and there take a picture of the famous copy of the 'Battle Cartoon,' after its recent cleaning; to Count Antoine Seilern, who presented me with an excellent photograph of the 'Dream of Human Life'; and also to the Directors and Keepers of the museums of Chantilly, Vienna, Florence, Haarlem and Oxford, who, in a very obliging way, had many drawings photographed or re-photographed for this book.

London, Autumn 1965 L.G.

---

[1] See Appendix to the Bibliography, p.70.
[2] Volume IV: The Tomb of Julius II (1954); Volume V: The Final Period (1960).
[3] Authentic drawings, Nos. 1 to 266. – Drawings rejected as apocryphal or as copies, Nos. 1-A to 52-A.
[4] Dussler discusses 243 sheets as 'certainly by Michelangelo's own hand' (and 122 'attributions', and 456 'apocryphal drawings'). This judgement is very different from Wilde's and Parker's who counted 228 genuine Michelangelo drawings just in the three large English collections – the Royal Library, the British Museum, and the Ashmolean Museum. Nor is Paola Barocchi in agreement with Dussler; she catalogues 339 sheets as by Michelangelo's own hand, merely in the three public collections of Florence.
[5] A large part of this new Introduction was first printed in the *Neue Zürcher Zeitung* (Beiblatt 'Literatur und Kunst', 16 February 1964), and this was translated into English by Heinz Norden.

CONTENTS

FOREWORD TO THE FIRST EDITION	*page* 5
NOTE TO THE PRESENT EDITION	6
INTRODUCTORY ESSAY	11
CONCORDANCE	25
CATALOGUE OF THE DRAWINGS	27
BIBLIOGRAPHY	67
SUPPLEMENT TO THE BIBLIOGRAPHY	70
PLATES	73
APPENDIX OF PLATES	185
INDEX OF COLLECTIONS	210

INTRODUCTION

MICHELANGELO AS A DRAUGHTSMAN

An artist paints with his brains and not with his hands.

MICHELANGELO, 1542

INTRODUCTION

'EVERYONE OF MICHELANGELO'S WORKS IS AN IDEA', wrote the youthful Romain Rolland in a letter to Malvida von Meysenbug. It is the drawings of Michelangelo, above all, that are ideas, works of the brain rather than works of the hands. For in drawing, as every artist knows, the technical obstacles to capturing an idea are reduced to a minimum; and during the brief span taken up by the execution of a drawing, the artist's memory is able to maintain intact his inward vision in its entirety.

'Michelangelo did never sketch', wrote another poet, William Blake. 'Every line of his has meaning.'

Michelangelo was anything but a naive artist, depicting reality – the world as it can be seen. He looked neither near nor far to delineate the shape of life, as did Raphael, with serenity, and Leonardo, meticulously. He was after the meaning of all form, ransacking his ever-agitated mind for symbols. And the images he found within, and projected without, make up a world that resembles reality no less than do dreams, which are equally bound up with the sense of vision.

Michelangelo was a religious artist. He inquired after the meaning of things. The world of things is fleeting – we must seek its meaning and its transcendence. Man's body is part of the mortal world of things; but since man is created in God's image, we may be certain that his body reflects that everlasting image. What a revelation this is to the artist! The movements of the human body, passionately enhanced, were to Michelangelo a language in which he could express anything – even the invisible, which alone matters, even the movements of the immortal soul, even the vast orbits of the universe, which never rests.

In Greek art of the best period movement invariably held a purpose – a youth donning the victor's wreath, drawing a thorn from his foot or hurling a discus, or a faun thrumming the castanets. In late Greek art expressive movements make their appearance – the response of a body to some external event. Fear and the expression of fear are fundamentally the same in ancient Niobid reliefs as in Michelangelo's battle cartoon, and the mother of the Niobids – to keep to one example – expresses her grief with the self-same gestures as the Mother of God in Michelangelo's Pietà (Plate 108). So long as an external cause is perceptible and the gesture is a comprehensible reaction to a single influence, it is an expressive movement.

In the Prophets and Sibyls on the ceiling of the Sistine Chapel, however, the movements become a language of the soul – they are emotional movements, having no purpose and provoked by no external cause; like the gestures of a dancer, they symbolize the inner life; they are elicited, not by events, but by states of mind, they are a silent dialogue between the human soul and its destiny, between the soul and eternity; they have no beginning and no end, and are as hard to understand and susceptible to as many interpretations as cries rising from the depths.

The emotional movement is the chief motive of Michelangelo's art; he was the first to render it, and down to his last works he continued to develop it, renouncing it only in the very last of all.

The main challenge to Michelangelo was to acquire the grammar of this language – anatomy. It was an anatomy of a very special kind. What he understood by it, he said quite plainly in his comment on Dürer's *Four Books on Human Proportion* : 'To tell the truth, Dürer deals only with the measurements and differences of bodies . . . He says nothing about the much more important subject of human movements and gestures'.

We know from Condivi, Michelangelo's disciple and biographer, that the master himself had meant to write a similar work, 'for the use of those engaged in sculpture and painting, a work that would treat of the human body and its skeleton in all their movements and attitudes'. 'I mean knowledge of anatomy', Condivi adds on his own, 'only as it affects painters and sculptors. Details appropriate to anatomy as a science are not in order here'. He might as well have said: I do not mean the kind of anatomy pursued by Leonardo.

Such knowledge Michelangelo could not have acquired in the studio of his teacher Ghirlandaio. He was compelled to become his own instructor.

Michelangelo's association with this studio stemmed from Granacci, one of Ghirlandaio's pupils, who, recognizing Michelangelo's 'great skill in drawing', brought him some of his teacher's work to copy. Michelangelo was thirteen at the time. Eager to recruit so talented a hand for his shop, Ghirlandaio agreed to a most extraordinary covenant of apprenticeship. Its term was set at three rather than the customary seven years; and although apprentices were ordinarily paid only after absolving such a term, having indeed to pay for their tuition before its expiration, Michelangelo was to be paid from the very first day. To judge by the reports that have come down to us from Vasari and Condivi, young Michelangelo's entry into the modest workshop of Ghirlandaio created intolerable trouble.

Among the things an apprentice had to learn in an artist's workshop in those days were pigment-grinding and the preparation of grounds for paintings; perspective, and the three varieties of drawing: copying from master drawings and paintings, drawing from sculpture and drapery models, and drawing from nature. The first subject to be learnt was copying.

But when Ghirlandaio one day gave one of his drawings to another apprentice to copy, Michelangelo seized the sheet and went over the contours *con penna più grossa* – i.e. strengthened them with bold strokes – to demonstrate the art of drawing to both pupil and master. Vasari, who still had this sheet, lost today, in his possession forty years later, comments: 'It is marvellous to see the difference in style and the greater skill and knowledge of the younger man.'

The nature of this improvement is readily envisioned from copies the youthful Michelangelo made of details of frescoes by Giotto and Masaccio. There are drawings of this description in Munich, in the Albertina in Vienna, and in the Louvre. Berenson, adopting something like Vasari's tone, pronounced this judgement on them: 'It is not surprising that his figures are better articulated and have more vibration and tremor of life than the originals, so much we expect from a boy of genius. . . . It is more remarkable that he has given these men all the corporeal existence, the full physical weight, the elemental sturdiness that Giotto [or Masaccio] imparted to them.'

From the purely technical point of view, these drawings do not differ too greatly from those of Ghirlandaio: they are drawn with a rather fine pen, the cross-hatching powerfully deepened in the shadows, while in the light portions dissolving into delicate strokes or missing altogether. In contrast to the styles of Ghirlandaio and Granacci, the pattern of this shading is neither uniform nor mechanical, rather changing with the form it models. Vigour marks the rounding of the figures – heralding the sculptor to come. Berenson saw in these strokes of the pen the same signature that spoke from the chisel traces of Michelangelo's early works in marble.

Even in the first year of his apprenticeship Michelangelo went beyond the copying of drawings and engravings by others that preoccupied his fellow students – he began to 'invent'. Ghirlandaio was working on the frescoes in the choir of Santa Maria Novella at the time – it is not clear whether his awesome prize-boy had any share in them – and during the master's absence one day Michelangelo indulged his whim to represent the whole show in a drawing – tables, scaffolding, painters' gear, assistants at work and all. It was a scene straight from everyday life, presumably quite in the manner of the later Netherlandish painters – the drawing is lost today. One may even conjecture that the heads of his fellows in Michelangelo's drawings were good likenesses, for the figures in Ghirlandaio's own religious frescoes were portraits of well-known Florentine citizens. In his maturity, Michelangelo had no time to waste on genre, portraiture and landscape; and perhaps this drawing was no more than a display of virtuosity. If so, it fulfilled its purpose. He succeeded, as he was to do often enough later on – he created a sensation.

'When Ghirlandaio saw this drawing [relates Vasari], he was completely taken aback with the novelty of its conception and representation and said: "That one in truth knows more about drawing than I do".' Michelangelo quite shared this view. When, more than sixty years later, Vasari showed him one of those early drawings, he remarked that he knew more about drawing as a boy than he did as an old man.

Soon Michelangelo the apprentice was no longer content merely to improve while copying. He began to forge with consummate skill. Given the drawing of a head to copy, Michelangelo did so, but by means of smoke and grime imparted an appearance of age to his drawing, which he returned in place of the original. Teacher and fellow students were deceived – and amazed.

In the circumstances it is not hard to understand that Ghirlandaio lost composure and even his temper with this terrifyingly talented student of his, and Condivi is probably telling the truth: One day the master refused young Michelangelo the use of his sketchbook, from which the boy wished to copy shepherds and horses and dogs, and landscapes with buildings and ruins.

Ghirlandaio was doubtless relieved when, even before the end of the first year, Michelangelo together with his friend and fellow student Granacci moved over to Bertoldo's school of sculpture.

Bertoldo's academy had its quarters in the Medici Gardens at San Marco. It enjoyed the patronage of Lorenzo de' Medici, who paid not only the teacher but the students as well, granting them stipends and allowing them to live in his house and dine at his table. Thus Michelangelo became a guest in the palazzo of the Medici. Lorenzo, surely not the meanest poet nor the unworthiest philosopher among the men of his Platonic academy, took a hand in his school of sculpture as well. The story goes that he was critical of Michelangelo's first carving, the head of a faun, copied from an ancient marble. Poliziano, chief luminary of this academy and responsible for setting the theme of young Michelangelo's Centaur relief, seems to have generally inspired the school with the spirit of humanism. In the main the students made drawings after ancient sculptures and engraved gems that were kept there, but they also worked from the models and cartoons of Donatello, Brunelleschi, Masaccio, Uccello and Fra Angelico that made a veritable museum of the Casino Medici, in the custody of Bertoldo. Brunelleschi and Uccello were apparently the standards for studies in perspective. Anatomy was studied from ancient statuary. Vasari reports that in this school too Michelangelo skipped all the preliminary stages. He watched Torrigiani working on clay statuettes – 'he watched and at once set about shaping such statuettes himself'. Vasari goes on to commend Michelangelo's 'close study of nature, day after day'.

This could scarcely have meant copying from the work of others; but no other Michelangelo drawings from this period have survived. The magnificent 'Philosopher', now in the British Museum, was drawn then, probably from a cartoon by Masaccio, and likewise the fine sheet in Chantilly, showing two drapery studies after Masaccio, two views of an ancient statue of a nude woman, and a study of another Greek or Roman statue. These drawings cannot be dated with certainty, for Michelangelo's technique did not change for a long time. He used the pen exclusively, and the kind of cross-hatching he had learnt in Ghirlandaio's workshop. Black chalk is added only at the time of the Battle Cartoon, about 1504. Red chalk was first used, I believe, in scattered sketches for the Sistine frescoes, about 1508. Michelangelo never used silver-point, with its delicate, gossamer line, but he used lead-point.

Even though Michelangelo remained faithful to his old pen-and-ink technique for perhaps fifteen years, he gradually modified his manner – just as his handwriting changed over the same period.

Michelangelo used the same pen for writing as for drawing. The margins of many of his drawings show notations which but rarely have anything to do with the drawing – obscure words and names, but also quotations from Petrarca and lines from his own poems. In the course of the years, Michelangelo developed his handwriting into a carefully designed style of calligraphy.

He was intent upon giving even his script 'form', i.e. the highest graphic perfection. As Valerio Mariani puts it, 'he was determined to master form even in handwriting'.

Proceeding from one of Michelangelo's sonnets, Robert Clements (in his book, *Michelangelo's Theory of Art*) has expounded this obsession with form, this calligraphy, as an art on its own, in the sense of the Neo-Platonists, resting his case on quotations from their writings. All form, including even the forms of art, was contained in nature, they contended. *Intelletto*, according to Clements a Neo-Platonist concept of great importance, constantly used in Michelangelo's circle, meant not so much reason and grasp as it did apprehension of reality and *truth* (in the literal sense of the German term *Wahr-Nehmung*). *Intellectus divinus* combined outward perception with inward vision.

A Neo-Platonist from the time of his apprenticeship at the Medici Gardens, Michelangelo submitted his every line in drawing and script to the discipline of *intelletto*. Upon first looking at these drawings and manuscripts, one is not, of course, aware of the artist's lofty concepts about perception and form; one merely sees that in Michelangelo drawing and script keep pace with each other in their development towards beauty and freedom.

In 1505, when Michelangelo, at thirty, was summoned to Rome by the Pope, he had already drawn admiration with a series of achievements in the realm of sculpture that were marked by grandeur and originality. Yet as a draughtsman he was still dependent on models, with only a single exception. He drew from ancient marbles, such as the Apollo Belvedere, which had belonged to Pope Julius II even when he was still a cardinal; he let the Horse Tamers of the Monte Cavallo stimulate him; he copied a statue of Mercury. The fact that his Bronze David (as shown on the drawing in the Louvre) follows Donatello's David is explained by the terms of his contract to do this figure; but at the same time, having seen Leonardo's first cartoon for 'St Anne with the Virgin and Child', he made a drawing that is almost equivalent to a copy. In contrast to Leonardo's own sketches, however, Michelangelo's approach is anything but that of a painter. The long pen-strokes utterly fail to convey any feeling of light and shade, merely emphasizing the orientation of the various surfaces in space, so that it has been thought this drawing may have been a study for a piece of sculpture. In other respects too the influence of Leonardo, or perhaps Michelangelo's rivalry with him, emerges in several drawings – representations of standing or crouching children and,

PORTRAIT OF MICHELANGELO, 1522. Pen-and-ink drawing (BB. 1598 D), attributed to Bugiardini. Paris, Louvre.

DESIGN FOR THE SECOND PROJECT FOR THE TOMB OF JULIUS, 1513.
Copy by Jacomo Rocchetti of a ruined Michelangelo drawing (BB. 1623B). Berlin Printroom.

even more strongly, two studies of horses and two equestrian battles which, if they were indeed drawn at this early time, must certainly be associated with his cartoon for the 'Battle of Cascina'. On the other hand, if they are of a later date (as I incline to believe), these studies of horses and horsemen testify that Michelangelo, whether consciously or not, wrestled with the challenge of Leonardo's art for many years, even down into a time when Raphael had long since supplanted Leonardo as his chief antagonist.

Leonardo and Michelangelo were the two greatest artists of Florence; and the city fathers, still new to republican government, wished to dramatize the rivalry between the two before all eyes, so to speak. In fame there was nothing to choose between them. Leonardo had come home from Milan, where he had left all of his works behind – the 'Last Supper', the 'Madonna of the Rocks', and the much-admired 'Great Horse', a huge plaster model for the equestrian statue of Francesco Sforza. Nothing of importance by his hand was to be seen in Florence, except for two cartoons, 'Adam and Eve', and 'St Anne with the Virgin and Child'. Michelangelo's early masterpiece too, the 'Pietà', had been left behind in another city, Rome; but his gigantic 'David', recently finished, stood before the entrance of the Palazzo Vecchio, the city hall of Florence.

It was in this building that a wall was to be decorated with two paintings showing scenes from the city's history. Leonardo was commissioned to do one, Michelangelo the other. Leonardo chose as his theme a cavalry battle, Michelangelo a more peaceful incident from the war against Pisa, a scene with bathing soldiers. This choice of themes is scarcely surprising, for Leonardo was the unexcelled master in the representation of horses, while Michelangelo had no peer in representing the nude human body. Leonardo finished his cartoon and actually painted the main scene, the Fight for the Standard. Then he gave up the work and returned to Milan. Michelangelo never got beyond the cartoon.

Michelangelo's cartoon was done in black chalk, charcoal and lead white. The representation was of lifesize nude men, in every possible attitude, contortion and foreshortened perspective. The 'cartoon', i.e. drawing to the same dimensions in which the fresco would have been executed (about 24 feet high), was destroyed even in Michelangelo's lifetime. But before it was gone two generations of artists drew from the figures in the cartoon, including Raphael, Daniele da Volterra, Andrea del Sarto, and Beruguete. In his autobiography, Cellini described Michelangelo's cartoon as 'a drawing-academy for the whole world'. The figures were so life-like, so true to nature, that the 'Cartoon' went far beyond anything that had been achieved in Italy hitherto in the representation of the nude. A direct continuation of classical art had been achieved, fulfilling a dream of the Renaissance.

Studies for the cartoon paved the way for the figures of the Sistine ceiling, the technique of which in turn presaged that of the later drawings. For the cartoon Michelangelo had chosen soft drawing materials, charcoal and chalk, with which pictorial effects may be achieved seemingly without effort. Highlights in lead white were added with a brush. With these rich black-and-white gradations in tone and by means of powerful modelling in grey (judging from the preserved studies for individual figures in the Albertina and the British Museum), the cartoon must have exerted the pictorial effect of grisaille.

In his Sistine drawings too Michelangelo used black chalk for the most part. Some of the finest drawings, however, are done in red chalk, a drawing material that lends itself even more to pictorial effects than black chalk. Three magnificent heads for Jonah, Zechariah and one of the *ignudi* are drawn in this technique, as is a study for the Libyan Sibyl.

The preliminary drawings for the Sistine frescoes must have been vast in volume; but virtually nothing has survived of these thousands of drawings for the Bible stories and individual figures, of the detail studies of heads, hands and other parts of the body, of the drapery and action studies, and none of the hundreds of cartoons. Michelangelo had the cartoons for the Sistine ceiling frescoes burned when he dissolved his household in Rome in February 1518. 'It is also known to me [says Vasari] that shortly before his death Michelangelo burned a large number of his drawings and cartoons, lest anyone should see the evidence of the immense pains he had to take, the countless designs his genius compelled him to try, so that he might enhance his creative power to the point of perfection'.

Cellini related he was able to testify that Michelangelo sometimes needed only a single day to complete the painting of one of his gigantic figures in the Sistine frescoes – 'again and again the furies of passion laid hold of him while he was at work and drove him on'. The report has the ring of truth. It is thus on record that Michelangelo did tolerate observers while he painted. But his drawings he kept hidden, writing his father not to let anyone see those he had left behind in Florence; and in the end he burned all on which he could lay hands, to keep even posterity from seeing them. We can only grieve over these bonfires; but from Michelangelo's own point of view this destruction made sense. Even the few drawings that have come down to us afford us the kind of insight into his creative processes which he sought to deny us. It was his ambition to remove all traces of effort and doubt, to let us see only the completed and perfect work, which was to appear as though it had come about effortlessly, a boon from heaven – as though he, the anointed, had given physical form to his visions out of hand. Vasari has an instructive passage: 'So powerful was Michelangelo's imagination that his hands were at times unable to give form to the tremendous visions of his mind'. Those visions often emerge more clearly in his drawings than in his finished works.

The style of the drawings for the statues of the Medici Chapel is less pictorial than that of the period that had gone before. The shading again describes the orientation of the planes in space rather than the modelling imparted by light. They are the drawings of a sculptor. Michelangelo even returned to pen-and-ink drawing, but he no longer used cross-hatching, drawing outlines instead, which he filled in with long parallel strokes, straight or curved.

About the same time Michelangelo began to make presentation drawings for his friends, compositions of religious or mythological content, finished with great care. These sheets are held in small esteem nowadays – precisely because of their painstaking perfection – although they are among Michelangelo's most valuable drawings, copied in contemporary engravings and widely admired by several generations.

The time from his forty-fifth to his sixtieth year was Michelangelo's erotic period. The chief artistic fruit of these penchants, illusions and heart-searchings was the marble group of 'The Victory', created at the same time as the last figures for the Medici Chapel. The metaphor contained in the 'Victory' is not difficult to interpret. We need only think of the self-portrait of Cristofano Allori as the head of Holofernes in the hand of the beautiful Judith, in order to be able to guess the meaning of Michelangelo's marble youth kneeling over a prostrate old man.

Gherardo Perini may have posed for the 'Victory'. Michelangelo made the acquaintance of this young man in 1522 and exchanged letters with him; he was on intimate terms with other young men and portrayed them – the only portraits by him. We have documentary proof that Michelangelo drew a portrait of Tommaso de' Cavalieri, whose acquaintance he made ten years after he met

Perini, and we also learn from a letter that he portrayed the boy Cecchino Bracci in a drawing. Mini, another of Michelangelo's favourites, was apprenticed to him in 1523 at the age of seventeen. Although the master never bought for him pink hose and capes of silver brocade, as Leonardo had done for his pupil Salai twenty-five years before, he seems to have been lavish in presenting him with drawings. The last of these youthful friends of Michelangelo's was Febo di Poggio, whom he met in Florence shortly before his departure for Rome, and who sent him a letter which is not far short of blackmail.

To this period belong the designs for the 'Samson and Delilah', 'Venus and Cupid', the 'Rape of a Woman' and the 'Leda', the erotic character of which need scarcely be pointed out; but at the same time Michelangelo also made his designs for the 'Noli me tangere', the 'Risen Christ', 'Christ in Limbo', the 'Three Crosses' and the 'Deposition', as well as the sketches for the 'Last Judgement'. This list documents a conflict between the erotic and the religious propensities of his mind.

In 1545 Aretino wrote to Michelangelo, reproaching him for failing to keep his promise to send him drawings – 'only the Gherardos and the Tommasos can expect favours from you'.

The three drawings Michelangelo gave to Gherardo Perini are still extant (Plates 50–52). One of them, showing Women's Heads executed with a pronounced sense for ornamentation and calligraphy, is interesting only on account of the unusual technique. The second, depicting a Fury, a head with fluttering hair and gaping mouth, symbolizes the frenzy of love. The third, 'Venus, Mars and Cupid', expresses that terrible form of love which resorts to cruelty and destruction.

The presentation drawings for Tommaso de' Cavalieri and an unknown friend owe their origin to the same state of mind. In these drawings the artist's thoughts are passionately engaged with the problem of temptation, sin and atonement.

From the point of view of religious symbolism, the drawings may be interpreted as follows:

The Archers : The invulnerability of the protected soul (Plate 74).

Tityus : The sin and punishment of illicit sexual indulgence, of the torments of a man who through sensuality has become godless (Plate 75).

The Bachanal of Children : The abasement of mankind through sin (Plate 89).

Phaëthon : The penalty of arrogance, or the fall resulting from desire for that which is not permitted (Plate 93).*

The Dream : The sins of passion, or the terrible awakening of the sinner to consciousness of himself (Plate 97).

A sixth drawing (Plate 73), *The Labours of Hercules* – his struggles with the lion, with the giant, and with the nine-headed hydra – coincides exactly with the three examples given in Landino's 'Dialogues', in which Hercules is the representative of the *Vita Activa* and fights against evil in the course of his journeys, as the Apostles did after him.

Some of these drawings were made in Florence, others in Rome. In the autumn of 1534 Michelangelo transferred his residence to Rome.

Florence, Venice, Ferrara and other Italian cities had their local schools of painting, differing clearly from one another and far less closely related than dialects of the same language. In this respect they may be compared with the schools of painting in the Germanic countries, where Cologne and Nuremberg, Colmar and Basle, the Tyrol and Vienna used completely different idioms in their art. In Italy, Rome occupied a place of its own as an artistic centre. It was the

*The lost drawing of 'Ganymede' and the above-mentioned nine presentation drawings (of which three were for Perini, three for Cavalieri, and three for unknown friends) are more fully discussed in the Catalogue.

only city which had witnessed a direct continuation of antiquity down to the days of the Renaissance. In the other cities the rebirth of the antique had a literary origin; in Rome where ruins and statues were visible to the eye of succeeding generations as tangible presences, the Renaissance was derived, not from books, but from stones. The Belvedere Apollo, the Laocoön and the River-gods had merely remained hidden in the earth until the descendants of those who once had owned, admired and imitated them, had proved themselves, by means of their own art, to be worthy of these treasures; and now they were restored to the hands of these descendants.

Rome was the city of the Popes, and the Popes were the heirs of the Caesars. Rome, the seat of the Catholic Imperium, had the ability to assimilate artists from the most varied cities and schools, to fill them with the Roman spirit – in both the old and the new sense.

When Michelangelo arrived in Rome for the first time, in 1496, there were in the city artists from many provinces who had just completed, or were still engaged upon, important works: there were to be seen new frescoes by Mantegna, Perugino, Signorelli, Pinturicchio, Filippino Lippi, and Antonio Pollaiuolo's bronze monuments to the Popes – great works of Roman Renaissance art.

Michelangelo's removal to Rome in 1534 and his work on the 'Last Judgement' were the foundations of the Roman school of 'Mannerism'.*

A new style heralds the dawn of a new period. The end of the pagan Renaissance had come and the Christian Renaissance now began, as a long prepared religious revival. Religion, like art, poetry, philosophy, fashions and morals, has a stylistic history of its own.

The spiritual laws of the Renaissance, the revival of pagan antiquity, were conceived in Florence, by enthusiastic humanists; the Counter-Reformation was an act of State and originated in Rome.

The religious revival in Italy, the course of which began about 1540, formed no part of the Reformation; it was a Catholic movement.

In 1541 Pope Paul III appointed Cardinal Pole, a distant cousin of King Henry VIII of England, to be governor of the Patrimonium Petri, the oldest part of the Papal States, with residence at Viterbo. Here Pole gathered around him those who shared his views, among them the priest Carnesecchi, who many years later was burned at the stake, and the religious poet Flaminio. The latter collaborated in the writing of a book which appeared at Venice in 1542, and was at once placed on the Index as heretical – Benedetto's 'Of the Mercy of the Crucified Christ', a work to which Flaminio gave its final stylistic form, and the mere possession of which was punished by the Inquisition with death.

Cardinal Pole and his circle, the 'Spirituali', were associated with a number of men who were working for a purification of the Catholic Church, men such as the Venetian Gasparo Contarini, and the preacher Ochino. Of the latter, who at the time was preaching in Rome, only a few miles from Viterbo, Agostino Gonzaga wrote to Ferrara: 'Ochino lives like a saint. . . . His convincing persuasiveness is seconded by a most magnificent voice. All Rome flocks to his sermons. . . . The Marchesa di Pescara never misses one of them. She is living in cloistral retirement with the sisters of San Silvestro and receives no visitors.' (1541)

In the autumn the Marchesa di Pescara, Vittoria Colonna, went to Viterbo in order to be near Pole and Flaminio. At that time Vittoria was a grey-haired widow, fifty years old, and very unattractive – to judge from the woodcut portrait in the 1540 edition of her poems. She had led a restless life, moving from city to city and from convent to convent, and – as Carnesecchi later testified

*A 'Roman School' without Roman artists. In a similar way, the great lights of the 'School of Padua' were Mantegna of Vicenza and Donatello of Florence; and the 'School of Milan' was the ingenious creation of Leonardo da Vinci.

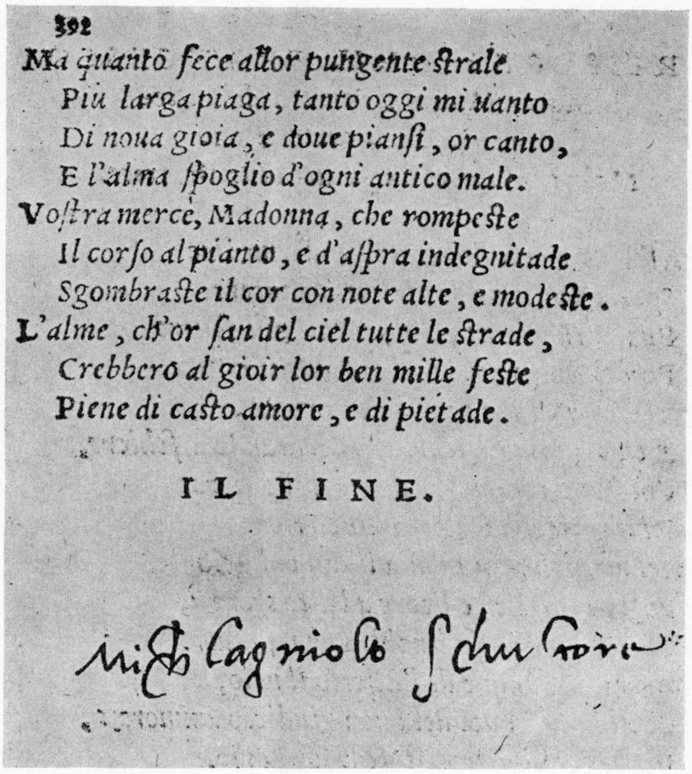

392

Ma quanto fece allor pungente strale
Più larga piaga, tanto oggi mi uanto
Di noua gioia, e doue piansi, or canto,
E l'alma spoglio d'ogni antico male.
Vostra mercè, Madonna, che rompeste
Il corso al pianto, e d'aspra indegnitade
Sgombraste il cor con note alte, e modeste.
L'alme, ch'or san del ciel tutte le strade,
Crebbero al gioir lor ben mille feste
Piene di casto amore, e di pietade.

IL FINE.

VITTORIA COLONNA. *Two pages from editions of her poems.*
(a) Frontispiece with her portrait, woodcut Venice, 1540. (Biblioteca Laurenziana). – (b) Last page, with Michelangelo's signature, from the complete edition Venice, 1558. (British Museum).

during his trial – she had reduced her body to skin and bone by wearing hair-shirts, by self-castigation and by fasting. 'Heavy with age, I have turned to ice', she says of herself in one of her poems. She enjoyed the reputation of being the greatest woman poet in Italy; but her poems are only echoes of Petrarca's and Bembo's. Her friendship with Michelangelo is now her only claim to celebrity.

Michelangelo, who since the time of his friendship with Cavalieri had passed through a long and severe spiritual crisis – a religious crisis in which all his thoughts were directed towards the concepts of sin and atonement, its artistic outcome being the cycle of presentation drawings and the mighty fresco of the 'Last Judgement' – found in Vittoria Colonna a friend who understood his fears and anguish.

Michelangelo made a new series of drawings, this time of purely religious significance, which he presented to Vittoria Colonna. Three of these sheets have been preserved – two of them, the 'Crucified Christ' and the 'Pietà', in the original (Plates 107, 108), and one, the 'Woman of Samaria at the Well', in engravings. Their import is as follows:

The Crucified Christ : Justification by Faith.

The Woman of Samaria : Justification by Works, or Salvation through the living water.

Pietà : Sacrifice for the sake of truth, or Salvation through the sacred blood.

In the Colonna drawings the style is even more miniature-like than in the earlier presentation sheets.

Cardinal Caraffa, afterwards Pope Paul IV, was at first favourably disposed towards the 'Spirituali' and on friendly terms with Cardinal Pole. In 1542 there was an abrupt change. In that year Ochino openly seceded to the Protestants and fled across the Alps; Vittoria Colonna, to whom he wrote, disavowed him. In the same year a feeble attempt was made to inaugurate the Council of Trent; on the other hand, the Roman Congregation of the Inquisition was successfully established, and Caraffa in his impatient zeal equipped a house at his own expense to serve as prison and tribunal. Three years later Pole was sent to the Council of Trent as Papal Legate. Vittoria Colonna died in 1547 in a Roman convent, and immediately after her death the suspicions which had been hushed during her lifetime in deference to her exalted rank, found expression. For fear of the Inquisition no one dared to make arrangements for her funeral, and her wooden coffin was left for weeks in a corner of the chapel of Sant'Anna dei Funari; Cardinal Pole refused to act as her executor. But a few years later Pole, too, was accused by Caraffa of heresy, though this brought no harm to the Cardinal. Against Michelangelo, who had shared the convictions of Pole and Vittoria Colonna, no voice was raised.

Through his association with this circle, Michelangelo became an exclusively religious artist. His friendship with Vittoria Colonna is well known, but it is not always correctly interpreted; his connexion with Cardinal Pole is confirmed by Condivi.

All the works of Michelangelo's last thirty years are of a religious nature. The religious tendency had been present from the beginning in Michelangelo's violent and restless character, but only in the latter part of his life did it free itself from the counterpoise of Classicism.

The three religious compositions of which he made gifts to Vittoria Colonna were succeeded by sheets of a similar character. These exert today a much more immediate effect, because they are unfinished – a 'Resurrection of Christ' (in several versions), a 'Descent from the Cross', a 'Christ Expelling the Money-Changers', an 'Annunciation' (likewise in several versions), and finally what is perhaps Michelangelo's greatest achievement as a draughtsman, six versions of a 'Crucifixion'.

Michelangelo felt old and close to death when he was only forty; and during the fifty years that were to be left to him, his fear of death grew, and even more his fear of Eternal Damnation. To be sure that he would be ever mindful of death, he had painted a skeleton and a coffin on the wall of the stair-hall of his house in Rome, and had written underneath these three lines of verse:

Io dico a voi, ch'al mondo avete dato
L'anima, e'l corpo e lo spir'to 'nsieme:
In questa cassa oscura è'l vostro lato.

I say to you, who to the world have given
Your soul, your body and, withal, your spirit:
In this dark chest there is a place for you.

Creation never came easily to Michelangelo. In his later years, his ideas seemed to emerge only as though from a heavy mist, scarcely recognizable at first, their meaning almost beyond grasp. He drew with his eyes closed, so to speak, his head and heart crowded with images, his vision that of a dreamer struggling to capture wisps as fleeting as thought. The visible world grew to be no more than a metaphor to him and the human form a hieroglyph, its true meaning known only to God.

In the last ten years of his life, Michelangelo no longer drew 'from nature', but solely 'by heart' – he put down what he saw with his mind's eye. In the end, he dispensed with all verisimilitude. He no longer had the least intention to draw 'correctly', he made no effort to achieve anatomical accuracy or clarity of detail. The vision is put down without elucidation, the expressiveness lying in the lines and blotches of the drawing itself. The last drawings have the solitary aspect of diaries and confessions never intended for the attention of strangers. They are monologues.

On 18th February 1564 the master died, almost ninety years old. His disciple Daniele da Volterra moved into his house at the Forum Traianum. To Michelangelo's nephew he wrote: 'I have had the laurel trees in the garden felled. They took the sun away from the smaller trees.'

It sounds like an allegory. Michelangelo's followers took possession of his manner, but deposed his great ideas. They stood in their light.

TABLE OF REFERENCES

BIBLIOGRAPHICAL ABBREVIATIONS

[BB]. Bernard Berenson, *The Drawings of the Florentine Painters*, Amplified Edition, 3 vols., Chicago, 1938. (Vol. II: *Catalogue.*) – Compare also the entries of the Italian edition, Milan, 1961.

[F]. Karl Frey, *Die Handzeichnungen Michelangiolos Buonarroti*. Berlin, 1909–11.
Erster Nachtragsband (First Supplement) von F. Knapp, Berlin, 1925.
Zweiter Nachtragsband (Second Supplement), Berlin, n.d., 45 plates without text.

[T]. Henry Thode, *Michelangelo : Kritische Untersuchungen*, Vol. III: *Verzeichnis der Zeichnungen, Kartons und Modelle*, Berlin, 1913 (Same as Vol. VI of Thode's complete work on Michelangelo).

[To]. Charles de Tolnay, *Michelangelo*. With a Catalogue of Drawings. (Vol. I: Youth, 1947, Vol. II: Sistine Ceiling, 1945; Vol. III: Medici Chapel, 1948; Vol. IV: The Tomb of Julius II, 1954; Vol. V: The final period, 1960).

[D] Luitpold Dussler, *Die Zeichnungen des Michelangelo : Kritischer Katalog*. Berlin, 1959.

[KdK]. *Klassiker der Kunst*, Leipzig, Deutsche Verlagsanstalt.

[*Ph.M.*] Ludwig Goldscheider, *Michelangelo : Paintings, Sculptures, Architecture*, Phaidon Press, 4th edition, London, 1964.

The first numbers in the following list correspond with the numbers of the Plates and the Catalogue numbers of the present volume.

The Wilde Numbers for the drawings at Windsor and in the British Museum, the Parker Numbers for the drawings at Oxford, and the Barocchi Numbers for drawings in the Florentine collections are not included in our Concordance because they are directly quoted in the captions of the following Catalogue.

References to 'Goldscheider' in the books by Berenson, Tolnay, Parker, Barocchi, and Dussler correspond with the Cat. Nos. of the 1951 edition, not of the present volume.

CONCORDANCE

1. BB.1587. F.1. T.481. To.2. D.212.
2. BB.1602*r*. F.23. T.525. To.4. D.235*r*.
3. BB.1602*v*. F.22. T.525*v*. T.5. D.235*v*.
4. BB.1544. F.11. T.380. To.3. D.186.
5. BB.1590*r*. F.88. T.498. To.15. D.214*r*.
6. BB.1588*r*. F.87. T.477. To.14. D.209*r*.
7. BB.1561*v*. T.406. To.10. D.193*v*.
8. BB.1561*r*. T.406. To.9. D.193*r*.
9. BB.1585*v*. F.25. T.474. To.13. D.213*v*.
10. BB.1585*r*. F.24. T.474. To.16. D.213*r*.
11. BB.1560*v*. T.405. To.12. D.192*v*.
12. BB.1560*r*. T.405. To.11. D.192*r*.
13. BB.1397*r*. F.2. T.7. To.17. D.4*r*.
14. BB.1522*r*. F.41. T.348. To.6. D.171*r*.
15. BB.1520. T.345. D.327.
16. BB.1481*r*. F.92. T.336. To.23. D.169*r*.
17. BB.1481*v*. F.91. T.336. To.21. D.169*v*.
18. BB.1479*r*. F.45. T.307. To.24. D.162*r*.
19. BB.1479*v*. F.46. T.307. To.25. D.162*v*.
20. BB.1590*v*. F.64. T.498. To.35. D.214*v*.
21. BB.1418. F.26. T.65. To.22. D.56.
22. BB.1656. T.18. To.26. D.253.
23. BB.1559. F.201a. T.403. To.27. D.344*v*.
24. BB.1604*v*. F.62. T.528. To.30. D.361*v*.
25. BB.1476*r*. F.103. T.335. To.31. D.324.
26–27. BB.1521. F.13. T.346. To.19,20. D.170.
28. BB.1579*v*. F.28. T.461. To.33. D.208*v*.
29. BB.1579*r*. F.27. T.461. To.32. D.208*r*.
30. BB.1588*v*. F.63. T.477. To.34. D.209*v*.
31. BB.1400. F.52. T.11. To.45. D.48*r*.
32. BB.1522*v*. F.42. T.348. To.43. D.171*v*.
33. BB.1483*r*. F.43. T.310. To.36. D.163.
34. BB.1519A. T.517. To.6A. D.580*r*.
35. BB.1598B. T.507. D.680*r*.
36. BB.1599B. T.218. To.42*r*. D.147*r*.
37. BB.1661C. T.33. D.261.
38. BB.1399E. T.221. D.509*r*.
39. BB.1544D. F.4. T.378. To.46*r*. D.339*r*.
40. BB.1562*r*. F.3. T.407. To.47. D.194*r*.
41. BB.1543*r*. F.36. T.372. To.86. D.182.
42. BB.2483. T.330. D.562.
43–45. BB.1558*r*. F.141. T.402. To.96. D.191.
46. BB.1556. F.132. T.400. To.106. D.190.
47. BB.1462A. T.1. D.359a.
48. BB.1555. F.133. T.398. D.343*r*.
49. BB.1552. F.172b. T.394. D.342.
50. BB.1628. (T.544.) To.150. D.493.
51. BB.1627*r*. T.204. D.492.
52. B.B.1626. T.206. To.149. D.491.
53. BB.1680. F.183. T.304. D.553.
54. BB.1482. F.184. T.289. To.90. D.307*r*.
55. BB.1502. F.251. T.314. To.88. D.149.
56. BB.1603*r*. T.526. To.141. D.360 (*verso*).
57. BB.1487. F.281. T.297. To.24a. D.313.
58. BB.1589. T.478. To.140. D.354*r*.
59. BB.1491. F.60. T.286. To.95. D.154*r*.
60. BB.1409A. F.114. T.40. To.98. D.53.
61. BB.1409E. F.263b. T.44. D.267.
62. BB.1401B. F.263a. T.19. D.255.
63. BB.1549. F.218. T.391. D.599.
64. BB.1498*v*. F.147. T.312. D.255*v*.
65. BB.1401. F.16. T.16. To.44. D. 49.
66. BB.1490. F.31. T.299. To.91. D.159.
67. BB.1472*r*. F.320. T.268. D.528.
68. BB.1414. F.126c. T.59. D.272.
69. BB.1472*r*. F.320. T.268. D.528.
70. BB.1610. F.212a. T.535. To.93. D.237.
71. To.52A. D.582.
72. BB.1718. T.434. D.624.
73. BB.1611. F.7. T.536. D.363a.
74. BB.1613. F.298. T.538. To.121. D.721.
75. BB.1615*r*. F.6. T.540. To.115. D.241*r*.
76. BB.1615*v*. F.219. T.115*v*. D.241*v*.
77. BB.1666. F.155c. T.54. D.444.
78. BB.1406. F.179. T.32. D.261.
79. BB.1665A. T.53. To.163. D.443*v*.
80. BB.1580. F.40. T.464. To.108. D.210.
81. BB.1612. F.19. T.537. To.109. D.239*r*.
82. BB.1507. F.59. T.328. To.110. D.168.
83. BB.1523. F.288. T.350. To.166. D.328*r*.
84. BB.1413*v*. To.172. D.55*v*.
85. BB.1493. F.270. T.341. To.101. D.583.
86. BB.2480. F.330. T.266. D.529*r*.
87. BB.2485. T.325. D.559.
88. BB.1564. F.51. T.417. To.107. D.195*r*.
89. BB.1618. F.187. T.543. To.120. D.365.
90. BB.1608. T.533. D.715*r*.
91. BB.1535. F.57. T.363. To.117. D.177.
92. BB.1601. F.75. T.518. To.118. D. 233.
93. BB.1617*r*. F.58. T.542. To.119. D.238*r*.
94. Detail of 92.
95. Detail of 93.
96. BB.1655. T.12. To.151. D.409.
97. BB.1748B. To.169. D.589.
98. BB.1536*r*. F.79. T.364. To.178. D.333*r*.
99. BB.1395B. T.512a. To.170. D.246.
100. BB.1413. F.20. T.57. To.171. D.55*r*.
101. BB.1468*r*. T.261. To.183. D.295*r*.
102. BB.1536*v*. F.80. T.364. To.179. D.333*v*.
103. BB.1416. F.15. T.61. To.182. D.274.
104. BB.1417. F.292. T.62. D.275.
105. BB.1514. F.258. T.326. D.320.
106. BB.1675. F.332. T.269. To.157. D.299.
107. (BB.1724A.) F.287. T.353. To.198. D.329.
108. BB.1623C. To.197. D.378.
109. To.196. D.336.
110. BB.1595. T.488. To.199. D.537.
111. BB.1582. T.469. To.201. D.355.
112. BB.1544A. To.554. To.203. D.187.
113. BB.1519. F.190. T.340. To.220. D.179*r*.
114. BB.1534*r*. F.259. T.362. To.221. D.176*r*.
115. BB.1470*r*. T.265*r*. To.215. D.297*r*.
116. BB.1470*v*. T.265*v*. To.209. D.297*v*.
117. BB.1537. T.552. To.236. D.178.
118. BB.1571*r*. F.157. T.441. To.211. D.200*r*.
119. BB.1544E. F.76. T.367a. To.207. D.188.
120. BB.1516. F.252a. T.324. To.233. D.165*r*.
121. BB.1515. F.253. T.323. To.231. D.166*r*.
122. BB.1517. F.255. T.322. To.235. D.167*r*.
123. BB.1572. F.239. T.442. To.246. D.201.
124. BB.1574. F.180. T.446. To.254. D.204*r*.
125. BB.1575. F.45. T.448. To.220. D.205.
126. BB.1621. F.129. T.547. To.252. D.236.
127. BB.1530. F.128. T.357. To.256. D.175.
128. BB.1518. F.257. T.305. To.266. D.161.
129. BB.1529. F.127. T.356. To.251. D.174.

CATALOGUE
OF THE DRAWINGS

'A critic with little experience suspects every painting he comes upon as a fake. A common malady amongst art critics of any standard. When I was young I condemned as forgeries or copies the finest pictures if they did not agree with my conception of the artist in question. Now I have changed; I proceed cautiously and reject only those pictures the authenticity of which I have the best reason to doubt.'

T'ANG HOU (a Chinese art critic of the 14th century)

The figures in brackets after the names of art critics refer to the Bibliography at the end of the present book (pp. 67–70).

There is a Concordance on p. 25, giving references to the numbers of the drawings in the Catalogues of Berenson, Frey, Thode, Tolnay and Dussler.

1. COPY OF TWO FIGURES FROM GIOTTO'S FRESCO OF THE 'ASCENSION OF ST JOHN THE EVANGELIST' IN SANTA CROCE, FLORENCE. Pen and (faded) brownish ink. 12½ × 8 in. (31·7 × 20·4 cm.) Paris, Louvre (No. 706).

Since Vicomte Both de Tauzia (*Dessins du Louvre*, Paris 1888, p. 39) attributed this drawing to the youthful Michelangelo, the only contradictory opinion has been Morelli's (12, p.39); C. H. Weigelt (in 'Giotto', KdK, p. LIV) is undecided. It is generally assumed that this is the earliest of all the drawings by Michelangelo that have been preserved. It dates from the time of his apprenticeship in Ghirlandaio's workshop, when Michelangelo was about fourteen years old.

There is, however, a pen and ink drawing of a *Boy on Horseback* which ought to be taken into consideration (Fig. 1). This drawing, drawn with courage, vigour and an enormous understanding of spatial values, though obviously a beginner's work, could be by young Michelangelo, dating from about 1488, when he had just begun his apprenticeship. On the other side of this sheet is an uninspired Drapery Study by Ghirlandaio (Fig. 2).

Drawing No. 1 forms part of a group which also comprises the following copies after Masaccio, Nos. 2–4 (all rejected by Morelli).

The drawing bears the mark of the collector Coypel.

The sheet has been cut on the left.

On the *verso* a small study of a left arm, in red chalk, attributed to Michelangelo.

2. COPY OF THREE FIGURES FROM MASACCIO'S LOST FRESCO OF THE 'CONSECRATION OF THE CHIESA DEL CARMINE,' FLORENCE. Pen and ink. 11½ × 7⅞ in. (29·4 × 20·1 cm.) Vienna, Albertina (Catalogue III, 129 *recto*; S.R. 150).

Vasari, in his life of Masaccio, gives a detailed description of the fresco, which was a chiaroscuro, painted in terra verde, in the Carmine at Florence, 'over the door within the cloister which leads into the convent'. It was destroyed during a reconstruction of the cloister about 1600. Vasari also says that Michelangelo made drawings after Masaccio's murals and Cellini goes into further detail on this point.

Tolnay assumes that the two figures in the background were added later, but this seems to me unlikely; the difference in

FIG. 1.—Michelangelo (?): *Boy on Horseback*. Pen and ink, about 1488. Berlin, Print room.

FIG. 2.—Domenico Ghirlandaio: *Drapery Study*. Pen and ink, about 1488. Berlin, Print room.

style is due to the fact that the figure in the foreground is executed more carefully, whereas those in the background have remained at the stage of sketches.

According to Vasari, Michelangelo made drawings 'in front of Masaccio's frescoes' while he was the guest of Lorenzo de' Medici, i.e. in 1490–92.

No. 3 (see below) is on the back of the sheet.

From the collections of Mariette and the Prince de Ligne.

3. KNEELING MAN, PROBABLY A COPY AFTER MASACCIO. Pen and ink. $11\frac{1}{2} \times 7\frac{7}{8}$ in. (29·4 × 20·1 cm.) Vienna, Albertina (Catalogue III, 129 *verso*; S.R. 150).

This drawing belongs to the same period as No. 2, being drawn on the back of the same sheet. It can be dated about 1491. So far no one has succeeded in identifying the fresco from which it was copied. Meder thought of Pesellino and there are, in fact, similar figures on the predella made by Pesellino for Filippo Lippi's altar-piece of the 'Madonna enthroned with Saints Cosmas and Damian', which was originally in Santa Croce, Florence. Nevertheless such figures are also found in Masaccio's works, e.g. in the 'St Peter invoking the Holy Spirit', a fresco in the Brancacci Chapel (Salmi, *Masaccio*, 1947, plate 96). The figure in No. 3 is of a monumental simplicity, the credit for which cannot be given entirely to the draughtsman who copied the fresco, and which is alien to Pesellino. We may therefore accept the opinion that the model must have been Masaccio.

4. COPY OF MASACCIO'S ST PETER FROM THE FRESCO OF THE 'TRIBUTE MONEY' IN THE BRANCACCI CHAPEL, FLORENCE. Pen and ink on red chalk. $15\frac{5}{8} \times 7\frac{3}{4}$ in. (39·7 × 19·7 cm.) Munich, Staatliche Graphische Sammlung (Inv. No. 2191).

This drawing is not so well preserved as the similar Nos. 1–3. Chronologically it belongs to the end of the series and must therefore be dated about 1493. According to Frey and Tolnay the red chalk lines on this sheet are not by Michelangelo's hand.

5. STANDING NUDE FIGURE, PERHAPS AFTER AN ANTIQUE SCULPTURE. Pen and ink. $13 \times 6\frac{1}{4}$ in. (31·4 × 16·8 cm.) Paris, Louvre (Inv. No. R.F. 1068 *recto*).

Usually dated about 1501 (by Baumgart and others), but this seems to me rather too late. Probably made soon after Michelangelo's arrival in Rome. The drawing dates from about the same time as the 'Bacchus' (*Ph. M.*, Plate 9, datable 1496–97).

Bears the marks of the collectors Mariette and Gatteaux. There is a copy in the Royal Library at Windsor Castle (Catalogue No. 461).

No. 20 (see below) is on the back of the sheet.

6. MERCURY-APOLLO AND FIGURE CARRYING A LOAD. Pen drawing in brown and grey ink. $15\frac{3}{4} \times 8\frac{1}{8}$ in. (40 × 21 cm.) Paris, Louvre (Inv. No. 688 *recto*).

Only Giovanni Morelli has doubted the attribution of this drawing to Michelangelo; Baumgart dates it 'about 1496–1501', i.e. during Michelangelo's first stay in Rome. There is much to be said for this dating, since the master seems here to have been copying antique sculptures in Rome. The model for the figure in the lower left corner was a sculpture on a fountain in the Giardino Cesi,[1] namely, a putto carrying a large vase on his shoulder, and the Mercury is likewise derived from an antique statue, probably the Mercury of the 'Horti Farnesiani' on the Palatine (cf. F. Perrier, *Icones et segmenta* 1634, plate 43); the same statue was used by Raphael (1518) for the Mercury in the Farnesina fresco of 'Psyche in Olympus'.

The Mercury was transformed into an Apollo by subsequent over-drawing in grey ink. In this second version the right arm is laid across the breast and the left arm is holding a viola.

The paper (Briquet 5543) comes from Pistoia. (Berenson wrongly maintains that the drawing is on parchment.)

On the *verso* of this sheet are some sketches (No. 30) which can be dated about 1505.

Nos. 6, 11 and 13 form a group of drawings derived from sculptures and apparently dating from the years 1501–03. I think that No. 6 was made in 1500–01, while the master was still in Rome, and the other two only after his return to Florence.

From the Coypel collection.

7. NUDE SEEN FROM THE BACK AND FIVE HEAD STUDIES. Pen and brown ink. $10\frac{1}{8} \times 6\frac{3}{4}$ in. (25·7 × 17·2 cm.) Oxford, Ashmolean Museum (Cat. No. 291 *verso*).

This drawing belongs to the same period as No. 8 (which is on the *recto* of the sheet, datable 1501.

The inscription beneath the head of the bearded man has been read as 'Leonardo'—by Thode, Baumgart and Tolnay, who relate the style of the drawing to Leonardo da Vinci. (Compare e.g. A. E. Popham, *The Drawings of Leonardo da Vinci*, 1946, plates 22–24.)

In parts of the drawing even Leonardo's left-handed hatching lines are imitated—e.g. on the neck of the bearded head in the centre of the sheet, and also on the cheek and nose of the seated youth in the upper right corner, but not on the trunk. This figure reminds us of the Master of the Manchester Madonna, but the drawing is certainly by Michelangelo's own hand. Baumgart (16, pp. 36–37) rejects the attribution to Michelangelo.

From the Crozat, Lagoy, Dimsdale, and Lawrence collections.

8. STUDY FOR THE 'ST ANNE WITH THE VIRGIN AND THE INFANT CHRIST'. Pen and brown ink. $10\frac{1}{8} \times 6\frac{3}{4}$ in. (25·7 × 17·2 cm.) Oxford, Ashmolean Museum (Cat. No. 291 *recto*).

In 1501 Michelangelo returned from Rome to Florence, probably arriving just in time for the exhibition of Leonardo's cartoon for his 'St Anne with the Virgin and Child'. This cartoon, since lost, caused great excitement in Florence at that time, and Fra Pietro da Novellara described it in a letter to Isabella d'Este.[2]

There are few Michelangelo drawings concerning which the critics are so much in agreement as they are about this one. Firstly, it is generally agreed that it is a free copy of Leonardo's

---

[1] A. Grünwald, *Über einige Werke Michelangelos im Verhältnis zur Antike*, in *Vienna Yearbook*, XXVII, 1907–1909, p. 125 f.
In the Glyptothek at Munich (Nos. 232 and 233) there are two similar Roman statues of Satyr boys, one carrying a wine-skin, the other a vase, both originally used as fountain figures.

[2] A translation of this letter, in *Leonardo da Vinci*, by L. Goldscheider (Phaidon Press, 1964), p. 37. The letter is dated 5 April 1501.

Florentine cartoon.[3] Secondly, almost all critics date it 'about 1501' (Berenson, Baumgart, Tolnay; only Thode dates it about 1504). Thirdly, the authenticity of the drawing has never been disputed, despite the fact that its style does not differ in any way from that of the drawing on the back (No. 7) or from No. 9.

9. MAN DIGGING, NUDES SEEN FROM THE BACK, *and other Studies from the Nude*. Pen and ink. 10½ × 7¼ in. (26·5 × 18·8 cm.) Paris, Louvre (Inv. No. 714 *verso*).

This drawing dates from the beginning of Michelangelo's second early period, which begins with the completion of the Pietà in St Peter's and the return of the young master to Florence, and ends immediately before the Cartoon of the Battle of Cascina, thus comprising the years 1501–1504.
The lines of verse in the upper left-hand corner are written in the same hand as the lines on the *recto* of the sheet, Plate 10.
Valentiner (in *Art Quarterly*, V, 1942, and also in *Studies of Italian Renaissance Sculpture*, London, 1950, p. 209), thinks that the nudes seen from the back are studies for the marble David and dates them 1502. For the digging man he ventures the hypothesis that Michelangelo was here thinking of a relief of Adam, and suggests a counterpart in the form of a spinning Eve; these suggestions are interesting, but cannot be substantiated. There is an almost identical study of a man digging, on a sheet of small sketches by Leonardo da Vinci in the Royal Library, Windsor (No. 12644 *verso*).[4]
Baumgart (16, pp. 37–38) does not think that No. 9 is by Michelangelo's own hand, and also rejects Nos. 7 and 12.
Formerly in the collections of Crozat, Mariette, Lawrence, King William II of Holland.

10. ARM STUDY FOR THE MARBLE DAVID AND SKETCH FOR THE BRONZE DAVID. Pen and ink. 10½ × 7¼ in. (26·5 × 18·4 cm.) Paris, Louvre (Inv. No. 714 *recto*).

Most critics maintain that the sketches on this sheet do not both date from the same period; the arm study for the over-lifesize marble David cannot be later than the drawing on the *verso* (Plate 9) of about 1501;[5] the freer sketch for the bronze David is perhaps a year later.[6]
Noteworthy is the master's signature on this early drawing.[7]
Meder assumes that the sketch for the bronze David was not a creation of fantasy, but drawn 'from the living model'.[8]

11. MERCURY-TRITON AND THREE HEADS. Pen and brown ink. 9⅝ × 7⅝ in. (24·4 × 19·4 cm. Parts of the blank margins are covered by the mount.) Oxford, Ashmolean Museum (Cat. No. 292 *verso*).

This drawing appears to be derived from an antique statue of Mercury; the Triton's fins were an afterthought and were added later by Michelangelo, as can be seen especially from the left arm. The bearded heads differ hardly at all from the bearded head in No. 7.
No. 12 (see below) is on the *recto* of the sheet.
From the Wicar and Lawrence collections.

12. STUDIES OF THE NUDE. Pen and brown ink. 7⅝ × 9⅝ in. (19·4 × 24·4 cm.) Oxford, Ashmolean Museum (Cat. No. 292 *recto*).

Raised left arm, seen from the front and the back; nude, seen from the back; right knee and shank.
Tolnay and Baumgart date the drawing correctly about 1501, but Baumgart doubts its authenticity (16, p. 37).
On the back of the sheet is a drawing of a Triton (No. 11).

13. STUDIES AFTER ANTIQUE SCULPTURES AND AFTER MASACCIO. Pen and ink. 10¼ × 15¼ in. (26·3 × 38·7 cm.) Chantilly, Musé Condé (No. 29 *recto*).

The figure in the long mantle in the centre seems to have been drawn from Masaccio's St John,[9] or perhaps, as Berenson supposes, from a female figure in the 'Consecration of the Carmine' (cf. No. 2). The study of draperies on the right is more likely to have been taken from a figure in a fresco, perhaps by Masaccio, than from an antique Herm. The nude female figure, shown in two attitudes, is derived from an antique statue, either a Venus (cf. e.g. the Venus in the Museo Nazionale, Rome, No. 236) or one of the Graces. The same figure in four attitudes occurs in a drawing by Passarotti (Casa Buonarroti No. 28F; photo Brogi No. 1242); there are other copies at Oxford and in the Louvre. The 'Faun' (as Berenson calls it) on the left is after an antique statue (copies in Windsor, Cat. No. 438, and in the Albertina, Cat. III, 135). The right knee of the Faun and the profile head of the Venus were pasted over by Michelangelo for retouching purposes.
Various dates have been assigned to the drawing, between 1492 and 1504.
The back of the sheet contains a drapery study,used about a year later for the *Pitti Tondo*. (Tolnay I, p. 161, dates the *Pitti Tondo* from the same time as the *St Matthew*, i.e. about 1504.) Another drapery study on the *verso* of No. 13 can be connected with the *Bruges Madonna* and be dated about 1503. This is, probably, also the date of the *recto*.

14. A 'PHILOSOPHER'. About 1503. Pen and two shades of brownish ink. 12⅞ × 8¼ in. (33 × 21·5 cm.) British Museum (Cat. No. 1 *recto*).

Robinson (28, p. 23, No. 58) mentions that this drawing was at one time held to be a self-portrait of Michelangelo. Emil Möller[10] interpreted it as a portrait of Leonardo, which would support a dating after 1501. To judge from the type, however, it is not a portrait, but a very generic representation of a learned man, such as Raphael later used for his philosophers

[3] This 'copy' by Michelangelo supports Suida's hypothesis that in the lost cartoon the figures were turned towards the left (*Leonardo und sein Kreis*, p. 131). Baumgart (16, pp. 11–13) gives the most thorough analysis of the differences between Leonardo's cartoon and Michelangelo's new version of it.
[4] Leonardo's drawing dates from the same period as Michelangelo's. There is, of course, no other connection between the two drawings—they show only that both artists were, at the same time, interested in the study and the rendering of straining and bulging muscles. A few years later, when commissioned to paint side by side the 'Battle of Anghiari' and the 'Battle of Cascina', Leonardo and Michelangelo benefited from such studies.
[5] Michelangelo began work on the marble David on 13 September 1501.
[6] The contract for the bronze David was made on 12 August 1502.
[7] *Dauicte cholla fromba/e io coll archo* (David with the sling/and I with the bow); and underneath: *Michelagniolo*.
[8] Joseph Meder, *Die Handzeichnung*, 2nd edition, Vienna, 1923, pp. 364–65. Tolnay (17, p. 183) misunderstood Meder and speaks of 'a small wax model', whereas Meder is referring to a young man whom Michelangelo often used as a model. L. Dussler (1959, p. 135) misunderstood again Meder, who says nothing about a wax model but speaks of 'well considered poses of the living model' and of 'indefatigable study of nature'.

[9] In the 'St Peter distributing Alms', a badly preserved fresco in the Brancacci Chapel (S. Maria del Carmine, Florence).
[10] '*Wie sah Leonardo aus?*' in *Belvedere* IX, Vienna, 1926, p. 29 f.

in the 'School of Athens'. But the man in this drawing is wearing a pilgrim's hat with shell, and is thereby characterized as 'coming from the East'. Moreover, he strongly resembles the various representations of the old King (Caspar) in the numerous Florentine versions of the Adoration of the Magi painted from the time of Masaccio on. Compare, for instance, the figure on the extreme left in Leonardo's unfinished 'Adoration of the Magi' in the Uffizi, and the drawing in the British Museum.[11]

According to J. Wilde (1953) the style of the hat indicates a Greek philosopher, probably Aristotle holding a skull and lecturing on anatomy.

Baumgart dates the drawing 1493–96, i.e. about the same time as the copy after Masaccio (No. 4). Frey dated it from the time of the frescoes in the Sistine Chapel, about 1508–09.

On the *verso* of the sheet is No. 32, which dates from about 1505–8.

Tolnay, in his catalogue of the drawings, under No. 6 describes the drawing on the *verso* as 'not by Michelangelo', which is a mistake, since under his No. 43 he describes the same drawing as authentic.

From the Lempereur, Constantine, Dimsdale, Lawrence, and Malcolm collections.

15. HEAD OF A SATYR. Pen and two shades of brownish ink. $5\frac{1}{8} \times 5\frac{1}{8}$ in. (13 × 13 cm.) London, British Museum (Cat. No. 2).

Robinson, Loeser, Berenson and Thode maintain that this drawing is authentic; but see also Popp (45, LIX, 1925, p. 174). In technique it is very closely related to the drawing in Chantilly (No. 13), especially to the figure on the left. Early drawings by Sebastiano del Piombo (Pallucchini, 60, plates 84b and 85) seem to have originated from this or similar drawings by Michelangelo. The main difference lies in the fact that Sebastiano used his pen in a free and almost impressionistic way, whereas in this drawing the forms are evolved out of a uniform network of lines, which is a characteristic of all Michelangelo's early drawings.

Frey, Baumgart and Tolnay tacitly exclude the drawing from the genuine works.

The sheet has been so drastically cut that one may call it a fragment.

From the Richardson, West, Lawrence, Woodburn, Robinson, and Malcolm collections.

16. RUNNING YOUTH, WITH LEFT ARM EXTENDED. Pen and brown ink. $14\frac{3}{4} \times 9$ in. (37·5 × 23 cm.) London, British Museum (Cat. No. 4 *recto*).

Frey and Tolnay assume a relationship to some antique sculpture; Frey, to one of the Monte Cavallo horse-breakers; Tolnay, to the Belvedere Apollo; the points of contact are slight.

In its general pose the figure reminds us also of the 'Hypnos' in Madrid; or of Dürer's drawing of the so-called Poynter Apollo, L. 179, W. 262; and also of the *Man with the cornucopia* in Mantegna's 'Bacchanal' (engraving, B. 19).

Robinson, Thode, Berenson and Baumgart think that it was a sketch for the Battle Cartoon, which would at least agree with the date, fairly unanimously considered to be about 1504.

Below, obliquely across the sheet, a lead-point sketch of a right leg.

From the Mariette, Crozat, Lawrence, Woodburn collections.

There is a copy at Oxford (Cat. No. 346).

No. 17 (see below) is on the back of the sheet.

17. EIGHT NUDE CHILDREN. Pen and brown ink. $14\frac{3}{4} \times 9$ in. (37·5 × 23 cm.) London, British Museum (Cat. No. 4 *verso*).

The drawing dates from the same period as that on the front of the sheet (No. 16), or not much later. Brinckmann related the figures to the Child Christ of the Bruges Madonna (1503–1504) and the infant St John of the Taddei tondo in London (about 1504–05). The relationship to the Bruges Madonna had already struck the collector who, about 1600, twice wrote 'chosse de bruges' on the sheet.

The sheet also contains some sketches in lead-point which have almost disappeared, e.g. on the left, beneath the outline sketch of the little St John, the profile of a woman, and on the right a repetition of the infant St John.

No. 16 (see above) is on the *recto* of the sheet.

18. STUDIES FOR THE 'BRUGES MADONNA' AND THE 'BATTLE CARTOON'. Black chalk and pen. $12\frac{3}{8} \times 11\frac{1}{4}$ in. (31·5 × 27·8 cm.) London, British Museum (Cat. No. 5 *verso*. From the Casa Buonarroti).

There are no documents enabling us to determine exactly when the Bruges Madonna was executed. If we accept the assumption of Brinckmann (7, p. 22) and Valentiner (*Studies of Italian Renaissance Sculpture*, p. 216 f.) that the work was carried out between 1504 and 1506, we may consider this sketch to have been a first idea and date it about 1504.

Brinckmann has given the correct explanation of the three nude figures: On the right, a man with a sword in his left hand (corresponding approximately to the nude seen from behind in No. 19); in the centre, a man making a beckoning gesture (similar to the gesture in No. 16); on the left, a crouching man doing up the sandal on his left foot. Brinckmann believes the figure group to be a sketch for the Battle Cartoon (1504). Popp (20, pp. 161–162) dates the whole sheet about 1530.

Doubts have been cast on the authenticity both of the chalk drawing and of the pen and ink sketch; as regards the Madonna, by Frey; as regards the group of three figures, by Baumgart (16, p. 32 f.). Baumgart believes that some mannerist from the entourage of Pontormo or Rosso has here combined three separate figures from the Battle Cartoon. This supposition is supported by the very unusual style, almost reminding us of El Greco. This chalk drawing of three figures may be classed with some manneristic drawings by Michelangelo, of a similar style though of a much later date—e.g. the 'Study for the Brazen Serpent' (Plate 90), the figures in the centre of the lower row, as Berenson has first pointed out (BB. 1564), or with some of the sketches for the 'Resurrection' (see Plate 82).[12]

[11] Ludwig Goldscheider, *Leonardo da Vinci* (Phaidon Press, seventh edition, 1964), Plate 49.—A. E. Popham, *The Drawings of Leonardo da Vinci* (London 1946), Plate 49.

[12] A. E. Popp and Baumgart dated the group in black chalk between 1525 and 1530, and, I used to share their view. But J. Wilde's explanations in the British Museum Catalogue of Michelangelo Drawings, 1953, p. 12 f., have convinced me that *all* the sketches in chalk, and those in pen and ink, contained in Plates 18 and 19, ought to be dated about 1504.

19. NUDE SEEN FROM BEHIND, TWO PUTTI, LEG STUDY. Black chalk and pen. 12⅜ × 11¼ in. (31·5 × 27·8 cm.) London, British Museum (Cat. No. 5 *recto*).

According to Baumgart the standing nude man is a study for the Battle Cartoon (1504), but was not used. The two Putti, still revealing the influence of Leonardo,[13] are related to the Pitti tondo (about 1504). The leg study, according to Tolnay, was drawn later (about 1520–25). Popp (20, p. 161 f.) dates the whole sheet from this period. This late dating was rejected by Thode (49, p. 268, No. 51), who dates the four lines of poetry written in the same dark-grey ink as the leg study 'about 1504'.
The four lines of poetry beneath the drawing (Frey, XXII) run as follows:

'Sol' io ardendo all' ombra mi rimango,
Quand' el sol de suo razi el mondo spoglia,
Ogni altro per piaciere, e io per doglia,
Prostrato in terra, mi lamento e piangho.'

('Alone I remain burning in the shadows,
When the sun withdraws his rays from the earth,
Others go to their pleasures, but I, prostrate with grief
Upon the ground, must mourn and weep.')

20. NUDE YOUTH, STUDY FOR AN ARM, HEAD OF A BEARDED MAN. Pen and ink. 12¾ × 6⅝ in. (34 × 16·8 cm.) Paris, Louvre (Inv. No. R.F. 1068 *verso*).

This drawing is on the back of No. 5. Thode, who dates it from the time of the Sistine Chapel frescoes, i.e. about 1508–10, thinks that the nude youth was a preliminary study for the Haman, influenced by the Belvedere Apollo. (This relationship to the Belvedere Apollo, which is not very clear, was subsequently transferred by Tolnay to No. 16.)
Panofsky (50, col. 23) accepts Thode's dating. Tolnay (*Münchener Jahrbuch*, 1928) at first interpreted the figure as a sketch for one of the Captives on the tomb of Pope Julius, a supposition which was emphatically rejected by Baumgart (16, p. 44); subsequently (17, p. 191) Tolnay described this nude as a sketch made from memory of one of the youths in the Laocoön group (which, as is well known, was excavated in 1506 in the presence of Michelangelo). He thinks that the arm was a partial sketch for the St Matthew, commissioned in 1503. The bearded head is, according to Berenson, a sketch for the 'Moses'. Baumgart compares No. 20 with No. 10, especially as regards the arm studies, and dates both about 1501.
I think it quite possible that both the arm and the bearded head may have had some connexion with the Piccolomini altar. The contract concluded with Michelangelo in 1501 (and renewed in 1504) stipulates expressly that sketches shall be made. The arm and the face, looking downwards, have points of similarity to the St Peter; the arm of St Paul might also serve for purposes of comparison.[14]
The sketch of the nude youth belongs to the same period as the 'Battle Cartoon'. J. Wilde sees in it a sketch for a 'Ganymede'. Dussler does not agree with Thode, Berenson and Panofsky that this drawing was made as a first study for the 'Crucified Haman' of the Sistine Frescoes, but admits that Michelangelo may have returned to this concept when he designed the Haman several years later. The figure has also a strong resemblance to the 'Bad Thief' (bronze, part of a 'Golgotha group', designed by Michelangelo, Metropolitan Museum, New York; Tolnay, V, figs. 330, and 332).

21. MALE NUDE SEEN FROM THE BACK. (Study for the Battle Cartoon.) Pen and ink. 16⅛ × 8¼ in. (41 × 28·5 cm.) Florence, Casa Buonarroti (Cat. No. 6 *recto*).

J. Wilde has proved that this figure is a free copy from one on a Roman sarcophagus relief (46, pp. 41–64). A female figure in the same pose, though reversed, appears on the Amazon Sarcophagus in the Vatican (reprod. Plate IX, 16, in *The Renaissance and Mannerism : Studies in Western Art*, Vol. II, Princeton 1963). Thode, Berenson and Dussler believe it was directly intended for the 'Battle Cartoon'; Tolnay thinks there is no direct connection. Baumgart calls it a copy. On the *verso* of the sheet is a note in Michelangelo's handwriting, dated 24 September 1528.

22. NUDE SEEN FROM THE BACK. Pen and ink; below, two sketches in black chalk. 11¼ × 8¼ in. (28·4 × 21 cm.) Florence, Casa Buonarroti (Cat. No. 5).

Sketches for the Battle Cartoon (1504).
There is another version of this drawing in Oxford (BB. 1559 *verso*), showing a further elaboration of the same figure. Berenson calls the Oxford drawing 'one of Michelangelo's best pen and ink sketches', but Tolnay describes it as a copy; Baumgart, too, excludes it from the genuine drawings. (See note on 23.)

23. NUDE MAN MOUNTING A HORSE, AND ANOTHER MAN HOLDING THE STIRRUP FOR HIM. Black chalk. 10¼ × 6¾ in. (26·2 × 17·3 cm.) Oxford, Ashmolean Museum (Cat. No. 296 *verso*).

On the *recto* of this sheet a carefully elaborated study, for which our No. 22 is a sketch.
Tolnay and A. E. Popp rejected *recto* and *verso* of this sheet; Baumgart ascribed the *verso* to Daniele da Volterra; but Berenson, Thode, Panofsky, Wilde, Parker and Dussler regard this sheet as authentic. I am convinced now that my former doubts were not justified.
From the Lely, Gibson, Richardson sen., West, Lawrence, Woodburn collections. The inscription in the (restored) upper right corner is by the former owner of the drawing, William Gibson, about 1690.

24. MALE TORSO, SEEN FROM THE BACK. Black chalk, heightened with white. 7¾ × 11 in. (19·4 × 26·6 cm.) Vienna, Albertina (Catalogue III, No. 130 *verso*; S.R. 157).

Study of a lance-thrower, for the 'Battle Cartoon'. On the *recto* of this sheet are pen and ink studies of two male nudes (Fig. 3). Berenson, Frey, Thode, Popham, Weinberger and Wilde have accepted them as genuine; Tolnay doubts both sides of the sheet, he finds the drawings 'completely retouched by a modern hand' which makes it difficult to pass judgment. Dussler agrees with him but emphasizes 'the outstanding documentary characters of these drawings' and is inclined to judge them favourably.

[13] Windsor Castle, No. 12562. Emil Möller (in *Belvedere*, Vienna, 1926, IX, p. 18) reverses the relationship and ascribes the 'heroic' style of the Leonardo drawing to the influence of Michelangelo (about 1503–06).
[14] *Ph. M.*, Plates 29 and 32.

FIG. 3.—*Studies for the 'Battle Cartoon'*. Pen and ink. Vienna, Albertina.

In my opinion, No. 24 is at least as good as No. 25, and one cannot accept the one and reject the other.

25. NUDE MAN, SEEN FROM THE BACK. Pen, brush and warm-grey ink; washes on torso and background; heightened with white. 16⅝ × 11¼ in. (41·2 × 28·7 cm.) London, British Museum (Cat. No. 6 *recto*. From the Casa Buonarroti).

Study for a figure of the 'Battle Cartoon'. In Agostino Veneziano's engraving (B. XIV) the figure is bending much more towards the right, and the left arm is also shown (Fig. 4). This fine drawing is not generally accepted as authentic, but Berenson, Panofsky, Wilde and Dussler have voted for it.

FIG. 4.—*Copy of a part of the 'Battle Cartoon'*. Engraving by Agostino Veneziano, 1523.

26–27. STUDIES FOR AN APOSTLE; CAVALRY BATTLE.—ORNAMENT SKETCHES. Pen and brown ink. 7¼ × 7⅛ in. (18·6 × 18·3 cm.) London, British Museum (Cat. No. 3 *recto* and *verso*).

All the sketches on the front and back of this sheet date from the same time. The ornaments are sketches for a relief on the base of the pillar on the extreme left of the tomb of Pope Julius, as Frey (13B) already suggested (cf. Laux, *Juliusmonument*, pp. 109 and 189). The contract was made in March 1505, and the drawing must have been made soon afterwards, either in 1505, while Michelangelo was still in Rome, or, more probably, in the summer of 1506 in Florence.[15]

On 2 May 1506, Michelangelo wrote to Giuliano da Sangallo offering to continue in Florence his work on the tomb of Julius; judging from a letter of Balducci's dated 9 May 1506 (Gotti, II, 52), about this time he seems to have resumed work on the Battle Cartoon (Thode, I, 349); simultaneously, i.e. during the summer of 1506, he was also working on the 'St Matthew' for Florence Cathedral (Valentiner, *Studies of Italian Renaissance Sculpture*, p. 219; Baumgart, 16, p. 17).

In April, 1505, Michelangelo had received the last payment from the Opera del Duomo for four figures of Apostles (Frey, Vol. II, p. 9; Valentiner, *op. cit.*, p. 219). Thode and Meder have already pointed out that the two sketches for an Apostle on the front of this sheet should not be identified as sketches for the St Matthew, as they frequently are; we must assume that they were for another figure of an Apostle, which Michelangelo never began in sculpture.[16]

Lastly, I believe that the sketch of a battle of horsemen, which has always been held to be a first design for a part of the cartoon of the Battle of Cascina, is really a free copy of Leonardo's Battle of Anghiari.[17] In Florence during the same year, 1506, Raphael copied another portion of Leonardo's cartoon,[18] and a few years earlier Michelangelo himself had copied in the same free manner Leonardo's cartoon for the 'St Anne' (No. 8).

Berenson is the only critic who has disputed the authenticity of the sketches of ornaments (which he describes as 'grotesques and arabesques not by Michelangelo').

The sheet has been cut on the left.

From the Lempereur, Dyce and Malcolm collections.

A drawing in the Uffizi showing the same figure of an Apostle, similar ornaments, the figure seen from the back in No. 19,

[15] For the ornament sketches see *Ph. M.*, Plate X.—But I am now doubtful whether this connexion is correct. The sketches could have been meant for the frame of the 'Doni Madonna'; designed, I believe, by Michelangelo himself. See note on Plate XV of *Ph. M.*, p. 261; and the Plate XIV of the present volume.

[16] The cancellation of the contract for the twelve Apostles on 18 December 1505, may not have deterred Michelangelo from carrying on with the work during the summer of 1506. Valentiner believes the sketch of an Apostle to be a preliminary drawing for a *St Thomas* for the Piccolomini altar, in connexion with a contract concluded in October 1504 (*op. cit.*, p. 220). I am here discussing merely the date, not Valentiner's hypotheses.

[17] I have just realized that this idea is not new; see Kenneth Clark, *Leonardo da Vinci*, 1939, p. 139; revised edition 1958, Penguin Books, p. 126.—But Berenson thought: 'It is highly probable that the skirmish was for the background of the cartoon of the Bathers'.

[18] Fischel, *Raphael*, 1948, plate 53 (F. IV, 210). This composition appears in a similar form, but partially inverted, in the left half of the 'Victory of Constantine' (Gronau, *Raphael*, 1923, KdK 204).

etc., which Frey (233F), Brinckmann (pl. 8) and Valentiner (*Studies of Italian Renaissance Sculpture*, 1950, fig. 224) reproduce as authentic, is recognized as an imitation by Berenson (1645A), Thode (No. 215) and Baumgart (16, p. 31); Tolnay (17, p. 185) describes this drawing as an old forgery. Wilde, Dussler, and Paolo Barocchi declared it genuine; but Dussler still believes that the drawing is a (composite?) copy by a pupil, dating from 1515 or a little earlier. On the other hand, Berenson has revised his view (1961 edition, II, p. 376) and declared himself inclined to regard *recto* and *verso* as authentic. This Uffizi drawing may not be a fake, but it is certainly not by Michelangelo's own hand.

There seems to be a lingering echo of the Apostle on No. 26 in Raphael's pen and ink sketch for the Dante in his 'Parnassus' (Fischel, V, 247).

28. SALOME WITH THE HEAD OF THE BAPTIST (?). Pen and ink. $12\frac{3}{4} \times 10\frac{1}{4}$ in. (32·5 × 26·1 cm.) Paris, Louvre (Inv. No. 685 *verso*).

This drawing has been variously dated—by Baumgart as early as 1501–02, by Anny E. Popp as late as about 1524.

Frey dated the drawing 1513 (Berenson a little earlier), and there is apparently a good reason for such a dating. In January, 1512, Michelangelo's brother, Buonarroto di Simone, came to see him in Rome, probably in connexion with his project of acquiring a partnership in the banking house of Donato di Bertini in Florence. Officially, the partnership agreement was not concluded until 1513, *but it may well be that the collaboration between Donato and Michelangelo's brother began before* 1513. These dates are important, because the drawing we are discussing is on a page from a ledger of the firm of Donato and Buonarroto.[19]

At the top on the left, underneath the seven lines of entries made by the bank clerk, we see, drawn upside-down, the head and upper part of an eagle next to a slender Greek vase, a so-called Loutrophoros. There are similar eagles on the base of a pulpit in Pisa Cathedral, between the statues of Prudence and Fortitude (A. Venturi, *Giovanni Pisano*, 1927, plate 102), and on the Palazzo Comunale at Bologna; the latter was at one time wrongly attributed to Michelangelo (KdK. p. 186). There is an antique prototype of this eagle, namely, that belonging to the *Ganymede statue* in Naples (No. 186, from the Farnese collection; reprod. W. Klein, *Praxiteles*, p. 129).

Close to the eagle in the drawing there are two words in Michelangelo's handwriting, which I read *Andraqu* [aratesi].[20] This could be used as a further argument for the dating 1512–13, as Andrea Quaratesi was born on 13 November 1512.

The subject of the drawing is far from certain. It has also been called 'Judith with the Head of Holofernes'. It is impossible to decide whether the figure is kneeling on a clod of earth in the open air, or on a step in front of the table of Herodias, presenting the head on a salver. There is a similar figure in a fresco by Fra Filippo Lippi in Prato Cathedral. Matthew 14, 6–11: 'And the king . . . sent, and beheaded John in the prison. And his head was brought in a charger and given to the damsel: and she brought it to her mother.'

FIG. 5.—Fra Filippo Lippi: *Salome*, detail from 'The Feast of Herod', c. 1464. Prato Cathedral.

Baumgart (16, p. 46 f.) thinks that only the front of this sheet is authentic (No. 29), and attributes the back (No. 28) to the Master of the Manchester Madonna.

From the Mariette collection.

29. ST ANNE WITH THE VIRGIN AND CHILD. Pen and ink on black chalk. $12\frac{3}{4} \times 10\frac{1}{4}$ in. (32·5 × 26·1 cm.) Paris, Louvre (Inv. No. 685 *recto*).

No. 28 is on the back of the sheet, and what has here already been said about the dating is also applicable to No. 29.

As Johannes Wilde (46, p. 60 f.) has pointed out, the Virgin in this drawing is a free copy of Giovanni Pisano's Sibyl on the pulpit in Pistoia. The ductus of the pen in the nude figure (below, across the sheet) is similar to that of the sketches of the putto and the captive in No. 30.

30. SKETCH OF A CAPTIVE, A PUTTO, A WINGED HEAD OF AN ANGEL, ETC. Pen and ink. $15\frac{3}{4} \times 8\frac{1}{4}$ in. (40 × 21 cm.) Paris, Louvre (Inv. No. 688 *verso*). On the back of No. 6.

The Mercury-Apollo here appears traced in black chalk, but in the original attitude, with one arm hanging down free, not laid across the breast; the attributes, the winged hat and the viola, are also omitted. According to Berenson, this tracing is not by Michelangelo; nor can the profile head, in the exact middle of the sheet, be by him, since its technique is identical with that of the Madonna drawing in Berlin (BB. 1396; by the Master of the Manchester Madonna; see Figs. 6–7). Frey

---

[19] Previously I followed Frey and accepted the fact that the sheet comes from the banking house Donato–Buonarroto as a definite proof for the date 1513. I am inclined now to a more orthodox dating. There is, however, no agreement among scholars about the dating of this drawing. Dussler dates it 1504–05; Tolnay 1505–06, Berenson 1509–11.

[20] For Andrea Quaratesi and his family see J. Wilde in his *Catalogue of the Michelangelo Drawings* in the British Museum, 1953, p. 97.—A similar inscription—*Andra Quar . . .*, and also *andrea*—is on No. 48 *verso*.

Details from drawings by the Master of the Manchester Madonna

FIG. 6.—From a drawing in Berlin (see Plate No. IX–c).
FIG. 7.—From a drawing in Paris (see Plate No. 30).

rejected the attribution to Michelangelo of the head of a man with a feather in his hat; the leg study and the little nude lying obliquely below on the right are likewise by the hand of the same assistant. On this side of the sheet there thus remain only two authentic sketches—the putto and the Captive. The winged head of an angel is (*pace* Frey) most probably also by Michelangelo; it is drawn in the same ink as the sketch of a Captive, and it appears in similar form on the head-dress of the 'Pitti Madonna'.[21] Michelangelo used sometimes such a winged head of an angel (*Angelo*) as a rebus to sign his letters with; e.g. the letter he wrote to Gherardo Perini in February 1522, is signed with this rebus.

The putto, a sketch by Michelangelo's own hand, was used by the Master of the Manchester Madonna—to whom, in my opinion, altogether five of the sketches on this sheet ought to be attributed—for the infant St John in his large picture of the Madonna (London, National Gallery, No. 809).

The Captive sketch, which has some connexion with the contract for the tomb of Pope Julius signed in 1505, enables us to date the sheet. Here we must remember the letter which Michelangelo wrote from Florence on 2 May 1506, to Giuliano da Sangallo, asking him to obtain the Pope's consent to Michelangelo's continuing his work on the tomb of Julius in Florence instead of in Rome.

The lines of poetry near the Captive, a stanza of Petrarch's, are in Michelangelo's handwriting.

From the Coypel Collection.

31. HEAD STUDY. Red chalk. $8 \times 6\frac{3}{4}$ in. (20 × 17·2 cm.) Florence, Casa Buonarroti (Cat. No. 8 *recto*).

Tolnay was the first to describe this drawing as an inverted study for the head of the Prophet Jonah, which demands a dating of about 1511. Most other writers—including Berenson, Thode, Frey, Bertini, Dussler, Barocchi, and Hartt—regard it as a study for the 'Doni Madonna',[22] although one characteristic feature of this head—the open mouth showing the teeth—does not correspond with the Madonna but with the Jonah. For this reason I accepted formerly Tolnay's view without reservation; but I believe now in the possibility that the study may have been used twice, first for the 'Doni Madonna', and about seven years later for the 'Jonah'.

On the *verso* of this sheet are two caricatures of the *recto*, by some ungifted pupil.

32. HEAD OF A YOUNG MAN. Red and black chalk over a sketch with metal-point, partly gone over with pen and brown ink. $12\frac{7}{8} \times 8\frac{1}{4}$ in. (33·1 × 21·5 cm.) London, British Museum (Cat. No. 1 *verso*).

Colvin (1895) thought that this head was an inverted study for the 'Adam' of the Sistine frescoes; but posture and shading are very different. None the less Brinckmann, Tolnay, Wilde and Dussler maintained that the drawing was at least 'near to' the head of Adam in the fresco. Berenson felt himself reminded of the head of 'Lazarus' in Sebastiano del Piombo's picture in the National Gallery, London. At one time I followed Berenson in believing that Michelangelo had reworked here a drawing by Sebastiano; but I can see now that the relation between the two heads is not strong and a dating of about 1516 much too late. For the general concept of No. 32 compare the head of the 'Taddei Madonna',[23] or the turbaned head of a soldier at the utmost right in the Holkham copy of Michelangelo's Battle Cartoon. The probable date of No. 32 is between 1505 and 1508, the time between the Battle Cartoon and the inception of work for the Sistine frescoes.

The faint black chalk sketch of a hand in the lower left corner of the sheet corresponds more or less with the right hand of 'Moses';[24] but this gives no clue to the dating.

On the *recto* of the sheet is No. 14.

33. SKETCH FOR THE DECORATION OF THE SISTINE CEILING; HAND AND ARM STUDIES. Pen and brown ink, and black chalk. $10\frac{7}{8} \times 15\frac{1}{8}$ in. (27·5 × 38·6 cm.) London, British Museum (Cat. No. 7 *recto*).

This pen drawing is connected with Michelangelo's original plan for the frescoes in the Sistine Chapel, viz., that the twelve Apostles were to be painted in the spandrels and the remaining surfaces filled with ornaments.[25] On 10 May 1508, Michelangelo received the first payment, and this is approximately the date of the sketch. The Apostle may possibly have been drawn from a lay figure.[26]

The arm and hand studies are probably of later date, about 1509 or 1510. The study for the left hand was used three times: for the Adam, the Amon and the Jesse. The studies for the right hand and right arm were used twice, for an Ignudo and for a figure in the Ezechias lunette.

On the *verso* are the brush drawing of a seated figure; another seated figure in metal-point, hardly visible (both not by Michelangelo); and a drapery study, drawn in brown ink with the brush over light-grey preparation, possibly by Michelangelo's own hand.

The drapery may have been used (inverted) for the Jesse lunette.

Formerly in the Casa Buonarroti.

---

[21] *Ph. M.*, Plate 45, datable about 1505.

[22] *Ph. M.*, Plate 44.—Woelfflin, Poggi, Tolnay, and Hartt date the 'Doni Madonna' 1503–04; Baumgart and Dussler date it 1505–06, which seems too late.—The drawing No. 35 is in *red* chalk, which is unusual for genuine Michelangelo drawings before the time of the Sistine frescoes; it could be used as an argument for Tolnay's dating.

[23] *Ph. M.*, Plate 45.

[24] *Ph. M.*, Plate 147.

[25] Heinrich Wölfflin in *Jahrbuch der preussischen Kunstsammlungen*, XII, 1892, p. 178 f

[26] Cf Filarette, Book XXIV (ed. Oettingen, p. 654).

34. STUDY FOR THE FIGURE OF ADAM IN THE SISTINE FRESCO. Red chalk. $7\frac{1}{2} \times 10\frac{1}{4}$ in. (19·3 × 25·9 cm.) London, British Museum (Cat. No. 11 *recto*).

This beautiful drawing is regarded as an original by Thode, and Wilde, but not by Panofsky, Tolnay, and Dussler, who declared it a copy. Berenson was undecided.
On the *verso* of the sheet is a sketch for the head of an *ignudo*, apparently not an original drawing.
From the Reynolds, Ottley, Lawrence, Woodburn, Locker-Lampson collections.

35. HEAD STUDY FOR AN IGNUDO. Black chalk (heightened with white by another hand). $12 \times 8\frac{1}{2}$ in. (30·5 × 21 cm.) Paris, Louvre (Inv. No. 860 *recto*).

Study for the Ignudo on the left above the Isaiah on the Sistine Chapel ceiling. In the fresco the head has a fillet fixed round it, and there are also other minor modifications of the sketch. The treatment of the hair and the spotty forms of the shadows remind us of No. 31; the long, oblique lines of the hatching are found again in No. 36.[27] Retouching by another hand, consisting especially in the addition of reflected lights in white chalk, have impaired the quality of the drawing. None the less, like Thode, Berenson, and recently Wilde, I believe that this drawing is authentic.
On the other side of the sheet: the same Ignudo, in full length; black chalk, badly rubbed and consequently difficult to judge; probably not by Michelangelo.
From the Jabach and Coypel collections.

36. STUDY OF A HEAD IN PROFILE; TWO SKETCHES OF A LEFT KNEE. Black chalk. $17\frac{1}{8} \times 11$ in. (43·2 × 28 cm.) Florence, Uffizi (18718F. Cat. No. 21).

This drawing was made for the 'Zechariah' of the Sistine Ceiling Frescoes.[28]
K. A. Laux (*Michelangelos Juliusmonument*, Berlin 1943, p. 342) maintains that it represents Pope Julius II and he dates the drawing 1513, which is certainly too late. But if it were a portrait of Julius II, the drawing would have to be dated *after* 1510, since the Pope—as all his portrait medals that can be dated prove—wore no beard before 1511.
The leg studies in metal-point on *recto* and *verso* are probably also by Michelangelo.

37. FIRST SKETCH FOR THE IGNUDO AT THE LEFT OVER JOËL. Black chalk. $11\frac{3}{4} \times 8\frac{3}{8}$ in. (30 × 21·2 cm.) Casa Buonarroti (Cat. No. 17).

Berenson is the only authority who doubted this drawing; he thinks it might be by Silvio Falconi. Thode, Wilde, Dussler, and Barocchi have no doubts in the authenticity of this rapid and excellent sketch.
Steinmann regarded it as intended for the *ignudo* at the left over Daniel. Thode, as for the *ignudo* at the left over the Cumaean Sibyl; but the position of arms and legs corresponds only with the figure at the left over Joël.

38. FIRST SKETCH FOR THE IGNUDO AT THE RIGHT OVER ISAIAH. Metal-point and black chalk, $13\frac{3}{4} \times 10\frac{1}{8}$ in. (35 × 25·5 cm.) Florence, Uffizi (Cat. No. 11 *verso*).

Tolnay and Dussler rejected *recto* and *verso* of this sheet; Berenson, Wilde, and Barocchi rightly accepted them as authentic.
The sketch of a thigh is for the *ignudo* at the left over Daniel (not over Joël).

39. STUDIES FOR THE LIBYAN SIBYL. Red chalk. $11\frac{3}{8} \times 8\frac{1}{2}$ in. (28·8 × 21·3 cm.) New York, Metropolitan Museum.

Drawn from a male model, although intended for a female figure of the Sistine Ceiling frescoes.
The large head in the lower left corner is not of the same high quality as the main figure or the other sketches on the *recto*; but I believe now that it can be accepted as autograph. (A copy of No. 39 in the Uffizi, Cat. No. 268, does not include this large head, but in the right lower corner a sketch for the left foot of the Libyan Sibyl, apparently copied from a Michelangelo drawing, not from the fresco.)
The sketches in red chalk on the *verso* (of 39) are for the lower part of the Libyca, drawn from a female model, not much better than the large head on the *recto*, and no doubt by the same hand.
In spite of this criticism, this is one of Michelangelo's most important drawings.
From the collections of Jabach, Paris, and of Don Aurelio Beruguete, Madrid.

40. STUDIES FOR THE SISTINE CHAPEL CEILING AND THE TOMB OF JULIUS. Red chalk and pen with brownish ink. $11\frac{3}{8} \times 7\frac{7}{8}$ in. (28·6 × 19·4 cm.) Oxford, Ashmolean Museum (Cat. No. 297 *recto*).

Sketches in red chalk for the boy holding a roll of paper, in the fresco on the left behind the Libyan Sibyl, and right hand of the Sibyl. At the top on the left, drawn with the pen, part of a cornice, presumably for the tomb of Julius, and six pen and ink sketches of shackled Captives for the tomb.
The red chalk drawings were made about 1511. The pen and ink sketches, which are invariably dated 1513, may have been a little earlier, since Michelangelo began to busy himself again with the tomb of Julius, at the latest in October 1511, although the second contract was not concluded until after the death of the Pope on 6 May 1513. (This means that the *whole* drawing may possibly date from 1512.)
On the back of the sheet are leg studies in pen and black ink.
From the Mariette, Lagoy, and Lawrence collections.

41. SKETCH FOR THE RISEN CHRIST MADE FOR METELLO VARI. Pen and ink on red chalk. $9\frac{3}{8} \times 8\frac{1}{4}$ in. (24·7 × 21·3 cm.) London, Brinsley Ford collection.

The statue was commissioned on 14 June 1514, and this sketch of a torso was probably made about that time. The first version of the Christ, since lost, was at one time in the possession of Metello Vari. The second version was completed in 1521 and is now in Santa Maria sopra Minerva in Rome.
The sketches on the back of the sheet are—according to A. E. Popp—by the hand of Silvio Falconi (cf. B.B. 1702).

[27] Dussler (70, 299) makes the same comparison between the present drawing and the two at Florence, quoted above, but he arrives at a different result; he rejects No. 35 which he dates about 1530.
[28] Paola Barocchi (66, 33) has pointed out that there is a certain resemblance to the Ezekiel. In my opinion it resembles even more the profile of Moses. But, no doubt, it is not a portrait, and it was intended for the fresco of Zecchariah, although in the painting the receding forehead and the different form of the nose are at once noticeable.

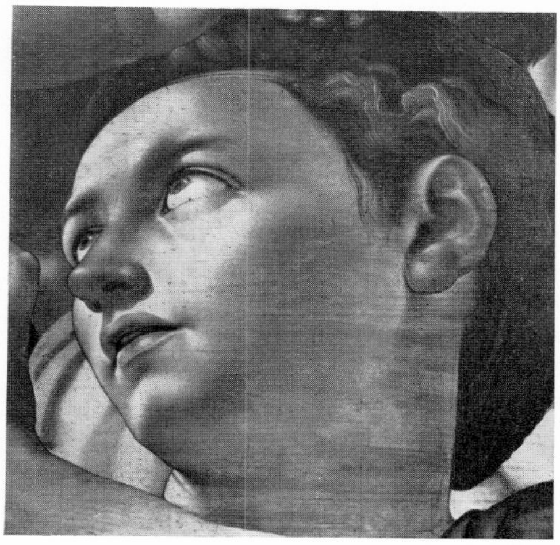

(a) The head of the Prophet Jonah, about 1511, detail of a fresco in the Sistine chapel.—(b) Detail of Plate 31, about 1504. Florence, Casa Buonarroti.—(c) The head of the Doni Madonna, about 1504. Florence, Uffizi.

(d) The head of the Prophet Zechariah, about 1509, detail of a fresco in the Sistine chapel.—(e) Detail of Plate 36, about 1509. Florence, Uffizi. (f) The head of Moses, 1513–16, detail of the Julius monument in S. Pietro in Vincoli, Rome.

(g) Cornice with masks in the courtyard of the Palazzo Farnese, Rome, about 1550.

a

A capital in the Medici chapel, about 1524: Bearded Mask.

b

Mask on the keystone of the Porta Pia, Rome, about 1562.

c

Mask on the back-plate of Giuliano's cuirass. About 1533–34. Florence, Medici chapel.

Formerly in the Lempereur, Heseltine and Henry Oppenheimer collections.

42. STUDY FOR SEBASTIANO DEL PIOMBO'S RAISING OF LAZARUS. Red chalk. 10 × 4¾ in. (25·2 × 11·9 cm.) London, British Museum (Cat. No. 16).

Vasari, who knew both Michelangelo and Sebastiano del Piombo well and had personal contact with them, says in his Life of Sebastiano that the *Raising of Lazarus* was 'painted by Sebastiano under the direction of Michelangelo and partly after drawings made by the latter'.[29] During the last sixty years, various critics from Franz Wickhoff to Berenson, Tolnay, and Dussler have rejected the attribution to Michelangelo of this and a number of related drawings, and have assigned them to Sebastiano. Sebastiano's latest biographer, Pallucchini, accepts their views. Charles Loeser condemned No. 42 as an imitation. Wilde rightly defends the attribution to Michelangelo.

The clumsy studies of feet at the bottom of No. 42 are probably by Sebastiano.

From the collections of the Casa Buonarroti, Wicar, Lawrence, King William II of Holland, and Woodburn.

See also Karl Frey, *Sammlung ausgewählter Briefe an Michelagniolo Buonarroti*, Berlin, 1899; letter from Rome, dated 19 January 1516, from Leonardo Sellaio to Michelangelo. For additional references see Pallucchini (60, p. 124, note 52).

43–45. THREE STUDIES OF HORSES AND A BATTLE SCENE. Pen and ink. 16¼ × 11⅛ in. (42.7 × 28.3 cm.) Oxford, Ashmolean Museum (Cat. No. 293 *recto* and *verso*).

Most critics have related these sketches to the Battle Cartoon and dated them about 1504–05. Miss A. E. Popp (20, p. 159) attempted to establish a relationship between this drawing and a projected lunette fresco in the Medici chapel, and suggested dating it about 1525; Tolnay agrees with her on this date.

In 1520, after the death of Raphael, a commission for frescoes in the Sala di Costantino in the Vatican was to be assigned. On 12 April Sebastiano del Piombo wrote to Michelangelo asking for his support against the assistants of Raphael.[30] Michelangelo tried to have the commission given to Sebastiano by writing to Cardinal Bibbiena, but it was finally assigned to Raphael's workshop.[31] On 3 July 1520, Sebastiano wrote to Michelangelo concerning the projected frescoes in the Sala di Costantino: 'I believe that they want to have painted there a lot of battle pictures, and that is not a job for young men.' He goes on to say: 'To tell the truth, that is not a job for beginners, it is more suited to you.... If you are willing to undertake the work, there is much money and honour to be gained.'

Did Michelangelo, who for many years had been jealous of Leonardo and Raphael, take Sebastiano's suggestion seriously and draw these sketches at that time?

In any case, I find it impossible to assign an early date to this drawing (or to No. 46), and on this point am in agreement with Popp and Tolnay. Nevertheless, it seems to me that to date it about 1520 accords better with the development of Michelangelo's draughtsmanship than dating it from the later period of the work on the Medici Chapel.

On the back of the sheet are a sonnet (Plate 45) and four love-poems (Frey 48, poems II–VI), which likewise do not seem to fit in with an early dating.

Frey dates the sonnet about 1511 and assumes that it was addressed to Julius II; but he adds (p. 306): 'The sonnet, it is true, does not contain anything which definitely points to Julius II; one should rather think of Clement VII, whose "omo" Michelangelo called himself in 1518.' I believe that the sonnet can be connected with the quarrel Michelangelo had in 1520 with the Cardinal Giulio de' Medici, the later Pope Clement VII.

In the sonnet (Frey III) Michelangelo says '*I' sono e fui gia tuo buon seruo antico*' (I am and was your good old servant). But in 1505 Michelangelo was not an 'old servant' of Pope Julius II, as he had received from him the first commission only in March of that year. Five years later, in March 1520, Michelangelo wrote a letter of bitter complaints to a Florentine notary (Ramsden, *The Letters of Michelangelo*, London 1963, I, 128 f.) in which he counted up all the wrongs done to him—the old servant—who had worked for already six years for the Medici Pope Leo X and for his cousin the Cardinal Giulio de' Medici. (The contract for the façade of S. Lorenzo was cancelled on 10 March 1520.) 'I complained bitterly,' says Michelangelo in this letter. 'Now the Cardinal (Giulio de' Medici) told me to account for how much money I received and how much I spent . . . I am not charging for the wooden model of the façade which I sent him to Rome; I do not charge for the time of three years I have wasted over this work; I am not charging to his account that I have been ruined over my work for San Lorenzo; I am not charging to his account *the enormous insult* of having been brought here to do the work and then see it taken away from me; and I still do not know why.' '*Del mie tempo non tie incresce o dole*' (You do not worry about the time I have lost), says Michelangelo in the sonnet, reproduced as Plate 45.

There is no *definite* proof that Michelangelo made any studies of horses and cavalry battles for his Cartoon of 'The Bathers' (also called 'The Battle of Cascina') in 1505.[32] The sheet of studies of horses in the Casa Buonarroti (Cat. 206), attributed by Tolnay, Wilde, Parker and Dussler to Michelangelo, was by Paola Barocchi rightly recognized as a drawing by Raffaello da Montelupo, moreover, the drawing at the Casa Buonarroti has no resemblance whatever to the one in Oxford; the latter being called by Berenson '*studi dal vero*', and by Parker '*literal renderings from nature*'. Berenson adds: 'I question whether in the whole range of Italian art, not excepting even Leonardo, we shall find another horse so like the real animal.' But he describes Michelangelo's other few genuine sketches of horses as 'drawn in a conventional and perfunctory fashion'. This must include the famous sketch of a calvary battle on the sheet in the British Museum (Plate 26).

---

[29] *Vasari*, Milanesi edition, 18, Vol. V, p. 570: '. . . Sotto ordine e disegno in alcune parti di Michelagnolo.' The painting is now in the National Gallery, London.

[30] All the documents relating to this are most easily accessible in Vincenzo Golzio, *Raffaello nei Documenti*, 1936, p. 125 f.

[31] Raphael's pupil, Giulio Romano, executed the fresco. He painted *The Battle of Constantine against Maxentius*, a picture full of fighting horses and falling men, not unlike Leonardo's *Anghiari Cartoon*. It seems that even before Raphael's death it had been decided that this wall in the Sala di Costantino should be decorated with such a representation of a Cavalry Battle (Gronau, *Raffael*, 1929, KdK 204).

[32] The copy from the 'Cartoon' in the British Museum is certainly not 'a reliable document'; see Wilde, 64, 1953, Cat. No. 85, p. 123.—The only drawing of a horse by Michelangelo, comparable to this one, is the early sketch of a marching horse, Plate 23. But this horse is of a very different type, inspired by the antique, reminding us of the bronze horse of Marcus Aurelius and of the horses on S. Marco in Venice.

All indications justify a fairly late dating, i.e. about 1520, of the drawing No. 43.
The sheet (Plates 43–44) has been folded in the middle so that four sides were available. The two inner sides are covered with the verses, while the two outer sides have been used for the upper and lower drawings, which are here reproduced facing each other in their original sizes.
From the Casa Buonarroti, Ottley, Lawrence, and Woodburn collections.

46. COMBAT OF CAVALRY AND FOOT SOLDIERS. Pen and brown ink. $7\frac{1}{8} \times 10$ in. ($18{\cdot}3 \times 25{\cdot}2$ cm.) Oxford, Ashmolean Museum (Cat. No. 294).

I date this drawing, too, about 1520—cf. the text to Nos. 43–45.
Baumgart suggested that the drawing was made with the help of lay figures. A comparison with woodcuts in Erhard Schön's *Unterweisung der Proportion und Stellung der Possen* (i.e. of manikins), Nuremberg, 1538 and 1542, supports this assumption (cf. the battle scenes, D. IV and E. I, and the rearing horse, F. III).
From the Casa Buonarroti, Ottley, Lawrence, and Woodburn collections.

47. TRITON. Charcoal drawing on a wall on the first floor of the Villa Michelangelo at Settignano. About $3\frac{1}{2} \times 5$ ft. (c. 1 m. $\times$ 1·5 m.).

This almost lifesize charcoal drawing appears to be derived from Mantegna's two engravings of the 'Battle of Tritons' (B. 17–18; about 1490; Kristller, p. 394). It was first discussed in detail and claimed for Michelangelo by C. H. Wilson (1876). Tolnay holds it to be the oldest work by Michelangelo that has been preserved, executed before he entered Ghirlandaio's workshop, that is to say, when the artist was thirteen years old! Thode stressed the bad state of preservation of the 'fresco' and thought that it 'could not possibly be a youthful work'; he does not, however, venture any opinion as to whether it is authentic or not. Frey said of it: 'Today a rough, much reworked drawing, the original form of which is barely recognizable; if it is really by Michelangelo, it must belong to a late period in his work.' Johannes Wilde (46, p. 46) and Baumgart (16, p. 11) refrain from expressing an opinion, on the ground that they have not seen the original. Berenson assigns it to the period between the Sistine Chapel ceiling and the 'Last Judgement', that is to say, between 1512 and 1534; but he tightened the time bracket by pointing out a relationship between the *Triton* and the *Anima Dannata* (Plate 50) which dates from 1522. I think that Michelangelo drew the *Triton* during the period when he worked on the San Lorenzo façade, i.e. between December 1516 and Spring 1520—rather towards the end of this period.
I have seen this drawing at least twice, and could detect Michelangelo's original and unadulterated work only in the back of the head and ear, the arms, and in the draperies. Although for this reason I can understand Frey's doubts, I am nevertheless inclined to believe that the drawing is authentic.

48. A DRAGON. Pen and brown ink (drawn over four profile drawings by some pupil). $10 \times 12\frac{1}{4}$ in. ($25{\cdot}4 \times 33{\cdot}8$ cm.) Oxford, Ashmolean Museum (Cat. No. 323).

Berenson suggested that this was drawn for the ornamentation of a marble candelabrum in the Medici Chapel.[33] But he dated the drawing about 1507, which date would rather connect it with one of the reliefs on the tabernacle of the Julius Monument, where two similar dragons can be seen.[34] (In my opinion either connexion is slight.)
Berenson calls the drawing 'one of Michelangelo's greatest and most artistic creations'. This justified judgment is almost a proof against the opinion that the drawing was intended as a design for ornamentation. (Compare the sketches on Plate 27.)
The *verso* of the sheet contains three profiles, fifteen studies of eyes, some sketches of locks of hair, and an ear. Three or four of these sketches are by Michelangelo, the others are copies by a not very skilful pupil, who is usually identified with Antonio Mini.[35]
Very interesting are the inscriptions on the *verso* (although it is uncertain whether all of them are in Antonio Mini's handwriting, or some of them are in Michelangelo's). One of the inscriptions reads *Andra Quar* . . .,[36] and below *Andrea qar* . . . and *Andrea q* . . .—in red chalk. In the lower right corner, in black chalk—*andrea abbi patientia/ame me chonsolatione assai*. (Cf. Wilde, 64, p. 77.) Andrea Quaratesi was born in 1512.
From the Vivant-Denon, Sir Thomas Lawrence, and Woodburn Collections.

49. PROFILE WITH ORIENTAL HEAD-DRESS. Red chalk. $8\frac{1}{8} \times 6\frac{1}{2}$ in. ($20{\cdot}5 \times 16{\cdot}5$ cm.) Oxford, Ashmolean Museum (Cat. No. 315).

This drawing, judged by its style, belongs to the same group as those presented to Perini (Nos. 50–52).
The drawings presented to Perini were attributed by Morelli to Bacchiacca, and the same writer and Loeser added several other drawings to the group, among these being the sheet in Frankfurt (Berenson, figs. 775 and 784), the 'Two Heads' in the Uffizi (Berenson, fig. 783), the so-called Count of Canossa and the so-called Marchesa di Pescara in the British Museum (Berenson, figs. 780 and 786).[37] Berenson attributes all these drawings to his 'Andrea di Michelangelo'. They are of uneven quality, and I believe that we can here draw a distinction between Michelangelo's originals and drawings of similar content made by an imitator. Authentic are the three drawings for Perini, the 'Marchesa di Pescara' (BB. 1689) and the drawing we are discussing. As regards the remainder, I follow Morelli's opinion; Bacchiacca frequently used similar heads in his paintings. No. 49 differs more markedly in quality from the latter than a copy normally does from its original, and the attribution to Bacchiacca (Tolnay, II, No. 15–A) is acceptable only if one also rejects the three presentation drawings for Perini, which are among Michelangelo's best achievements; this has actually been done, but quite wrongly. Recently by Paola Barocchi in her Catalogue of the Michelangelo drawings in Florence, 1962, Nos. 185, 186, 187. It should be noted that the strongest argument in favour of such an attribution is the

33 *Ph. M.*, Appendix, Plate IV–b. (Cf. Tolnay III, p. 32.)
34 *Ph. M.*, Appendix, Plate X–c.
35 Mini lived in Michelangelo's house from autumn 1522 until November 1531, when he left for France.
36 For *Andrea Quaratesi* see No. 28 and footnote 19.
37 Morelli, in *Kunstchronik*, new series, III (1891–92) and IV (1892–93). Loeser, in *Archivio Storico dell'Arte*, new series, III, p. 352 f.

FIG. 8.—Michelangelo: Detail of No. 49.

FIG. 9.—Bacchiacca: Salome, detail of a painting in Berlin.

fact that Bacchiacca used a similar head for his Salome in the 'Beheading of John the Baptist' in the Berlin Museum (see Figs. 8–9).

The only genuine Bacchiacca drawing that might be compared with this one is a red chalk study in the Albertina (BB.189, reproduced by A. E. Popham in *Italian Drawings*, Oxford, 1931, Plate 199–B); here, too, the figure is turned in such a way that we can see the back, but the head is in profile. Despite all this external resemblance, Bacchiacca's completely different technique stands out—his superficiality, his lack of plastic feeling, his striving after elegance and decorative values.

Anny Popp (in *Belvedere*, VIII, Forum, p. 75) ascribes No. 65 to a pupil of Michelangelo named 'Carlo', and believes that the drawing is a free copy of the slave on the left above the Prophet Joel. In my opinion this theory of Popp's leads to only one positive result, namely, that the model was a young man, as were the models for the Sibyls, and not a woman (cf. No. 39).[38]

[38] Of drawing No. 49 there are two copies—one in the Ashmolean Museum (Cat. No. 348) attributed to Salviati or alternatively to Battista Franco; the other, in the Uffizi (Cat. No. 188), seems to me to coincide in technique with BB. 1688, 1630 and 1669, for which reason I think that it is a copy by the hand of Bacchiacca. (Delacre, 8, 1936, figs. 85 and 86.)

The Danish poet, Jens Peter Jacobsen—who knew only the copy in the Uffizi—in his poem entitled 'Arabesque on a drawing by Michelangelo', senses the erotic atmosphere pervading this drawing, and writes: '*That is innocence, enchanted by thy glance,/which seeth not, yet wildly sucks/the stormy flood of the veins' red stream,/as the moon sucks up the ocean's frigid water . . . /Mighty blind Maenad,/ strange waves glitter in the darkness and foam with strange sounds . . ./ and the full-throated bellowing of madness.*'

At this point I would like to bring forward a supposition which cannot be proved. Twice in his life Michelangelo made portraits of young men—Tommaso de' Cavalieri, 'in a cartoon in life size', as Vasari informs us; and Cecchino Bracci, as we learn from a letter written by Luigi del Riccio in August 1544: 'I beseech you, try to find again a certain drawing of which I have already spoken to you, so that you may carve the head of Cecchino from it.' If we admit the relationship of No. 49 to the presentation drawings for Perini, then we may suspect that the model for this head was Perini himself.

Formerly in the Casa Buonarroti and the Wicar, Ottley, Lawrence and Woodburn collections.

50. 'DAMNED SOUL' (FURIA). Black chalk on grey paper. $11\frac{5}{8}$ × 8 in. (29·8 × 20·5 cm.) Florence, Uffizi (Cat. No. 187).

This is the most important of the three sheets which Michelangelo, according to Vasari, presented to Gherardo Perini. The Florence drawing was held to be a copy, and a version in Windsor Castle the original, until Johannes Wilde (41, p. 264) established the correct relationship.

At the top the drawing bears the inscription GHERARDUS DE PERINIS with the words MICHELAN. BONAROTI FACIEBAT below. Under this there are three intersected circles, Michelangelo's stonemason's mark (placed on all blocks of marble as soon as they had been purchased on his behalf at the quarries.

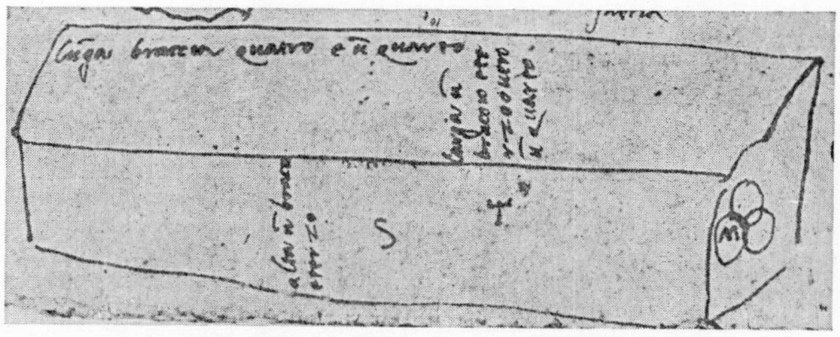

FIG. 10.—Michelangelo: Sketch of a marble block, bearing his stonemason's mark. Florence, Archivo Buonarroti.

The head is usually called 'Anima Dannata', the Lost Soul. Bernini called a very similar sculpture 'Testa di anima dannata.'[39] (On the derivation of these works from a Medusa head, see Appendix, Plate V.)

[39] In the Palazzo di Spagna, Rome (Photo, Anderson 17846).—Dussler (70, p. 232) has adopted my references to the head behind Minos, and to Bernini's *Anima Dannata*; but he regards No. 50 as a copy.

Michelangelo inserted an almost identical head in the 'Last Judgement', behind the right shoulder of Minos. The question arises, however, whether the correct designation would not be 'Furia'.

The following conjecture which, since I believed it for a long time, I present with the greatest confidence; but it must be taken with reserve, it is nothing but a hypothesis.

In February 1522—i.e. in the same month in which Michelangelo wrote the only letter to Gherardo Perini that has been preserved—there appeared the second edition of Ariosto's 'Orlando Furioso', the most important poem of the High Renaissance and a victory for Romanticism over Classicism.[40]

In the most impressive part of this poem madness is represented by love; indeed love itself is explained as being madness. I will quote a few passages:

'And when he found that he was all alone, with cries and groans opened the doors of grief./His eyes were sunken in his head, his face was pale and like a dried-up bone, his hair dishevelled, awesome and forbidding./I saw him . . . uttering fearsome howls and loud laments; he has gone mad./Various are the effects, but that wild madness which brings them out, is ever just the same. . . . And in conclusion I would say to you that he who, though old, still loves, the penalty deserves that he be bound and chained.' (XXIII, 124; XXIX, 60; XXXI, 45; XXIV, 2.)

In addition to this, the poet says of himself that he has been gradually losing his reason since arrows from the eyes of his beloved have been piercing his heart (XXXV, 1).

Is it not legitimate to suppose that this screaming head was intended to be a symbol of Michelangelo's infatuated love for Gherardo Perini, since it is after all generally admitted that the Ganymede drawing symbolizes his love for Tommaso de' Cavalieri?

In his Life of Michelangelo, Vasari wrote: 'To his close friend, the Florentine nobleman Gherardo Perini, Michelangelo gave three folios with several heads in black chalk (*a suo amicissimo . . . in tre carte alcune teste di matita nera . . .*). After his death they came into the hands of the illustrious Signor Francesco de' Medici'. Aretino, in his venomous open letter of 1545, refers to these drawings: 'You should have kept your promise [to send a drawing] and with the greatest punctiliousness, in order thus to refute the calumny which asserts that no one can obtain favours from you, unless he be a Gherardo [Perini] or a Tommaso [Cavalieri]'.[41]

[40] Ariosto, in the first edition of his 'Orlando Furioso' of 1516, had already made laudatory mention of Michelangelo's name.

[41] This is clear enough. But I have to enlarge on it, because drawings like the *Anima Dannata* (Plate 50) for Perini, or the *Tityus* (Plate 77) and the *Ganymede* for Tommaso de' Cavalieri, cannot be fully understood without acknowledgement of Michelangelo's anomalous inclinations (which have been emphatically denied by some writers). Shortly before Michelangelo moved to Rome for good he met Febo di Poggio, and in September 1534 he wrote him an excited letter, which—*pace* Miss Ramsden—can only be called a love-letter. On 14 January 1535 Febo di Poggio answered him in a way that is not far short of blackmail: 'When you left you told me that, if I needed anything, I was to apply to that friend of yours. Now I need money and Signor G[ti] is not here. I want to buy myself new clothes in order to go to the horse-races at Monte, where Signor G[ti] is also. I went to the bank, but there they told me they had no instructions from you. . . . I must ask you to be so good as to provide a little for me . . . and don't fail to answer me.' To him, as to Cavalieri, Michelangelo wrote passionate poems. After the death of Cecchino Bracci, a youth who died in 1544, Michelangelo wrote fifty short poems in memory of him. One of these quatrains '*stamps the boy as a homosexual adolescent used by older men*', as Robert J. Clement puts it (1963).

51. THREE FEMALE PROFILES WITH FANTASTIC COIFFURES. Black chalk on brownish paper. $13\frac{3}{8} \times 9$ in. (34 × 23·5 cm.) Florence, Uffizi (No. 599E *recto*. Cat. No. 186).

I date the three drawings (Nos. 50, 51, 52) presented to Gherardo Perini 1522. In November 1522, Antonio Mini entered Michelangelo's workshop, and although it does not make a continuance of the friendship with Perini impossible, the absence of any subsequent correspondence is striking.

On the lower edge of the sheet we read in very blurred characters: '*Gherardo, io non ò potuto oggi ve[nire]*'—Gherardo, I could not come today.

On 51 *verso* are three slight sketches—a half-figure of a woman, and two heads; probably also by Michelangelo's hand.

The three presentation drawings for Perini were identified by Johannes Wilde (in the Catalogue of Italian Drawings at Windsor Castle, 1949, p. 264). The attribution to Michelangelo has been rejected by Dussler (1959) and by Barocchi (1962). Dussler calls them copies by Antonio Mini; Paola Barocchi attributes them to Bacchiacca, as Morelli did seventy years before her.

52. VENUS, MARS AND CUPID. Black chalk on brownish paper. $14\frac{1}{8} \times 9\frac{7}{8}$ in. (35·7 × 25·1 cm.) Florence, Uffizi (No. 598E. Cat. No. 185).

This is the third of the drawings presented to Gherardo Perini (cf. the text to Nos. 50 and 51). The only reason why its authenticity has been questioned by critics is the fact that the back of the sheet is covered with insignificant sketches by the hand of a pupil.[42] Thode steadfastly maintained that it is authentic, despite the objections of Wölfflin, who had declared it to be a copy; of Morelli, who attributed it to Bacchiacca; and of Berenson, who for this drawing, too, suggested the name of 'Andrea'. Its authenticity has recently been defended once again by Johannes Wilde (41, p. 265).

There is a copy by Giulio Clovio at Windsor Castle, probably identical with the drawing mentioned in the 1577 inventory of Clovio's property as 'Il combattimento di Marte e Venere fatto da Do. Giulio et inventione di Michelagnolo'.[43] (Since the bearded head behind Venus wears a helmet, it probably does represent Mars; not Vulcan, as Wilde suggested.)

The popular name for the drawing is 'Zenobia', but this was already discarded by Berenson.

According to Dussler *recto* and *verso* of this sheet are 'no doubt Mini's work'; according to Barocchi, 'più probabile' by Bacchiacca.

Like the 'Furia' (No. 50), the drawing deals with the dark side of the realm of Venus, the 'sweet bitterness of love', as Sappho puts it. Here Venus appears, not smiling and persuasive, but armed, as she used to be represented in Sparta; her diadem has become a helmet, she is the violent goddess, the consort of the blood spirit Mars, triumphing over all pride and all power. She is a fateful goddess who tears the lover out of his concealment, discipline and reverence and drives him on 'with the whip of Peitho'—Verticordia, who transforms not only

[42] Two bearded heads, skulls, etc. The bearded head on the left, in faint black chalk, much better than the other sketches, is by Michelangelo himself; the apparently same head on the right is certainly a copy by a pupil.

[43] 'Battle between Mars and Venus, copy by Don Giulio Clovio after Michelangelo'.

hearts, but destinies, and leads them to fear, shame and destruction.[44]

About the same time as Michelangelo made this drawing, he created his marble group of 'The Victory'—a handsome young man triumphing over an old man crouching like a slave—a work which admits of the same erotic interpretation.

53. YOUNG GIRL WITH DISTAFF.[45] Black chalk. $11\frac{1}{4} \times 7\frac{1}{8}$ in. (28.8 × 18.2 cm.) London, British Museum (Cat. No. 40).

Cursory, but unusually beautiful sketch; in its technique, e.g. the long hatching lines, akin to Nos. 52 and 55; may be dated about 1524. Although Thode doubts its authenticity and Berenson attributes it to the assistant 'Andrea',[46] the British Museum has very rightly placed it among the authentic drawings of Michelangelo.

The figure is seated on a high-backed chair or throne, her right arm and the distaff being merely indicated. The wide, decorative girdle and the ornaments on her bosom seem to point to her representing a figure from classical mythology—probably Clotho, one of the three Parcae, who is always depicted holding a distaff.

It is much less probable that the figure could be a representation of Arachne, the Lydian princess who challenged Athene to a contest in weaving (Ovid, *Metamorphoses*, VI).

No. 53 was bought in 1859 from the Casa Buonarroti.

54. SIBYLLINE HALF-LENGTH FIGURE. Pen and brown ink, over red and black chalk. $12\frac{5}{8} \times 10\frac{1}{8}$ in. (32·3 × 25·8 cm.) London, British Museum (Cat. No. 41 *recto*).

Accepted as authentic by nearly all critics, recently also by Tolnay,[47] and Dussler. Berenson ascribes it to his 'Andrea di Michelangelo', Anny Popp to Mini. A small pen sketch of a man bending forward was on the sheet before it was used for the drawing of the female half-length. This little man appears now between the right hand and the lap of the woman; he does not belong to the composition.

No. 54 may be a first attempt for a presentation drawing, of which a final version is not known.

On the *verso* is another female half-length, an unfinished sketch by Michelangelo's own hand.

From the Casa Buonarroti.

55. TWO MADONNA SKETCHES. Pen and brown ink. $16 \times 10\frac{5}{8}$ in. (39·6 × 27 cm.) London, British Museum (Cat. No. 31 *recto*).

This sheet forms part of a group of pen-and-ink drawings (Nos. 55–62) illustrating Michelangelo's later style in this technique. The dating of this particular sheet is certain, since on the back, in Michelangelo's handwriting, there are several *ricordi*, i.e. notes of payments made between the 4th and 8th October 1524 (see Fig. 11). The contemporaneity of No. 55

---

[44] It is surprising that the import of this drawing was not grasped during the Romantic period. Henry Fuseli drew a similar Venus Philomeda, whose bosom is bound with the same high girdle as in Michelangelo's drawing, and whose countenance has the same mask-like stare; Aubrey Beardsley drew this terrible figure as Salome and as Lysistrata. Carl Justi came very near the truth when he said that the figure seemed to him to be a 'Bellona'—the Roman goddess of war.

[45] A somewhat similar figure of a woman holding a distaff is represented in a fresco by Perino del Vaga in the Vatican (Loggetta di Raffaello; reprod. D. R. de Campos, *Raffaello e Michelangelo*, Rome, 1946, plate 26).

[46] Panofsky identified this pupil with Antonio Mini, Michelangelo's least gifted pupil.

[47] See Tolnay V (69, 166; and fig. 115).

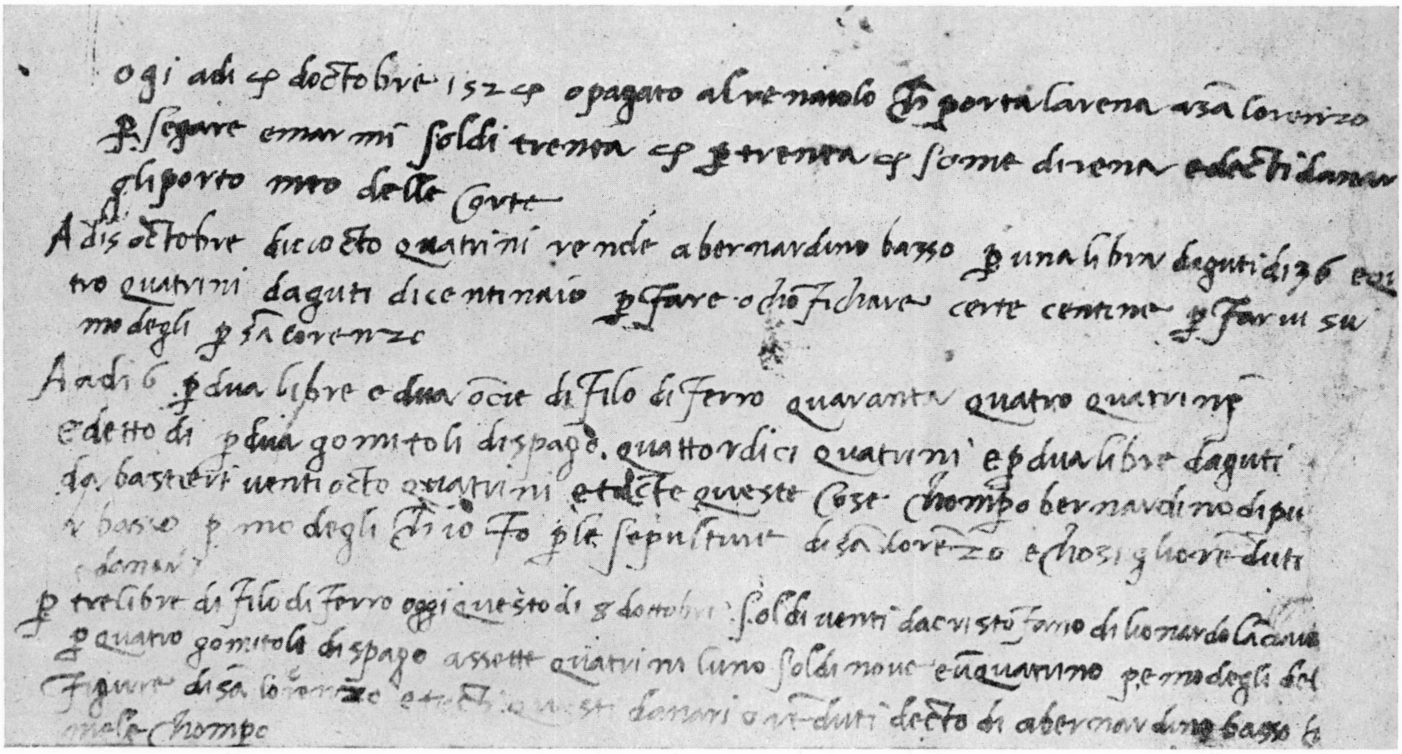

FIG. 11.—*Ricordi* in Michelangelo's handwriting, dated 1524; *verso* of Drawing No. 55. A transcription and translation in Fagan (27, p. 99 f.).

with Nos. 56 and 58 was first demonstrated by A. E. Popp (20, p. 141).
No. 55 was 'probably drawn as a model for Antonio Mini', as Berenson puts it. Mini entered Michelangelo's workshop in November 1522, at the age of sixteen, and remained there nine years. If we ignore all the drawings and paintings which Berenson, Popp and others have been only too willing to attribute to him, and consider only those drawings which can be proved to be his, Mini seems to have been one of the most ungifted artists who ever entered Michelangelo's entourage. At the bottom of the present drawing is an inscription in Michelangelo's handwriting: 'Disegnia antonio disegnia antonio, disegnia e non perder tempo'—Draw, Antonio, draw, Antonio, draw and don't waste time! Antonio would thus seem to have spent his time in making clumsy copies of Michelangelo's drawings.
The Madonna in profile is 'squared', i.e. covered with a quadrangular network of lines (which, as is well known, serve as an aid to an artist when he makes an enlargement or a cartoon).
Formerly in the Casa Buonarroti.

56. MADONNA AND CHILD. Pen and ink. $15\frac{3}{8} \times 7\frac{5}{8}$ in. (39 × 19·4 cm.) Vienna, Albertina (Cat. No. III, 132*r*; S.R. 152).

A. E. Popp (20, p. 141) was the first to attempt to prove the contemporaneity of Nos. 56 and 55; Wickhoff (37, 152), without investigating the style, arrived at the same conclusion. Thode and Brinckmann dated it about 1504, the latter holding it to be a study for the Bruges Madonna. The first to deny its authenticity was Morelli; Baumgart (16, p. 48) gives exhaustive reasons in support of this, but I do not find them convincing.
Tolnay (*The Sistine Ceiling*, 1945, p. 212, and vol. V, No. 141) shares Baumgart's opinion.
Panofsky, Berenson and Wilde regard the drawing as genuine. On the back of the sheet is a nude study of a standing man, seen from behind, without arms, which is reminiscent of the studies for the Battle Cartoon; it is, however, probably but a copy of uncertain date.
The question of the authenticity of No. 56 depends to no small extent on the dating. It would be idle to deny that the drawing has a certain stylistic resemblance to sketches like No. 26, datable c. 1504, and also to the drawing made in 1514 (No. 41) for the Risen Christ. The chief difference—clearly shown by a comparison with the earlier pen-and-ink drawings—seems to be that the ductus of the pen has become far more calligraphic, the straight and curved hatching lines being arranged as if they were handwriting; moreover, it seems to me that the ductus in the pen-and-ink drawing we are discussing is far more similar to Michelangelo's handwriting of about 1524 than it is to his writing of about 1504–14.
I myself (on the basis of the character of the pen strokes, which to me seem to be the same as in Nos. 55–62) date the drawing about 1524, and have no doubts as to the authenticity of any of the drawings in the whole group.
From the Mariette collection.

FIG. 12.—Michelangelo: Detail of Plate 57, c. 1524. British Museum.

FIG. 13.—Leonardo: Sebastian, c. 1481. Hamburg, Kunsthalle.

57. TWO STUDIES OF A CRUCIFIED MAN. Pen and brown ink, over metal-point. $9\frac{3}{4} \times 6\frac{1}{4}$ in. (24·9 × 16 cm.) London, British Museum (Cat. No. 12).

Georg Gronau (*Mitteilungen des Kunsthistorischen Instituts in Florenz*, III, 1919, p. 38 f.) recognized that No. 57 belongs to the same period as Nos. 56 and 58. Tolnay, who denies that the drawing is by Michelangelo, also rejects the old title ('Study for the Haman on the Sistine Chapel ceiling') and suggests a different designation—*Thief on the Cross*.[48]
The man on the left is standing among the branches of a tree, and the figure undoubtedly has some resemblance to one of the unfinished Boboli Captives, the so-called awaking giant.[49] But it also reminds of Leonardo's pen-and-ink study for a *Sebastian* (Fig. 13).
The figure on the right, on the other hand, coincides with a bronze statuette in Berlin (Fig. 15), which is attributed to Michelangelo and known as the 'Crucified Thief'. In my opinion, the bronze in the Berlin Museum is a cast from a (now lost) wax model by Michelangelo. (See Goldscheider, *A Survey of Michelangelo's models in wax and clay*, Phaidon Press, 1962, figs. 58, 59.)
No. 57 is a controversial drawing.
Baumgart rejected Nos. 55 and 56, and Tolnay, agreeing with him on this point, had logically to exclude also No. 57. Bertini (15, p. 114) regards No. 57 as genuine and dates it about 1510–12. Panofsky rejected it; Berenson and Wilde accepted it and dated it about 1510–12; Dussler, too, accepts it, but is doubtful about the dating. Tolnay, who does not accept it, dates it about 1530.
In my opinion the drawing can be dated by comparing it with Nos. 55, 56, and 58–62, i.e. about 1524.
Formerly in the Casa Buonarroti.

---

[48] Thode had already noticed the difference between the two figures in No. 57, and whereas he thinks that the figure on the left, standing 'on the stump of a hewn-off branch', like the crucified Haman in the spandrel fresco on the Sistine Chapel ceiling, is a study for this fresco, he says of the figure on the right that it has 'something of the pose of a Thief on the Cross'. On this point he anticipated Tolnay.
[49] *Ph. M.*, Plate 225. The most characteristic feature of No. 57, the crossed right leg, appears in a very similar form in this figure of a Captive, but is lacking in the crucified Haman on the Sistine Chapel ceiling.

FIG. 14.—Detail of No. 57. (Reprod. in reverse.)

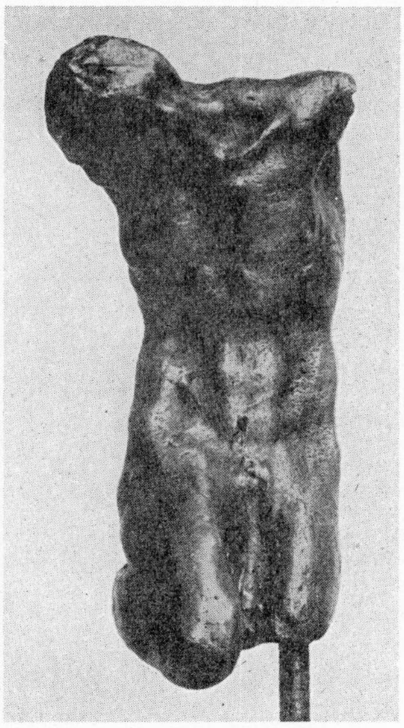

FIG. 15.—*Thief on the Cross* Bronze. Berlin.

58. TWO STUDIES FOR A MADONNA AND CHILD. Pen and ink. 10¾ × 7⅝ in. (27·5 × 19·5 cm.) Paris, Louvre (No. 689).

See text to No. 55. The sketches in No. 58 are perhaps shorthand notes made for the Medici Madonna.
On the back of the sheet is a pen-and-ink drawing, a male nude seen from the front, probably by the hand of the same assistant who drew the study of a nude on the back of No. 56.
From the Jabach Collection.

59. THREE SKETCHES FOR A RIVER-GOD IN THE MEDICI CHAPEL. Pen and brown ink. 5¼ × 8¼ in. (13·7 × 21 cm.) London, British Museum (Cat. No. 35 *recto*).

Frey recognized that these sketches are connected with the four river-gods which were to have been placed beneath the 'Phases of the Day'. Two of the sketches contain measurements. The third, in the right-hand lower corner, which is upside-down, has no measurements.[50] Michelangelo made the sketches with measurements about 1525, either for his own use or for the masons in Carrara. The River-Gods were never executed in marble, as originally planned, but a large clay model of one of them is preserved in the Accademia at Florence.[51] This model was probably made for a River-God on the tomb of Lorenzo, but these pen-and-ink sketches, as A. E. Popp has demonstrated, must have been intended for another River-God, forming part of the tomb of Giuliano. We are indebted to Joseph Meder[52] for the observation that the sketches are all of the same figure, shown in different attitudes.
On the back of the sheet are a number of parallel broken lines, and a few words.
Formerly in the Casa Buonarroti.

60. LEG STUDY FOR A RECUMBENT STATUE IN THE MEDICI CHAPEL. Pen and ink. 6 × 7½ in. (14·5 × 19·3 cm.) Florence, Casa Buonarroti (No. 44F; Cat. No. 74).

Drawn after a male model, as Michelangelo usually did for all his figures, male or female.
Anny E. Popp held that this drawing was a preliminary study for the 'Leda', made about 1530; to this Brinckmann made the amusing rejoinder that 'the tucked-in right foot of Leda would have made her inaccessible to the swan'.
Thode dated the sheet correctly about the time of the Medici tombs, and Brinckmann pointed out the resemblance to the statue of 'Night'. Thode thought that it was a sketch for a river-god, which is most probably correct.

61. LEG STUDY FOR A RECUMBENT STATUE IN THE MEDICI CHAPEL. Pen and ink. 7¾ × 4¾ in. (19·4 × 12·2 cm.) Florence, Casa Buonarroti (No. 48F; Cat. No. 72).

According to Thode, a first *concetto* for one of the River-Gods.

62. LEG STUDY FOR A RECUMBENT STATUE IN THE MEDICI CHAPEL. Pen and ink. 6¾ × 7¾ in. (17·2 × 19·6 cm.) Florence, Casa Buonarroti (No. 11F; Cat. No. 73).

Belongs to the same group of drawings as 60 and 61 (and also 59). Thode connected all of them with the models for the River Gods of the Medici Chapel; A. E. Popp, with the Leda painting. No. 62 is the only drawing of this group where Popp's hypothesis seems to click.

63. SKETCH FOR THE 'DAY' IN THE MEDICI CHAPEL. Black chalk. 6¾ × 10⅝ in. (17·6 × 27 cm.) Oxford, Ashmolean Museum (Cat. No. 310).[53]

Several sketches in black chalk for the 'Phases of the Day' have been preserved; the authenticity of all of them has been doubted and is, in fact, doubtful. Their quality, however, is so high that I have reproduced one of them here. Brinckmann, Popp and Tolnay ignore these drawings, obviously because they consider them to be copies after the finished statues. Robinson has suggested that they may be drawings by Michelangelo after his own wax models. Berenson, Frey and Thode believe that this and the following drawing (No. 64) are authentic, and date them about 1525.
On the back of the sheet there are some unimportant sketches in black chalk—a right arm, etc.
Formerly in the Reynolds, Lawrence, and Woodburn collections.

64. SKETCH FOR THE 'LEDA' Black chalk on greyish paper. 6½ × 11¼ in. (17·8 × 29·6 cm.) London, British Museum (Cat. No. 48 *verso*).

Drawn from a male model, although intended for a female statue. Formerly regarded as a study for the 'Night'.
J. Wilde (*Saxl Memorial Volume*, London 1957, p. 272, 'Notes on the Genesis of Michelangelo's Leda'), explains No. 64 as

[50] The ductus of the pen in this figure, especially as regards the right arm, in so far as it is drawn, coincides exactly with that of the seated women in No. 58.
[51] *Ph. M.*, Plate 204.—The River-Gods were planned on an enormous scale, over 9 ft. long. The model in the Florence Accademia is only a fragment without head and shanks.
[52] *Die Handzeichnung*, 2nd edition, 1923, p. 366.

[53] A related study of a recumbent male figure (Ashmolean Mus. Cat., Cat. No. 309) is according to K. T. Parker (p. 150) for the 'Day', but according to J. Wilde (p. 83) 'certainly a study for the *Notte*.' This shows how difficult it is to determine beyond doubt for which statues the drawings Nos. 60–63 were made, or whether No. 64 is for the *Night* or the *Leda*. But it is fairly safe to date No. 63 about 1525, and No. 64 about 1530—just for stylistic reasons.

a study for the 'Leda' and dates it 1530—which is convincing. On the *recto* of the sheet is a walking male nude, seen from behind (not by Michelangelo).
Formerly in the Casa Buonarroti.

65. STUDY FOR THE HEAD OF 'LEDA'. Red chalk. 14 × $10\frac{5}{8}$ in. (35·5 × 27 cm.) Florence, Casa Buonarroti (No. 7F; Cat. No. 122).

This drawing has formerly been assigned to the period of the Sistine Chapel ceiling frescoes, and dated about 1508–11. Berenson was reminded of the Libyan Sibyl; Steinmann, Venturi, Brinckmann and Tolnay, of a figure in the Ozias spandrel fresco; Thode, of a female head in the Manasses and Amon lunette. Its real purpose was first established by Johannes Wilde (41, p. 247): the head is a study for the Leda cartoon. Drawn after a male model.
The sketch of the eye and nose, below on the left, in a lighter-coloured red chalk, is, as I think now, also by Michelangelo. In the summer of 1529, when Michelangelo went to Ferrara during the siege of Florence, he promised to make a painting for Duke Alfonso I d'Este. Condivi relates the story in detail in the fortieth paragraph of his biography of Michelangelo. In the autumn of 1530 the painting was finished—'a large chamber-picture, representing Leda lying with the Swan, and nearby the birth of the egg, from which Castor and Pollux were born; as may be read, written in the fables of the ancients'; to which Vasari adds: 'a certain large picture, delicately painted in tempera'. The envoy sent by the Duke to fetch the picture behaved very tactlessly and offended Michelangelo (as we read in Condivi and Vasari), who refused to hand over the painting.
A year later he presented it to his pupil Antonio Mini, before the latter's departure for France, together with the cartoon. Mini opened a workshop in Lyons for the production of copies of the 'Leda', his partner Benedetto del Bene doing most of the work. Vasari asserts that in 1568 Michelangelo's 'Leda' was in Fontainebleau,[54] whereas the cartoon had been sent back to Florence and was in the possession of Bernardo Vecchietti. It seems, however, probable that the Fontainebleau picture is identical with the copy on canvas in London (National Gallery, No. 1868), which is now considered to be a copy by Rosso Fiorentino.

66. FOUR MASKS, AND SKETCH FOR 'HERCULES AND ANTAEUS'. Red chalk (gone over with metal-point). 10 × $13\frac{3}{4}$ in. (25·5 × 35 cm.) London, British Museum (Cat. No. 33 *recto*).

For similar masks see *Ph. M.*, Plates 183, 193–195, and Plate XIV. But, as Wilde observed: 'In neither case is the resemblance close enough for any definite connexion to be established. Moreover, the grotesques in these drawings (No. 66) are alive and lack the essentially formal, mask-like qualities of architectural decoration.' The masks are in fact so much life-like that one writer thought that the mask in the upper left was a self-portrait of Michelangelo's.[55] The mask next to it, towards the right, is fairly close to masks on the capitals in the Medici chapel (*c.* 1524; cf. *Ph. M.*, Plate XIV–c).
The sketch of 'Hercules and Antaeus', in the lower right corner, is a study for a marble group which was planned as a companion of the 'David' at the entrance of the Palazzo Vecchio. In 1508 the Signoria bought a marble block, about 15 feet tall, for the purpose; but Michelangelo was painting the Sistine Ceiling and delayed the work on the 'Hercules group'. In 1524 the project was taken up again; but in the end the commission was assigned to Bandinelli (1525).
Two other studies of 'Hercules and Antaeus' by Michelangelo are on a sheet in Oxford (Cat. of the Ashmolean Museum, No. 317).
On the back of No. 66 are some slight sketches in black and red chalk—a shield, a male head, and two spearmen.
Formerly in the Casa Buonarroti.

67. TWO FIGURES STRUGGLING. Black chalk. $4\frac{1}{2}$ × $3\frac{3}{4}$ in. (11·6 × 9·7 cm.) Haarlem, Teyler Museum (No. 21B *recto*).

Two sketches for a similar group in London and Oxford (Plate 66; and pl. LXXVIII of the Oxford Catalogue) seem to me to be much weaker than this drawing, the authenticity of which is rejected by the more recent critics, with the exception of Berenson and Thode. The drawings in London and Oxford are called 'Hercules and Antaeus'.
About the project of a marble group 'Hercules and Antaeus' (or 'Hercules and Cacus') see note to No. 66.
Michelangelo subsequently used his sketches of the 'Hercules and Antaeus' for a rather different clay model of 'Samson Slaying the Philistines', which has been preserved in the Casa Buonarroti.[56] In the drawing we are discussing Michelangelo has transformed the subject once again; here, as Thode was the first to notice, the abduction of a woman is represented; either the Rape of a Sabine Woman or the Rape of Proserpina. Giovanni Bologna followed Michelangelo's composition in his well-known 'Rape of the Sabines' in the Loggia dei Lanzi (terracotta model in the Accademia at Florence). It is a striking fact that Giovanni Bologna also used the same idea for a small bronze representing 'Hercules and Antaeus' (L. Planiscig, *Piccoli Bronzi*, 1930, fig. 359). The theme was not new, even before Michelangelo, in Florentine art. See, e.g. Sergio Orsolani, *Il Pollaiuolo*, Milan 1948, pl. 19, 83, 116.
On the back of the sheet the outlines have been traced—'probably by a later hand', as Berenson noticed.

68. THREE MALE FIGURES IN VIOLENT MOVEMENT. Pen and ink (over lead-point). $4\frac{3}{8}$ × 5 in. (11·6 × 11 cm.) Florence, Casa Buonarroti (No. 68F; Cat. No. 128).

This small drawing is one of a group of seven; six of them are in the Casa Buonarroti (Cat. Nos. 125–130), and one is in the Ashmolean Museum, Oxford (Cat. No. 321).[57]
According to Thode, and Wilde, these drawings were made

[54] K. Kusenberg, *Le Rosso*, Paris, 1931, p. 45 f. The cartoon in the Royal Academy, London, is also attributed to Rosso (Appendix, Plate XI–a). The other copies of the 'Leda' to be found in various collections are inferior to the two in London.
[55] The wrapper of Professor J. Clement's book *Michelangelo: A Self-Portrait*, 1963, is decorated with a reproduction of another mask—the mask of the 'Night', as if this were a self-portrait of Michelangelo's.

[56] *Ph. M.*, Plate 26 and Appendix, Plate XXIII.
[57] There is a faint lead-point sketch on a piece of paper which is only $1\frac{1}{2}$ in. wide, probably a fragment, in the British Museum (Cat. No. 51). It shows a single small figure, similar in style to the lead-point sketches in the upper half and on the left of the sheet in the Casa Buonarroti (Cat. No. 126. Reproduced: Dussler, fig. 81).
A sheet in Haarlem (B.B. 1471) showing three clothed and three nude figures, does not belong to the same group of drawings (though this has been suggested by Wilde and Parker). The Haarlem drawing is not in pen and ink like the others, but in red chalk; and (according to Dussler) it is apocryphal (see 70, Cat. No. 533 and fig. 240).

by Michelangelo for his friend Bugiardini to help him with the altarpiece 'The Martyrdom of St Catherine' in Santa Maria Novella, Florence (p. 56 below). Vasari (in his 'Life of Giuliano Bugiardini') relates that 'Bugiardini began a *Martyrdom of St Catherine*, but after keeping it in hand for twelve years he could not finish it, for lack of invention and skill'. Later on 'he begged Michelangelo to tell him how to make the eight or ten principal figures of the soldiers in the act of flight, fallen, wounded or dead, because he did not know how to foreshorten them in a row and in such narrow space. Michelangelo picked up a piece of charcoal and sketched a row of naked figures foreshortened in various attitudes . . .'. But this was still not enough help for Bugiardini, as the sketches were only in outline without modulation and shadowing. 'To help him, Tribolo made some rough clay models copied from Michelangelo's drawings . . . Bugiardini finished then the work in such a manner that no one would have suspected that Michelangelo had ever had anything to do with it.'

In fact, it is difficult to believe that he had. None of the figures in the front row do really tally with any of Michelangelo's drawings, which by the way are not in charcoal. Some of the figures on the balcony are to some extent a little closer to Michelangelo's sketches.

It remains doubtful whether these sketches are connected with 'The Martyrdom of St Catherine', or rather with the 'Resurrection of Christ', for which Michelangelo made designs at the same time (see Plates 82–84).

69. DESIGNS FOR SMALL PLASTIC WORKS. Black chalk. $6\frac{1}{8} \times 6\frac{1}{4}$ in. (16 × 16 cm.) Cambridge (Mass.), The Fogg Museum of Art (No. 1932–152).

The fantastic head of an animal with a helmet[58] in the upper right corner was intended as a model for a lamp. There are two similar bronze lamps by Riccio in the Museo Estense at Modena (Bode, *Bronzestatuetten*, small edition, 1922, plate 55). The faun, below on the left, with a hod on its shoulders, is likewise a model for a lamp, or perhaps for a small censer. Another lamp by Riccio, in the Museo Nazionale, Florence, is more or less a combination of these two sketches of Michelangelo's—it consists of a fantastic animal's head with a boy crouching on top of it (Bode, *op. cit.*, plate 54).

On the same sheet are also four slight sketches. Below, on the right: an eye and a man with his head between the horns of a lyre; below, on the left: a man with raised right arm (reminiscent of background figures in No. 91); above on the left: a woman with head thrown back and arms raised in lament (reminiscent of BB. 1415 and 1409).

A kindred drawing by Michelangelo, of somewhat later date, in the British Museum, shows a design for a richly ornamented vessel with a lid (Plate 71).

The two designs of lamps (No. 69) and the design of a salt-cellar (No. 71) were made by Michelangelo for the craftsman who had to execute the works in metal, and for this reason they are painfully exact, drawn with slow strokes. This lack of verve induced some writers (Berenson, Dussler, Tolnay) to regard them as copies or assistant's work.

No. 69 has passed through various well-known collections, among them those of Jonathan Richardson, Earl Spencer and Charles Loeser.

70. DECORATIVE MASK. Red and black chalk. $9\frac{3}{4} \times 4\frac{3}{4}$ in. (24·8 × 11·9 cm.) Windsor Castle, Royal Library (Cat. No. 425). Sketched in red chalk and executed in black chalk. To judge by the style, about 1530 (cf. also Plate 66, which is earlier).

Silvio Cosini's marble frieze of masks behind the 'Phases of the Day' in the Medici chapel shows only a superficial resemblance to this drawing; one of the two capital masks to the right of the statue of Lorenzo de' Medici is more closely related to it; it should, however, be compared with the mask on the back of the Giuliano, in which the headgear and the two drops beneath the chin are found as they are in No. 70. This mask was executed by Montorsoli (Milanesi, *Les Correspondants de Michel-Ange*, I, 114), perhaps after this sketch, which in the course of the execution was simplified and coarsened. (See illustration on p.38.)

Johannes Wilde has pointed out that No. 70 was used again thirty years later for the keystone mask on the Porta Pia. Similar masks were also used in the decoration above the windows in the upper storey of the courtyard of the Palazzo Farnese.[59]

On the back of the sheet are sketches by the hand of a pupil, whom one can without misgivings identify as Antonio Mini. The latter left Michelangelo towards the end of 1531 and went to France and died there in 1533.

A similar headgear is found in the Leda cartoon, and this, too, points to the year 1530.

Plate 70 reproduces only the upper part of the sheet; the lower half, which virtually contains nothing, has been omitted.

71. DESIGN FOR A SILVER SALT-CELLAR. Black chalk. $8\frac{1}{4} \times 6\frac{1}{8}$ in. (21·7 × 15·5 cm.) London, British Museum (Cat. No. 66).

In 1537 Michelangelo undertook for Francesco Maria della Rovere, Duke of Urbino, one of the heirs of Pope Julius II, two minor works—a model for a small bronze horse (lost) and the design of a salt-cellar.[60] The Duke's agent in Rome reported on 4 July 1537 that the model was finished and the execution in silver already in hand. Michelangelo supplied the silver-smith, who had to work from it, with a very careful drawing, partly made with a ruler and showing clearly every detail of the ornamentation. It is exactly this precision of the drawing, this 'lack of spontaneity', which induced A. E. Popp, Parker, Tolnay and Dussler to regard the drawing as a copy; in Popham's and Wilde's opinion—and in my own—this is the original design. (It differs in some details from the model, as it was described by the Duke's agent.)

From the collections of the Earl of Dalhousie (collector's mark Lugt, Supplement, No. 717a); Henry Oppenheimer, Capt. N. R. Colville, and Colnaghi.

72. SAMSON AND DELILAH. Red chalk. $10\frac{5}{8} \times 15\frac{1}{2}$ in. (27·2 × 39·5 cm.) Oxford, Ashmolean Museum (Cat. No. 319).

[58] Berenson and Wilde rightly compared this grotesque head with the mask on the armour of a *Warrior*, the so-called Conte di Canossa (London, Cat. No. 87, copy; the lost original dates from about 1525–1528).

[59] See Plate p. 37–(g).

[60] Vasari-Milanesi, VII, pp. 383–84.—Georg Gronau, *Prussian Yearbook*, 1906, Beiheft, p. 7 f.—Thode III, p. 668.

FIG. 16.—*Sketch for 'Venus and Cupid'*, pen and ink drawing, 1531–32. British Museum (BB. 1504).

At one time wrongly attributed to Montelupo[61] and Mini; mentioned by Johannes Wilde (41, p. 250) among the authentic drawings and described as a 'presentation sheet'.
The stylistic relationship of this drawing to the two following, Nos. 73 and 74, strikes the eye. It has already been correctly dated 1530 by Thode and Berenson.
There is a fragmentary copy of this drawing, by Antonio Mini, at Windsor Castle (Cat. 425 *verso*) and another one, probably by the same weak hand, completely finished in black chalk and pricked for transfer, in the British Museum (Cat. No. 90). This composition was the immediate source of another, namely a *Venus and Cupid*, for which there is a small sketch in the British Museum (Fig. 16). The cartoon[62] for Venus and Cupid was drawn by Michelangelo about 1532 for his friend Bartolomeo Bettini. Pontormo's painting after Michelangelo's cartoon is now in the Uffizi (see Appendix, Plate VI–b).
From the Casa Buonarroti; Wicar, Lawrence, Woodburn collections.

73. THREE LABOURS OF HERCULES. Red chalk. $10\frac{3}{4} \times 16\frac{5}{8}$ in. (27·2 × 42·2 cm.) Windsor Castle, Royal Library (Cat. No. 423).

Presentation drawing for an unknown friend, about 1530. The subjects are: the slaying of the Nemean lion, the wrestling match with Antaeus, and the fight with the Lernaean Hydra.[63]
The authenticity of the drawing has been doubted by Anny Popp, who considers it to be a forgery, and by Erwin Panofsky, who thinks it is either a forgery, or a copy by Antonio Mini. Tolnay, too, suspected it.
This is one of Michelangelo's most important drawings, and symbolizes the virtue of the 'Vita activa'.
In Cristoforo Landino's 'Quaestiones Camaldulenses',[64] one of the speakers, Lorenzo de' Medici, mentions Hercules as the representative of the Active Life: 'Wise was Hercules, but he was not wise for his own sake alone, but helped mankind with his wisdom. On his wanderings, which led him over the greater part of the earth, he destroyed loathsome beasts, slew dangerous monsters, subdued dreadful tyrants, and restored law and liberty to many a nation. . . . Had he devoted all his labour to idle wisdom, he would have stood before us as a sophist, instead of a hero, and none would venture to call him the son of Jupiter, who likewise (in so far as we, following the Platonists, can hold him to be an earthly soul) is never idle.'
The three parts of this drawing—the struggles with the lion, the giant and the nine-headed Hydra—correspond with the three categories of deeds for which Hercules is praised in Landino's dialogue—the overcoming of beasts, evil men and monsters.

74. ARCHERS SHOOTING AT A HERM. Red chalk. $8\frac{5}{8} \times 12\frac{3}{4}$ in. (21·9 × 32·3 cm.) Windsor Castle, Royal Library (Cat. No. 424).

Goeth[65] (who, be it noted, did not know the original, but saw only the fresco copy which was then in the Villa Raffaelle) understood the import of this work and described it[65] as 'a mysterious, allegorical picture, probably depicting the power of the fleshly lusts'. In this case the figure of Herm, protected by a shield, would symbolize the soul. In a sonnet by Michelangelo (Frey, CXIX) we read: 'Chè l'alma, quasi giunta all'altra riva/Fa scudo a' tuo' di più pietosi strali'—'the soul, which has all but reached the further bank, is as a shield against the most fervent arrows of Love.' Conze, Thode and Panofsky quote passages from Lucian, Cristoforo Landino, Mario Equicola

[61] Montelupo was left-handed and his drawings are therefore easily distinguished; like the drawings of Leonardo and Holbein, they have hatching lines running from top left to bottom right.
[62] Lost. An excellent 16th century copy is in the Naples Museum (ill. Tolnay III, fig. 287).
[63] The three groups in this drawing are derived from sculptures. A bronze by Michelangelo's teacher Bertoldo (about 1480) in the Victoria and Albert Museum shows the upper body and arms of Hercules in the struggle with the lion in the same position as in Michelangelo's drawing (reproduced by Planiscig in *Piccoli Bronzi*, Milan, 1930, plate XI, fig. 16). The middle group has two different sources. First, an antique cameo, 'Hercules fighting with Antaeus' (Furtwängler, *Antike Gemmen*, Plate XXVII, 15), and an antique marble group in the Uffizi, formerly in the Belvedere (Hekler, *Michelangelo und die Antike*, p. 222). Secondly, as far as the composition itself is concerned, it has been developed out of an Etruscan cameo (e.g. Lippold, *Gemmen und Kameen*, plate XXXVII, 2); this cameo in its turn is derived from Greek coins (G. F. Hill, *Select Greek Coins*, Plate XLVII, 3 and 5), and was repeatedly copied by the masters of Renaissance plaquettes. The third group is, as Frey was the first to notice, derived from the Laocoön. Similar to Mantegna's engraving (B. XIII, 11), which Michelangelo is also held to have taken as a model, is a sketch by Dürer of Hercules slaying the Nemean lion, made about 1511 (Lippmann 765, Winkler 491), but there the figures are turned more towards the left; the composition is almost identical with Dürer's woodcut of 'Samson killing the Lion' (B. 2).
[64] *Landini Quaestiones Camaldulenses ad Federicum Urbinatum Principem*, Florentiae, *c.* 1470. In these dialogues, after Hercules, 'the men who have propagated the Christian faith', i.e. the Apostles and, above all, St Paul, are exalted as representatives of the Active Life. The same may be said both of Hercules and St Paul, viz., that they fought against evil and journeyed 'over the greatest part of the earth'. The problem of the Vita Activa also engaged the attention of Cardinal Pole, with whom Michelangelo came into contact at the time when the Cardinal, as administrator of the Patrimonium Petri, was residing at Viterbo (after 1541; at the same time as Vittoria Colonna). This contact with Cardinal Pole is confirmed by Condivi, who writes: 'He (Michelangelo) has therefore gladly entertained the friendship of those from whose virtuous and learned conversation he might draw some profit, and through whom he might reflect some ray of excellence: as of the very reverend and illustrious Monsignor Pole, for his rare virtues and singular goodness.' In Thomas Starkey's 'Dialogue' (written about 1534) a conversation between Cardinal Pole and Thomas Lupset is quoted, in the course of which the Cardinal gives his opinion on the conflict arising from the choice between the Vita Contemplativa and the Vita Activa; in the end he decides in favour of the Vita Activa. (W. Schenk, *Reginald Pole*, London, 1950, p. 32 f., p. 77; Starkey's *Dialogue*, ed. Miss Kathleen Burton, London, 1948).
[65] *Reisejournal*, under 14 March 1788. The painting is now in the Galleria Bôrghese (photo Alinari, No. 7983).

and Pico della Mirandola, in their efforts to explain the drawing.[66] Many elements in the drawing have remained unexplained. It contains, among other figures, five putti, one of whom has wings and is lying asleep by his quiver; except for the faun, above on the left, he is the only member of the group who has a bow; two more putti are hardening the points of their arrows (or burning the arrows?), and two others are running with the adults, two of whom are female and six male; two further figures are lying on the ground, one of them with hand raised in astonishment. Has it not some significance that the only winged putto takes no part in the action, but is asleep? Is there no meaning in the fact that not a single arrow has hit the Herm, but that all have remained impaled in the shield, the mantle or the socle? or in the fact that the attackers have no bows? If we take Goethe's brief explanation as a starting-point, we arrive at the conclusion that against the soul, which is able to protect itself, all the passions are powerless.

On the back of the sheet is a memorandum dated 12 April 1530, and a note to the effect that the drawing was in the possession of Giulio Clovio; according to Johannes Wilde this also proves that it was not a presentation drawing for Tommaso de' Cavalieri. The note on the back ('D. Giulio Clovio copia di Michiel Angelo') induced Anny Popp to reject the drawing as being a copy by Clovio; Panofsky, Tolnay and Dussler agree that it is only a copy. Johannes Wilde, however, has demonstrated its authenticity in a convincing manner.

A copy of this drawing by Bernardino Cesari (in the same collection, Cat. No. 456) reproduces it in its entirety, i.e. before it was cut on all four sides. Several other copies are known.

Formerly in the collections of Giulio Clovio and Cardinal Alessandro Farnese.

75. TITYUS. Black chalk. $7\frac{1}{2} \times 13$ in. (19×33 cm.) Windsor Castle, Royal Library (Cat. No. 429 *recto*).

Tityus, the giant son of Terra, fell in love with Latona, mother of Apollo and Diana. He attempted to do violence to her, but she summoned to her aid her children, who slew him with their arrows. He was cast into hell, where vultures perpetually fed upon his liver. Virgil mentions him in the *Aeneid* (VI, 595 f.): 'Likewise one might see Tityus, nursling of the Earth, the universal mother. Over nine full acres his body is stretched, and a monstrous vulture with crooked beak gnaws at his deathless liver and vitals fruitful for anguish; deep within the breast he lodges and gropes for his feast; nor is any respite given to the filaments that grow anew.' Ovid (*Metamorphoses*, VI, 457 f.) also devotes a few lines to the sufferings of Tityus; but Michelangelo's immediate source was perhaps only the short 55th fable of Hyginus.

Lucretius, in the third canto of his *De Rerum Natura*, says that the image of Tityus whose body is devoured by vultures must be interpreted as that of a man whose heart is continually torn by the pangs of love—'the pangs of a shameful amorous desire', as he says in amplification.

Tityus is the symbol of the penalty for illicit love.

According to Dante (*Inferno*, XXXII) the sons of Terra, among them Tityus, are in hell because they rebelled against the gods, and they are thus in the same position as heretics. In one of Savonarola's sermons we read: 'The sexual urge directs all the senses towards corporeal things. Do not therefore wonder that the lascivious become unbelievers . . . but there is no better remedy for sexual obsession than religious contemplation.'

This drawing thus represents not only the tortures of a lover, but the sin and its penalty, the punishment for a wanton desire which leads to the greater sin of defection from God.

No. 75 is a presentation drawing dedicated to Tommaso de' Cavalieri, whose acquaintance Michelangelo made during the winter of 1532, and to whom he sent love-poems, drawings and letters; their relationship lasted until the end of Michelangelo's life. In December 1532, at a time when Tommaso was ill, Michelangelo sent him by the hand of the sculptor Pierantonio Cecchini a letter and two drawings—the 'Tityus' and the 'Ganymede'. Tommaso answered him in a letter dated 1 January 1533: 'I hope . . . that in a few days I shall be restored to health and that I shall be able to visit you, should that be agreeable to you. Meanwhile I will comfort myself by contemplating for at least two hours a day your two drawings which Pierantonio brought me and which give me ever greater pleasure, the longer I look at them.'

The 'Ganymede' drawing has been lost and is preserved only in the form of a copy by the hand of Giulio Clovio (Windsor Castle, Cat. No. 457; see Plate p. 55). The counterpart to the mental anguish of Tityus is Ganymede's flight to heaven; we may remember a passage from one of Michelangelo's sonnets to Cavalieri: 'If one spirit, one will but dominates two hearts,/ If one soul makes itself immortal in two bodies/And bears them up to heaven on one wing'.[67]

Vasari (VII, p. 271) gives a list of the drawings presented by Michelangelo to Tommaso de' Cavalieri: 'More than to all the others and with the greatest tenderness was Michelangelo drawn towards the Roman nobleman Tommaso de' Cavalieri. The latter was still young and loved art. Wherefore, in order to instruct him in drawing, Michelangelo presented him with a number of most magnificent pages, among them divinely beautiful heads done in black and red chalk. He gave him also a Ganymede, whom the bird carries away to Zeus, a Tityus, whose heart the vulture is tearing out, and furthermore a fall of Phaëthon with his sun chariot into the Po, and a Bacchanal of Children; each single page was admirable and drawn with rare art such as was never seen before. Michelangelo also made a portrait of Tommaso, a cartoon in life size—the only portrait he ever created. . . . Ser Tommaso took such delight in these drawings that Michelangelo also gave him a number of others, originally destined for Sebastiano Veneziano, that he might execute them in colours. They are wonderful and Tommaso preserves them like relics; yet he is most friendly in allowing artists access to them.' (Karl Frey, *Die Briefe des Michelagniolo Buonarroti*, 3rd edition, 1961, pp. 252–262.)

At the time of the Tityus drawing Michelangelo was working on the composition of the 'Risen Christ'. This becomes clear if we examine the sketches on the back of the 'Tityus'; the sheet was held against the light and the outlines of the Tityus were traced on the back, in such a way as to produce a standing figure, looking like a first sketch for No. 83; the sarcophagus

[66] There is a good conspectus of the literature on the subject in *Antike und Renaissance* by Arnold von Salis, Zürich 1947, p. 241.

[67] For the erotic meaning of the *Ganymede* see Ludwig von Scheffler, *Michelangelo: eine Renaissancestudie*, Altenburg 1892, p. 53; or the more detailed study by E. Panofsky in *Studies in Iconology*, New York 1939, pp. 216–218. In a Greek vase painting by Duris (now at Berlin; reprod. Kurt Hildebrandt, *Platons Phaidros*, Kiel 1953, frontispiece) it is winged Eros, not an eagle, who carries Ganymede heavenwards: The soul ascending to God on the wings of Eros.

and its lid were then indicated by a few lines (Plate 76). Formerly in the collections of Tommaso de' Cavalieri and Cardinal Alessandro Farnese.

76–78. THREE SKETCHES FOR THE 'RESURRECTION OF CHRIST'. 76. Black chalk, on the back of No. 75 (only a detail of the *verso* is reproduced here).—77. Red chalk, 9 × 3½ in. (23·5 × 7 cm.) Florence, Casa Buonarroti (No. 62F; Cat. No. 134).—78. Red chalk, 5½ × 8½ in. (13·5 × 19·5 cm.) Florence, Casa Buonarroti (No. 32F; Cat. No. 138).

No. 76, which is on the back of 75 (see note on 75), is dated by Michelangelo's letter to Tommaso de' Cavalieri which he sent him towards the end of December 1532, together with the *Tityus* and *Ganymede* drawings and which was answered by Cavalieri on 1 January 1533.
No. 77. This drawing is probably a first sketch for the soldier at the utmost right of the 'Resurrection' composition (cf. Plate 82) and it would therefore be datable 1532–33. But it remains doubtful whether it was not drawn already in 1531, originally intended for the composition 'Noli me tangere', and later on used for the 'Resurrection' as well.[68]
No. 78. Sketch for the soldier raising the lid of the sarcophagus (Plate 81).

79. MOVEMENT STUDY FOR THE 'RISEN CHRIST'. Black chalk. 14⅜ × 9½ in. (38 × 25·2 cm.) Florence, Casa Buonarroti (No. 61F. Cat. No. 137 *verso*).

The sketch on the front of this sheet (Brinckmann 61) has been reproduced time after time; according to Steinmann and Thode it is a study for the 'Risen Christ'; according to Brinckmann, a study for Christ the Judge in the 'Last Judgement' in the Sistine Chapel.
The drawing on the back of the sheet, here reproduced for the first time, makes it clear that here and in a similar drawing (Brinckmann, 62; BB. 1167; Cat. Casa Buonarroti, No. 136) we have to do with sketches for the 'Risen Christ'.
From the summer of 1532 until the end of the year (cf. No. 76 *verso*), and perhaps until 1534, Michelangelo worked on several versions of the 'Risen Christ' and on the similar composition of 'Christ in Limbo'. The motive of the present sketch is not repeated either in No. 80 or in No. 81, in which the right arm is stretched out and the left arm raised. The present drawing is interesting because it is one of the few sketches by Michelangelo that have been preserved which represents a spontaneous first draft, giving nothing but the movement.
It was obviously this lack of definite form that led Berenson to doubt it. Anny E. Popp, Tolnay and Dussler rejected it emphatically; J. Wilde and Paola Barocchi accept *verso* and *recto* as authentic.

80. THE RESURRECTION OF CHRIST. Red chalk. 6¼ × 6¾ in. (15·5 × 17·1 cm.) Paris, Louvre (Inv. No. 691b).

Sketch for the following drawing, No. 81. Alexander Perrig *Michelangelo Buonarroti's letzte Pietà-Idee*, Bern 1960, pp. 128–129) declared Nos. 80 and 81 to be imitations. But Frey, Brinckmann, Thode, Tolnay, Wilde and Dussler accepted them without any doubt.
Formerly in the Jabach, Coypel, and Robert de Cotte collections.

81. THE RESURRECTION OF CHRIST. Black chalk. 9½ × 13⅝ in. (24 × 34·7 cm.) Windsor Castle, Royal Library (Cat. No. 427 *recto*).

Popp (20, p. 162) advanced the hypothesis that this drawing was intended for a lunette fresco on the entrance wall of the Medici chapel. In her opinion, No. 80 is of later date than the drawing we are discussing. Such theories can hardly be accepted.
The date of the drawing is 1532–33 (cf. the text to No. 79).
On the back of the sheet are sketches in soft black chalk, which Anny E. Popp attributes to Giulio Clovio, the former owner of the drawing.

82. THE RISEN CHRIST. Black chalk. 12⅞ × 11¼ in. (32·6 × 28·6 cm.) London, British Museum (Cat. No. 52).

The last and finest version of the theme. The composition is so monumental that it is easy to understand how Anny E. Popp arrived at her untenable theory that this drawing was intended for a lunette fresco in the Medici chapel. Christ has here assumed gigantic proportions. One of the foreground figures, the watchman, lying on his back on the lid of the sarcophagus, has not been completely finished, but only sketched in outline; on the left and right edges, too, there are lightly sketched-in figures. In general, the drawing can be regarded as not quite finished, for it was begun in hard chalk, and it can be seen that it was in parts continued and strengthened with soft chalk. The soldier with a shield on the right has a strong resemblance to a figure in Signorelli's 'Conversion of St Paul' in the Santuario of Loreto (KdK, p. 20); a similar figure with a shield in Michelangelo's 'Conversion of St Paul' in the Cappella Paolina still shows Signorelli's influence.
A painting by Marcello Venusti in the Fogg Art Museum, Cambridge (Mass.), mentioned by Francesco Scannelli (1657), Fagan (1883) and Frey (1911), is but an inorganic 'pasticcio', put together out of Nos. 80–82 (reproduced by Tolnay, 21, fig. 149).[69]
See also the notes on Plates 76–79.
Formerly in the Casa Buonarroti and in the Wicar, Lawrence, and Woodburn collections.

83. THE RISEN CHRIST. Black chalk. 16 × 10½ in. (41·4 × 27·4) London, British Museum (Cat. No. 54 *recto*).

The drawing is unfinished; it incorporates motives of attitude from two rough sketches in the Casa Buonarroti (reproduced

[68] A drawing, related to No. 77, is in the Archivio Buonarroti (Cat. No. 345). Tolnay regards it as the original from which No. 77 was copied. This drawing in the Archivio Buonarroti is on the *verso* of a *ricordo*, datable 1531 according to Paola Barocchi. (The first sketches for the 'Resurrection' were made a year later.)
The painting of the 'Noli me tangere' was commissioned at the beginning of 1531 by Alfonso Davalos, Marchese di Guasto, a general in the imperial army, through the good offices of Nicolaus von Schomberg, Archbishop of Capua and Governor of Florence. From a letter written by Figiovanni to the Master (Frey, 48, p. 507; dated 11 April 1531) we learn that Michelangelo was first to produce a 'schizzo di carbone', i.e. a charcoal sketch or cartoon. The cartoon was finished in the late summer of 1531, and after it Pontormo painted two panels in oil colours (B.B. 4–A, fig. 650). The cartoon was at one time in the art collection of Duke Cosimo I de' Medici (who also owned the cartoons of the 'Leda' and the 'Venus and Cupid') in Florence; but the three cartoons have since disappeared.

[69] On Venusti's paintings, based on Michelangelo drawings, see Hermann Voss (54, p. 116).

by Brinckmann, 61, 62). Twenty years later Michelangelo made use of this figure in his composition of the 'Expulsion of the Money-changers' (Nos. 120–122).

In the summer of 1532 Michelangelo was working simultaneously on a 'Christ in Limbo' and on several versions of the 'Risen Christ' (Nos. 76–82). The present drawing was intended for the 'Risen Christ'—Jesus is shown standing on the edge of the sarcophagus lid—but certain details, such as the lightly sketched-in banner of the cross in the left hand and the position of the right, remind us of the 'Christ in Limbo'.[70] This drawing represents a late version of ideas which Michelangelo had been turning over for a long time in his mind, and it may be dated about 1533. The technique coincides with that of No. 93.

On the back of the sheet are sketches by another hand (Frey, Thode, Popp, Dussler).

Formerly in the Casa Buonarroti, the Wicar, Lawrence, and Woodburn collections.

84. STUDY FOR THE 'RISEN CHRIST'. Black chalk. $16\frac{1}{2} \times 11\frac{3}{4}$ in. ($41{\cdot}8 \times 28{\cdot}8$ cm.) Florence, Casa Buonarroti (No. 65F; Cat. No. 142 *verso*).

A sketch for this drawing, but the raised arm differently posed, is to be found on the back of a letter from Bartolomeo Angiolini, dated 19 September 1532 (Archivio Buonarroti, Cod. VI, fol. 24; Cat. No. 346, illustrated).[71] On the other side of No. 84 is a general design for the 'Last Judgement' (No. 100; about 1534). No. 84 was, in fact, also used for several figures of the 'Last Judgement', with minor alterations.

Tolnay thought in 1948 (21, p. 220) that this drawing is a poor copy, based on the sketch on the *verso* of the Angiolini letter (mentioned above); but eight years later he changed his mind (69, p. 184, No. 172) and declared the present drawing '*a copy made by the master himself ca. February–March* 1534. *The purpose of the sketch was probably to prepare for the fresco of the Resurrection on the altar-wall of the Sistine chapel*'.

85. STUDY FOR A HOLY FAMILY. Black chalk. $12\frac{1}{2} \times 7\frac{1}{2}$ in. ($31{\cdot}7 \times 19{\cdot}1$ cm.) London, British Museum (Cat. No. 65).

To judge from its technique this drawing belongs to the same period as Nos. 84, 90, 93, 96 and 97; in other words, I date it about 1533. It also shares another peculiarity with No. 90—the unusually long neck. It seems hardly necessary to mention that here the motive of the Medici Madonna has been used again, though the proportions and pose of the figure are far more reminiscent of the statue of Giuliano de' Medici.[72] A strong affinity to this drawing is shown by one of approximately the same size, also in the British Museum (Cat. No. 58; BB. 2482; sometimes attributed to Sebastiano), dating from the same period.[73] In both these drawings, made by Michelangelo shortly before his departure for Rome (where he began working on the 'Last Judgement'), he shows himself as the initiator of a new style—a Florentine Mannerist.

The drawing has suffered badly from rubbing. In the upper right corner is a barely recognizable male head, looking downwards (Joseph); beneath it is the figure of a child (St John).

Formerly in the Mariette, Marquis de Lagoy, and Richard Payne-Knight collections.

86. THE 'DESCENT FROM THE CROSS' AND A 'DEPOSITION'. Red chalk. $10\frac{1}{8} \times 7$ in. ($25{\cdot}7 \times 18$ cm.) Haarlem, Teyler Museum (No. 19).

Nos. 86 and 87 belong together, a fact which would not be worth mentioning if Pallucchini (60, p. 191, and p. 177) had not attributed the two drawings to two different artists; in his opinion the London drawing is by Sebastiano del Piombo and the Haarlem drawing by Michelangelo. More logically, Berenson attributed both of them to Sebastiano, whereas Dussler deletes both from Sebastiano's œuvre.[74] According to Panofsky (26, p. 49) the present drawing is by Daniele da Volterra, about 1540. No. 86, however, has hardly any affinity to Daniele's authenticated drawings, and a comparison with his 'Deposition' in Santa Trinità dei Monti, painted in 1541, is particularly instructive. Despite all the borrowings from Michelangelo, Daniele's fresco is a manneristic work, in which theatrical gestures and an ornamental treatment of the draperies play a great part; Michelangelo's drawing (No. 86), on the other hand, is a monumental composition, sparing in its gestures, all of which serve to convey some definite expression, and above all, it is clearly the invention of a great sculptor. A notable tribute has also been paid to this drawing in that several generations of sculptors have made reliefs and plaques after it, in every possible kind of material—in wax, stucco, ivory, bronze and silver.[75] Such long-lived fame is reserved only for works designed by the greatest masters.

The style of the drawing is reminiscent of the figures in No. 88; in so far as they have remained at the stage of sketches, of the sisters in the 'Phaëthon' (No. 91; 1533) and of sketches for the 'Last Judgement' (e.g. No. 100; 1534). On the basis of these comparisons we may establish the date of the present drawing. The Virgin Mary collapsing beneath the Cross on the left has been drawn again separately in the upper right corner of the sheet. This 'group of three' was subsequently developed in a different way in No. 123.

On the back of the sheet are some heads, probably after Giotto; and a study of draperies, not by Michelangelo (cf. J. Wilde in *Belvedere*, XI, 1927, p. 145).

---

[70] Perrig (71, p. 101) has decided in favour of the latter theme (1960).

[71] Tolnay (21, p. 104) related No. 84 to a similar drawing in the Ashmolean Museum, Oxford (Cat. No. 311 verso; BB. 1713), on the *recto* of which is a design for the Relic Chamber in the church of San Lorenzo, datable about 1532. This led Tolnay to suggest that Michelangelo may have planned a fresco of the 'Ascension' for the lunette on the entrance wall of San Lorenzo, above the reliquary balcony.

[72] *Ph. M.*, Plates 174 and 177.

[73] A copy of this drawing (BB. 2482), though perhaps after a cartoon or a painting, is to be found on a page of a Heemskerck sketch book at Berlin, fol. 61 *verso* (see: *Die römischen Skizzenbücher von Marten van Heemskerck*, Berlin 1916, Vol. II, Plate 85, Text p. 38). Heinrich Egger (the main editor of the 'Heemskerck Sketch Books') does not attribute fol. 61 *verso* to Heemskerck himself, but to an anonymous Netherlandish artist, who is supposed to have copied here a painting by a follower by Giulio Romano or by some Dutch Mannerist.
BB. 2482 is not by Sebastiano del Piombo; it is close to Michelangelo; but whether it is an original remains questionable.

[74] He rejects No. 86 definitely and is very doubtful about No. 87 (*Sebastiano del Piombo*, pp. 190 and 182).

[75] Thode, V, p. 482; C. R. Morey, *Gli Oggetti di Avorio . . . del . . . Vaticano*, Vatican City, 1936, p. 43 f. Tradition attributed these reliefs to Michelangelo himself. Duke Maximilian of Bavaria, as we learn from a note which he wrote on it in 1623 with his own hand, thought that the wax relief in Munich was an original work of Michelangelo.
See also *Ph. M.*, Plate XXXI, reproducing a plaster (or stucco) cast from a lost wax model by Michelangelo (*Descent from the Cross*, relief, $12\frac{1}{2} \times 9\frac{1}{2}$ in., Casa Buonarroti). Wilde dates the drawing No. 86 and the relief about 1523–25; but a drawing (No. 105) which can be connected with the relief he dates about 1542.

From the collections of Queen Christina of Sweden, Cardinal Azzolino, Prince Odeschalchi, and the Duke of Bracciano.

87. THE THREE CROSSES. Red chalk. 15⅜ × 10⅞ in. (39·4 × 28·1 cm.) London, British Museum (Cat. No. 32).

See also the text to No. 86.

For the motive of the Thief on the left side of the cross Michelangelo made partial use of an older drawing, No. 57. The affinity to Daniele da Volterra, which Panofsky claimed for No. 86, may rightly be held to exist in this drawing, for the group of women beneath the Cross, as Fagan (27, p. 116) noticed, was used by Daniele for his 'Deposition' in Santa Trinità dei Monti.

Thode has already pointed out that we have here one of Michelangelo's most gifted creations. Compared with this drawing, Mantegna's 'Three Crosses', the beautiful predella panel in the Louvre, produces the effect of being little more than a 'veduta', for it has none of this drawing's visionary power. No. 87 can stand comparison with the most famous of all graphic representations of the 'Three Crosses'—Rembrandt's etching.

No. 87 was once in the Casa Buonarroti, and later in the collections of Wicar, Lawrence, King William II of Holland, and Woodburn. It was acquired by the British Museum at a Christie's sale in 1860.

88. TWO STUDIES FOR 'THE BRAZEN SERPENT'. Red chalk. 9¾ × 13¼ in. (24·4 × 33·5 cm.) Oxford, Ashmolean Museum (Cat. No. 318 *recto*).

In chapter xxi (6–9) of the Book of Numbers we are told how the people of Israel in the wilderness were assailed by fiery serpents, and how Moses made a serpent of brass and set it upon a pole, 'and it came to pass, that if a serpent had bitten any man, when he beheld the serpent of brass, he lived'. In the Gospel of St John iii. 14–15, the brazen serpent becomes the symbol of the Crucified Christ. In the four spandrels of the Sistine Chapel ceiling (1512) Michelangelo depicted 'the miraculous deliverances of Israel', by David, Judith, Esther and the Brazen Serpent. In this drawing, made more than twenty years later, he returns to the theme.

Popp (20, p. 159) thought that the sketches might be connected with a project for frescoes in the Medici chapel, a suggestion which is stimulating, but cannot be proved. The only thing which is clear is the monumental character of the drawing; despite the tiny dimensions of the figures, the impression produced is that of over-lifesize forms. Berenson and Popp observed that one group in the upper sketch ('Assault of the Fiery Serpents') goes back to figures with similar movements in No. 46, and individual motives in the lower sketch ('Salvation through the Brazen Serpent') to figures with similar movements in No. 18. Parker (Cat., 65, p. 158) has pointed out that the two groups of figures on this sheet were 'in fact conceived by the artist as one . . . to form the left-hand portion of a larger composition'.

The manner in which a mass of human figures in this drawing is combined to form an entity of movement, was something entirely new in Renaissance art. Even Leonardo, in his 'Battle of Anghiari'—as we can see from copies and engravings—built up his composition out of individual plastic elements, but was unable to achieve a fusion of the details in the picture and thus to give organic unification to the whole, though he jotted down these possibilities in his notebooks. The present drawing is an incunabulum of a new manner, subsequently developed by El Greco as far as his late painting of the 'Opening of the Fifth Seal', and used by Rubens in his 'Fall of the Damned'. Stylistically, No. 88 is akin to drawings such as No. 81 and, as regards certain of the background figures, to No. 97; but it is equally clearly related to the throngs of figures in designs for the 'Last Judgement' (No. 98). We may thus date it about 1533.—On the *verso* is a slight sketch of a male torso.

Formerly in the Casa Buonarroti and in the Wicar, Lawrence, King William II of Holland, and Woodburn collections.

89. BACCHANAL OF CHILDREN. Red chalk. 10¾ × 15¼ in. (27.4 × 38.8 cm.) Windsor Castle, Royal Library (Cat. No. 431).

Presentation drawing for Tommaso de' Cavalieri, mentioned by Vasari (see text to No. 75).

The motive of the putti carrying the dead animal is freely adapted from an antique sarcophagus (reproduced by Egger-Hülsen in *Die römischen Skizzenbücher des Marten van Heemskerck*, Berlin, 1916, Vol. II, Plate 93, text p. 40; the relief itself is now in the British Museum). The putti playing around the wine-butt are inspired by a Roman sarcophagus relief at Pisa, and the one looking into the barrel is directly copied from it (see G. de Nicola, in *Rassegna d'arte*, 1917, p. 157). An engraving by Battista Franco (Bartsch, XVI, 45, dated 1549) shows the same sarcophagus. The young man asleep in No. 89 reappears in a painting by Battista Franco, as the dead Christ in his 'Entombment' (Lucca, Pinacoteca; see Fig. 17). Montelupo, who entered Michelangelo's service late in the summer of 1533, copied one or two groups of figures from No. 89 (Oxford, Ashmolean Museum, Cat. No. 410).

The meaning of this drawing has not yet been completely explained. The scene is laid in a cave, the back of which is shut off by a curtain. Eating, drinking and sleeping are represented. On the left, above the cauldron, hang a boar's head and a hare, while a sucking pig is about to be thrown into the pot; in the centre, a dead animal is being dragged up; four goblets are shown in the drawing, of which one, at the top on the right near the wine-barrel, is being filled by a putto in the most improper manner. There are two sleeping figures—a putto in the left bottom corner and a young man on the right. A putto is endeavouring to suck milk from the withered breast of an

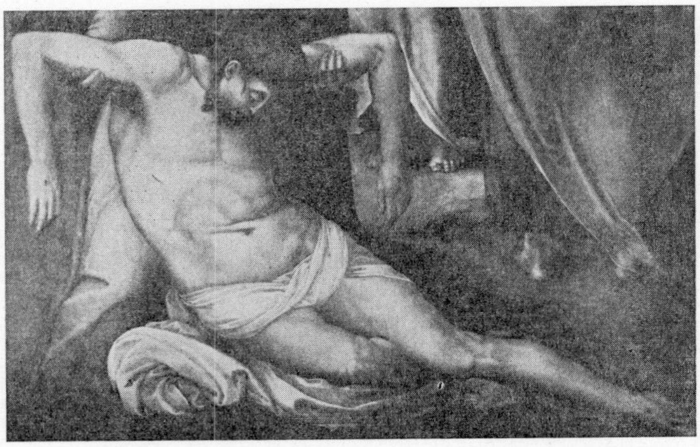

FIG. 17.—Battista Franco: Dead Christ, detail from 'Entombment'. Lucca, Pinacoteca.

aged Panisca. One of the boys on the left, standing with his hands on his knees, wears a mask. What this all means is not immediately clear, but we come a step further if we accept Panofsky's explanation, according to which this drawing symbolizes the lowest rung in the expression of human life, 'the sphere of purely vegetative existence, far below the real dignity of mankind' (Panofsky 47, p. 221 f.).

We may even arrive at a fuller interpretation if we bear in mind that a *Bacchanal* is here represented, that is to say, a drunken festival of love and wine, an orgy of excess wherein the bonds of shame are loosed. Savonarola says that 'all the activities of the intellect are confused and ruined by lewdness'; living sinfully 'suspends the working of all the spiritual forces, especially those of reason'. Are the personages in this drawing shown as children because their reason is undeveloped? Wine, which always plays the chief part in a Bacchanal, has a double meaning for Christians: it is a symbol of temptation and at the same time a symbol of salvation.[76]

No. 89 was formerly in the collections of Tommaso de' Cavalieri and Cardinal Alessandro Farnese.

90. UNFINISHED STUDY OF A HEAD. Black chalk. $8\frac{3}{8} \times 5\frac{5}{8}$ in. (21·2 × 14·5 cm.) Windsor Castle, Royal Library (Cat. No. 434 *recto*).

Here Michelangelo returns to a type of Madonna used by him in his early period, which received its most decisive stamp in the Bruges Madonna; the slit-shaped eyes, in particular, should be compared.[77] Michelangelo used probably a male model for this study.

In its technique the drawing agrees with No. 85, and still more with No. 96; we may date it about 1533.

According to Wilde, this drawing was perhaps intended as a gift for Cavalieri, but left unfinished.

Most scholars regard No. 90 as autograph; only Dussler, following Miss Popp, has rejected it. Sir Kenneth Clark suggested that it might be by Bugiardini.

The sketch of a female head on the *verso* is the work of a pupil.

91. THE FALL OF PHAËTHON. Black chalk. $12\frac{1}{4} \times 8\frac{1}{2}$ in. (31·3 × 21·7 cm.) London, British Museum (Cat. No. 55).

In the Allegory of the Sins (No. 97) 'Superbia' is omitted, which in Dante's *Inferno* is to be found in the lowest abyss of Hell.[78] The present drawing is an allegory of 'Superbia'.

The source of the composition is Ovid's *Metamorphoses* (I, 750; II, 400):

In his arrogance Phaëthon aspired to what no man could do, something which was reserved for the gods, namely, to drive the chariot of the sun for one day. He had an appetite for that which is forbidden. His father, Phoebus, in fulfilment of an oath he had imprudently made, granted his request. Phaëthon, through his rashness, brought misfortune upon the earth; and to himself, death, for the 'almighty father' struck him with a thunderbolt and hurled him into the river Eridanus.

The upper part of the drawing illustrates the following verses of Ovid (I, 319 f.): 'Phaëthon, fire ravaging his ruddy hair, is hurled headlong and falls with a long trail through the air; as sometimes a star from the clear heavens, although it does not fall, still seems to fall.' Below, we see the river-god Eridanus with his urn; the Heliades, Phaëthon's sisters, being changed into poplars, and Cycnus, his half-brother and friend, transformed into a swan.

Ovid's words, 'as sometimes a star from the clear heavens . . . seems to fall', reminds us of the fall of Satan, who was originally an archangel and 'Prince of Heaven' but rebelled against God—Lucifer, the morning star, which fell from heaven. 'How art thou fallen from heaven, O Lucifer, son of the morning!' (Isaiah xiv. 12); 'I beheld Satan as lightning fall from heaven' (St Luke x. 18); 'Lucifer, Prince of Hell, was created as a shining angel, but his pride and his rebellion against God were the cause of his fall' (annotation by Bishop Challoner to the Vulgate, Isaiah xiv. 12).

Shortly after finishing this drawing and before he began work on the 'Last Judgement', Michelangelo was thinking of making a Christian version of the fall of 'Superbia'. Vasari (VII, 204) relates: 'The Pope had also given him the task of painting on the entrance wall [of the Sistine Chapel] how Lucifer for his pride [superbia] was driven out of heaven and—together with all the angels who had sinned with him—cast into the depths of Hell. . . Michelangelo made sketches and several drawings for this composition.'

It never entered Michelangelo's mind to represent ancient myths for their own sake; all his presentation drawings made between 1530 and 1534 have a religious significance, clothed in the form of an antique allegory.[79]

No. 91 is a study for a presentation drawing for Tommaso de' Cavalieri (cf. text to Nos. 74 and 92). The writing on the lower edge is in Michelangelo's hand and says: 'Messer Tommaso, if this sketch does not please you, tell Urbino, so that I may have time to make another by tomorrow evening . . . as I promised; and if it pleases you and you want me to finish it, tell him so.' Francesco Urbino was Michelangelo's servant, whom he took with him to Florence, when he went back there for four months at the end of June, 1533. Urbino con-

---

[76] This double meaning is expressed in the clearest manner in the Greek Apocalypse of Baruch: 'I spake: Shew me the tree that once tempted Adam. The Angel spoke: This is the vine that the angel Sammael planted, wherefore God was angered and cursed it and its growth and forbade Adam to touch it. Then the Devil tempted him with his vine.' In the following verses we are told how Noah discovered the vine after the Flood, the waters of which had swept it out of the Garden of Eden, and how he, in obedience to the words of the angel Sarasael, planted it again: 'Then the Lord spoke: The bitterness of the vine is changed into sweetness, the curse upon it into blessing; for that which is won from it shall become the blood of God. . . . Even as Adam was once condemned on account of this plant, so it shall be with men today, if they drink of wine immoderately; for then they will all fall into sin worse even than that of Adam and will deliver themselves into eternal fire. . . . From wine come all evils such as murder, adultery and lewdness. . . .'
(This reference does not mean that Michelangelo could have read the Apocalypse of Baruch. It only shows the long-lived repertoire of symbolism.)

[77] *Ph. M.*, Plate 41.

[78] Arrogance, presumption, 'the root of all vices'. Cf. Hugo Delff, *Dante Alighieri und die Göttliche Komödie*, Leipzig, 1869, p. 140. Claudius Mino, in his commentary on Alciati's *Emblemata*, interprets the allegory of Phaëthon with the aid of quotations from numerous authors, among them Plato, Lucretius and Dio Chrysostomus (in the 1591 edition, p. 238 f.). A modern interpretation has been given by Erwin Panofsky, *Studies in Iconology*, New York 1939, p. 218 f.

[79] Wilde suggested that two sketches in the Casa Buonarroti (reprod. Barocchi, 66, Plates CCII and CCIII), originally studies for a 'Risen Christ', were in fact used for the Jupiter (Plates 91 and 92 respectively). The motives are indeed indentical, but so are those of the Christ in the studies for the 'Last Judgement' (Plates 99 and 100) or those of the Christ of the 'Expelling of the Money-changers' (Plates 118, 120–122). Michelangelo had a restricted repertoire of motives—of expressive movements made visible in human bodies—but he used his motives ingeniously.

FIG. 18.—(*a*) Detail from an antique marble group, called 'Hector and Troilus', formerly in the Farnese Collection, Rome (now Naples, Museo Nazionale, No. 150). From an engraving in F. Perrier's 'Segmenta nobilium signorum et statuarum', Rome 1638.
(*b*) 'Phaëthon', detail from Michelangelo's drawing, Plate 91.

veyed this first design for the 'Phaëthon' to Tommaso de' Cavalieri on his master's behalf before their departure for Florence.

After this Michelangelo made a second design (No. 92), which he executed only in part. An inscription in Michelangelo's handwriting, barely decipherable, seems to indicate that he was ready to make a third version. This final version (No. 93) is in the same format as the second (No. 92), but the execution is more complete than the first, sketch-like version (No. 91), though this does not imply that it is superior to it.

Tommaso de' Cavalieri acknowledges receipt of the drawing in a letter, dated 5 September 1533, to Michelangelo, who by that time was in Florence, and says: 'About three days ago I received my *Phaëthon*, which in every respect is well drawn; the Pope and Cardinal [Ippolito] de' Medici have seen it and everyone, I know not for what purpose, desires to see it. Cardinal de' Medici has asked to see all your drawings and they please him so well that he wishes to have the *Tityus* and the *Ganymede* cut in crystal.'[80]

No. 91 was formerly in the Crozat, Mariette, Lagoy, Dimsdale, Lawrence and Galichon collections.

92. THE FALL OF PHAËTHON. Black chalk. $15\frac{1}{2} \times 10$ in. (39.4 × 25.5 cm.) Venice, Accademia (No. 177).

Second version; not very well preserved.

See text to No. 91.

93. THE FALL OF PHAËTHON. Black chalk. $16\frac{1}{2} \times 9\frac{1}{4}$ in. (41·5 × 23·4 cm.) Windsor Castle, Royal Library (Cat. No. 430 *recto*).

Final version. See the text to No. 91.

On the *verso* is a red chalk drawing of a female half-length figure, a preparatory sketch for the 'Leah' of the Julius monument. (Not by Michelangelo; compare Uffizi Cat. No. 189.)

For the model for the *boy carrying a vase*, taken from an ancient Roman fountain in the Giardino Cesi, see *Die römischen Skizzenbücher von Marten van Heemskerck*, ed. Christian Hülsen & Hermann Egger, vol. II, Berlin 1916, pl. 85.

94–95. ERIDANUS AND THE HELIADES. Details of Plates 92 and 93.

No. 94 is a good example of Michelangelo's style when he limits himself to spontaneous, sketchlike indications. (Cf. the technique of Nos. 76–78, 87, or 98–100.)

No. 95 shows Michelangelo's work in completely finished presentation drawings. Beatrizet made a copper engraving after the Windsor version of 'Phaëthon'. About other copies of the final version, see Thode (3, 'Kritische Untersuchungen', vol. II, pp. 361 f.).

96. 'CLEOPATRA'. Black chalk. $9\frac{1}{8} \times 7\frac{1}{8}$ in. (23·2 × 18·2 cm.) Florence, Casa Buonarroti (Cat. No. 133 *recto*).

This is a well documented drawing. Vasari (in his *Life of Properzia de' Rossi*) mentions that Tommaso de' Cavalieri presented a 'Cleopatra drawing' to Duke Cosimo I; a fact which is confirmed by a letter from Cavalieri to the Duke, dated 20 January 1562 (see Paola Barocchi, 66, p. 164). Dussler pointed out that a 'Cleopatra' is listed in an Inventory of Michelangelo drawings in the Medici collections, which was compiled during the last years of Michelangelo's life. Many of the drawings named in that inventory were presented *c.* 1617 by Duke Cosimo II to the Casa Buonarroti, which at that time was being transformed into a museum.

In spite of the documentary evidence, most scholars regard No. 96 as a copy, though the best among a number of others (British Museum, Louvre, Boymans Museum). This rejection of the drawing is based on a hypercritical analysis of its 'quality'. Wilde and Barocchi regard No. 96 as the original. The drawing and No. 97 are on *a par* with the presentation drawings Michelangelo gave to Cavalieri in 1532–34.

No. 96 is pasted on paper-backing. Against the light one can see on the *verso* another female half-length.

97. 'THE DREAM OF MICHELANGELO'. Black chalk. $15\frac{5}{8} \times 11$ in. (39·6 × 27·9 cm.) London, Count Antoine Seilern.

As various critics have held Nos. 73, 74 and 81 to be *pasticci* or copies, it is not surprising that they also consider this drawing to be only a good copy.[81] To dismiss it as a *pasticcio* would hardly be possible, since it is well authenticated by an engraving of Beatrizet's (Passavant, VI, p. 119, No. 112, bearing the inscription MICHAEL ANGELUS INVEN).[82]

In addition to this there exist several copies in oil after this composition, the two best being those in the Uffizi and in the National Gallery, London.

If we want an explanation of the contents, we must first of all turn to Dante.[83] In his Hell we meet, in the second to the fifth

[80] By Giovanni Bernardi (Lippold, *Gemmen*, plates 138, 1; 144, 1). This lost engraving on crystal after the 'Phaëthon' was formerly in the Maffei collection. See Thode, V, p. 362, for the plaquettes, engravings and copies. He omits to mention a free copy by Frans Floris (reproduced by F. Winkler in *Flämische Zeichnungen*, 1948, p. 42). In his Life of Salviati Vasari says that in 1538 this artist executed Michelangelo's Phaëthon drawing in colour. See also Ludwig Curtius, in *Archaeologischer Anzeiger*, vol. 59–60, p. 12.

[81] Morelli, A. E. Popp, Frey, Dussler.—Berenson (1957) ascribed it tentatively to Marcello Venusti.

[82] Beatrizet's other engravings of the drawings in this cycle, viz., Tityus (Bartsch, XV, 39), the Bacchanal of Children (B. 40), Phaëthon (B. 38) and Ganymede (Passavant, VI, p. 119) have approximately the same format as 'The Dream'. Michele Lucchesi's engraving of 'The Dream' (Passavant, VI, 15) was not made direct from Michelangelo's drawing, but from Beatrizet's engraving.

[83] *Inferno*, Cantos V–VIII. The sequence of the sins in Dante is: Luxuria (Voluptuousness), Gula (Gluttony), Avaritia (Avarice), Ira (Anger) and Acedia (Sloth, Indolence of heart). Superbia (Vanity, Pride) is represented by the 'Fallen Angels' in Canto VIII.

a

b

c

The Rape of Ganymede.—(a) Roman stucco relief, about 100 B.C. Pompeii.—(b) Detail of a Michelangelo drawing, about 1504. Uffizi. (c) Copy of a lost Michelangelo drawing, 1532. Windsor.

Martyrdom of St Catherine. Painting by Bugiardini. Florence, S. Maria Novella.

circle, with the sinners who are undergoing punishment on account of their passions—the voluptuaries, the gluttons, the misers, the wrathful and, in the bottommost slime of the Styx, the indolent. All these have committed venial sins; the worst sins must be atoned for in the lower regions of Hell. In his *Convivio* Dante says of the sins of the passions that they all have their origin in intemperance; they are thus merely abuses of impulses which are harmless so long as they are held in check.[84]

These sinners from the upper circles of Hell form an arch around the awakening sleeper in the drawing we are discussing. Below on the left are the gluttons—a man turning a large bird on a spit, another waiting before an empty table, and a third drinking from a fat-bellied flask. Close to them are the carnal sinners—a naked couple on a bed, the man being smaller than the woman, a half-clothed figure rising from the bed, and a third figure, of which only the upper part of the body is visible, at the foot of the bed; behind this, a clothed couple kissing each other; in the background, heads and clouds.[85] On the right of the awakening sleeper are two hands, holding a purse; beneath, a man sucking his finger—avarice, and covetousness. Close by are two men attacking a third, who does not defend himself, and on the extreme right, a young man seizing an old man by his robe—anger. Below on the right, a group of three sleeping figures—indolence.

The youth in the middle of the drawing has been sleeping on a box-like seat, open at the front and containing numerous masks. These masks remind us of the mask of 'Night' in the Medici Chapel, where it symbolizes dreaming, and of those in the 'Venus and Cupid' (Appendix, Plate VI–b), which, following Cristoforo Landino's theory, express the false semblance and unreality of pleasure. The awakening sleeper has been resting his head on a large sphere, symbolizing the world; in the copies, a map of the world is painted on this sphere. The angel with the trumpet has just awakened the youth from his sleep.

The blowing of the trumpet is reminiscent of the 'Feast of Trumpets' (Joel ii. 15; Numbers xxix. 1), which Maimonides explains as signifying that the trumpets will awaken men from their spiritual slumber, to prepare them for the day of wrath and atonement before God.

Of the same date as our No. 97 is a tempera painting (now in the Louvre, No. 1118 B; painted about 1534 by Correggio for Isabella d'Este), called the 'Allegory of the Vices'. Here a female figure is blowing a flute into the ear of the sinner. Justi[86] gives the following platonic explanation of the drawing: 'The urge to create this representation of evil things, probably came from the last direction one would expect. According to Plato's dualistic theory of human nature, a base, animal element, having its roots in sensuality and licentiousness, is closely bound up with a spiritual, divine core. This base element is repressed, during the waking state of an ordered life, by consciousness and freedom, but during sleep it gains the upper hand. Its characteristics are folly and shamelessness, its symptoms murder and lewdness. But the chief of all the passions is Eros. . . . This platonic conception of the freeing of sensuality during dreams then became fused with the Christian idea of the death-sleep of sin. The worldly life of passion, amidst the impure flames of which one imagines that one is enjoying an enhanced existence, is in fact only a half-life. The rise of consciousness is therefore an awakening. . . . This awakening is here brought about by the blowing of a trumpet, the *mirus sonus* announcing the day of judgement.'

This platonic explanation coincides with that given in the Bible, where the sleeping state of sensuality is also contrasted with the waking state of consciousness. The drawing shows the moment of transition, when a loud sound—the voice of our hearts or the trumpet of the angel—summons us to awake from our drowsiness and pass judgement upon ourselves. Interpreted in this sense the drawing is, so to speak, the lyrical version of the theme, which Michelangelo soon afterwards depicted in dramatic form in his fresco of the 'Last Judgement'.

The content of the present drawing has points of contact with the ideas of the 'Spirituali', that religious association to which Cardinal Pole, Contarini, the poet Flaminio, Vittoria Colonna, the preacher Ochino and others belonged. Contarini finally evolved the formula of the twofold judgement ('duplex justitia'), of which the first part ('justitia inhaerens') consists in the moment *when Man*, inspired by the Holy Ghost, *becomes conscious of his sin* and turns to God, while the second part ('justitia imputata') is the justification by imputation, or justification through belief in the completeness of Christ's sacrifice upon the Cross. In the justification sense, which the explanations given above merely reduce to another formula, the 'Dream' illustrates the 'justitia inhaerens' and the Colonna Crucifixion (No. 107) the 'justitia imputata'.

Through his contacts with Cardinal Pole, and through his friendship with Vittoria Colonna, Michelangelo became familiar with the precepts of the 'Spirituali', which were gradually formulated and clarified between 1532 and 1542.

For the style of the figures in the background compare Plate 98.—The figures on the left have been reworked. In a copy of the drawing at Chatsworth, and in Beatrizet's engraving, those indecent details are clearly visible (Dussler, fig. 263; Tolnay V, fig. 306).

No. 97 was formerly in the Ottley, King William II of Holland and Robinson collections; and then in the private collection of the Grandducal Family, Weimar.

98. STUDIES FOR THE 'LAST JUDGEMENT'. Black chalk. $15\frac{1}{8} \times 10$ in. ($38{\cdot}5 \times 25{\cdot}3$ cm.) London, British Museum (Cat. No. 60 *recto*).

[84] Dante's definition of sin coincides with Plato's explanation of disease (in his 'Timaeus') as being due to 'a too much or a too little'. In this way he explains the urge towards 'licentiousness in the enjoyment of love', dejection, listlessness, etc. 'Incontinence in all pleasures' and 'wickedness' are, according to Plato, 'diseases of the soul', or, as he also puts it, afflictions of the soul, which have their origin in afflictions of the body.

[85] The representation of the sin of voluptuousness occupies a particularly large amount of space in this drawing. Savonarola, in a sermon which he preached on the second Sunday in Lent in the year 1496 in Florence Cathedral, said: 'The sin of fornication makes men blind. In the sensual portions of the soul there is no force which suspends to such a degree the activity of the other spiritual forces, especially those of reason, as the sense of touch during the sexual act. . . . You will find nothing which occupies the soul so much. The sexual urge is uncommonly strong, for it is given to all creatures for the preservation of their species, and as it operates in physical things, it draws all the senses towards them. Be not therefore surprised if the wanton become unbelievers, lose their natural judgement and defile all the activities of the intellect.' This sermon appeared in print in 1528.

[86] Carl Justi, *Michelangelo : Neue Beiträge*, Berlin 1909, p. 347 f. See also E. Panofsky, *Studies in Iconology*, New York 1939, pp. 223–225.

At the end of June 1533, Michelangelo, at the Pope's request, returned to Florence, to supervise the completion of the Medici tombs. At the beginning of November he went back to Rome. A few months later (the exact date is unknown) Pope Clement VII commissioned him to paint the 'Last Judgement' on the altar wall of the Sistine Chapel.[87] From June to September the preliminary work on the 'Last Judgement' was presumably interrupted, since Michelangelo was once more in Florence. He came back to Rome on 23 September 1534, two days before the death of Clement VII, but then devoted most of his time to continuing the work on the tomb of Julius. The drawings for the 'Last Judgement', of which only a limited selection is reproduced here (Nos. 98–103), were made partly in the spring of 1534 and partly during the winter of 1534–35, but in any case before 1 September 1535, since about this time (brief of Paul III: Gotti, II, p. 123) the cartoons for the painting had already been begun. Towards the end of April 1536, or a few weeks later, Michelangelo began the execution of the fresco, which was unveiled on 31 October 1541.
No. 98 is a design for the groups of the Martyrs and the mortal sins. Drawn in two kinds of chalk (soft and hard).
No. 102 is on the back of the sheet.
Formerly in various well-known collections, including those of Ottley, Lawrence and Galichon.

99. STUDY FOR THE 'LAST JUDGEMENT'. Black chalk. $13\frac{5}{8} \times 11\frac{1}{2}$ in. (34·5 × 29 cm.) Bayonne, Musée Bonnat (No. 1217).

The earliest of all extant drawings for this fresco. See text to No. 98.
Formerly in the Casa Buonarroti and in the Wicar and Lawrence collections.

100. STUDY FOR THE 'LAST JUDGEMENT'. Black chalk. $16\frac{1}{2} \times 11\frac{3}{8}$ in. (41·8 × 28·8 cm.) Florence, Casa Buonarroti (No. 65 F; Cat. No. 142 *recto*).

An early drawing, probably made in the spring of 1534. See text to No. 98.
Not quite perfectly preserved; the outlines of some of the figures have been overdrawn in ink.
Thode rightly drew attention to the fact that No. 99 is earlier than No. 100; whereas in the former the Apostles surround Christ, in this sketch the positions of the figures are nearer to those they occupy in the final version. The Virgin is given a more prominent position in the design and approaches Christ from the left (J. Wilde, in *Die Graphischen Künste*, new series, Vol. I, 1936, p. 7 f.).
On the *verso* is No. 84.

101. STUDY FOR THE 'LAST JUDGEMENT'. Black chalk. $9\frac{1}{2} \times 7\frac{1}{4}$ in. (24·3 × 18·3 cm.) Haarlem, Teyler Museum (No. 13 *recto*).

A relatively late study for the St Lawrence, drawn probably in the winter of 1534. See text to No. 98.
Knapp (in his first supplement to Frey's work), Thode, Berenson, Steinmann and Johannes Wilde support the authenticity of this drawing; Brinckmann is doubtful and Panofsky (*Repertorium für Kunstwissenschaft*, XLVIII, 1927, p. 43) rejects it. In technique and quality it is akin to No. 102.

[87] E. Steinmann, *Die Sixtinische Kapelle*, vol. II (Munich 1905), p. 479.

On the back is a sketch of a man's back and legs.
Formerly in the collections of Queen Christina of Sweden, Cardinal Azzolino, Prince Odeschalchi, and the Duke of Bracciano.

102. STUDY FOR THE 'LAST JUDGEMENT'. Black chalk. $10 \times 15\frac{1}{8}$ in. (25·3 × 38·5 cm.) London, British Museum (Cat. No. 60 *verso*).

The two head studies were probably intended for the figure of the Good Thief. A relatively late drawing. See text to No. 98 (which is the *recto* of this sheet).

103. STUDY OF A TORSO AND A RIGHT ARM. Black chalk. $15\frac{3}{4} \times 11\frac{1}{4}$ in. (39·8 × 28·2 cm.) Florence, Casa Buonarroti (69F; Cat. No. 143 *recto*).

Panofsky (*Festschrift für Julius von Schlosser*, 1927, p. 150 f.) took the sketches on the back as his starting-point and dated the whole sheet from the time of the 'Last Judgement', i.e. about 1534. Thode had already pointed out that 'the arm on this sheet reminds us of many of the arms in the *Last Judgement*'—e.g. the arm of Christ is similar, although inverted as if seen in a mirror. This study of an arm was connected with the arm of the 'Angel holding the sponge soaked in vinegar' in the right lunette of the fresco (Panofsky, Dussler).
The torso in No. 103, or a similar drawing, was used for the sleeping soldier at the utmost right in No. 81; but the Christ in Sebastiano's *Pietà of Ubeda* (Appendix, Plate III–b, 1534–37) is so close to it that we can assume that Sebastiano, too, made use of this drawing of Michelangelo's.
A related drawing in the Louvre (BB. 1586) which, in 1951, I described as by Michelangelo, is, as I believe now, a copy with variations, possibly by Sebastiano del Piombo; it was in fact attributed to him by Panofsky, Achiardi, Dussler, Palluchini, Tolnay, and Perrig.
The sketches on the *verso* of No. 103—a large head, a running man seen from the back, etc.—are by Michelangelo's hand.

104. THE SACRIFICE OF ISAAC. Black chalk. $16\frac{1}{4} \times 11\frac{3}{8}$ in. (40·8 × 28·9 cm.) Florence, Casa Buonarroti (70F; Cat. No. 140).

The drawing was begun in hard chalk and continued in a softer chalk. There are numerous *pentimenti* and traces of red chalk; some lines have been worked over with the pen.
Various dates have been suggested for this drawing—Thode, about 1530; Berenson, about 1535; Dussler, 1545–50. It cannot be much later than Nos. 92 or 103.
The technique of the figure of Isaac reminds us of the 'Risen Christ' in the Louvre (Plate 80). The Angel was used again by Michelangelo in his 'Annunciation' drawing in London (Plate 114) and he employed the same style; but despite these resemblances the London drawing with its flickering and vibrant figures must be at least ten years later.
Baumgart (Bollettino d'Arte, XXVIII, 1934), who ascribes No. 114 to Daniele da Volterra, suspects that No. 104 might also be by him. Both drawings are characteristic of a certain Mannerism of Michelangelo's, which was readily appropriated by Daniele and other imitators of the Master.

105. MOURNING WOMEN AT THE FOOT OF THE CROSS. Black chalk. $8\frac{1}{4} \times 5\frac{5}{8}$ in. (21·1 × 14·2 cm.) London, British Museum (Cat. No. 69).

FIG. 19.—Detail of a stucco, cast from a lost wax relief by Michelangelo. About 1540. Florence, Casa Buonarroti.

This drawing is of about the same date and in the same style as No. 104. According to Brinckmann it is a study for a group of figures of the stucco relief *Descent from the Cross* in the Casa Buonarroti (see Fig. 19).

Wilde's opinion that the relief is much earlier than the drawing is not the opinion of most other critics. Berenson dates the drawing about 1535, Frey 1538–40, and Dussler a little later. The stucco relief is generally dated about 1540. (Wilde dates it about 1524, and No. 105 after 1542.)

Panofsky and Baumgart ascribed No. 105 to Daniele da Volterra. But Berenson, Thode, Brinckmann, and Wilde regard it judiciously as a drawing by Michelangelo.

From the collections of Count Moriz Fries, Lawrence, Woodburn.

106. STUDIES FOR A CHRIST ON THE CROSS. Black chalk. $12\frac{1}{2} \times 8\frac{3}{4}$ in. (33·2 × 22·7 cm.) Haarlem, Teyler Museum (No. 22 *recto*).

Sketches for the earliest version of a 'Crucifixion', of which the finished original is lost.[88]

According to Tolnay, these sketches 'bear a close resemblance to a small bronze crucifix, attributed to Michelangelo—copy in the Metropolitan Museum, New York'.[89]

Tolnay dates the sheet about 1530–34; Wilde 1535–40; Dussler 1540 or a little earlier.

On the *verso* are two small sketches of a male figure, seen from the back (in black chalk); ten profiles of cornices (in red chalk); and an outline tracing of the crucified Christ from the *recto* (in hard black chalk; not by Michelangelo).

From the collections of Queen Christina of Sweden, Cardinal Azzolino, Prince Odeschalchi, and the Duke of Bracciano.

107. 'CRUCIFIXION' FOR VITTORIA COLONNA. Black chalk. $14\frac{1}{2} \times 10\frac{1}{2}$ in. (37 × 27 cm.) London, British Museum (Cat. No. 67).

Robinson (32, p. 87) discusses the copy of this drawing in Oxford without mentioning the original. There is another copy in the Louvre. Frey and Berenson believe that the present drawing is only a copy, but Thode maintains that it is the original. In more recent times only Johannes Wilde (41, p. 259) has accepted Thode's opinion.[90] In technique, it is close to the carefully executed drawings of the Cavalieri period (cf. especially No. 89), but the style in this case is more developed, in that the outlines are more sharply stressed and the shadows more subdued. Moreover, No. 107 actually belongs to a later period. Of the copious correspondence between Michelangelo and Vittoria Colonna only seven letters have been preserved, two of these being from Michelangelo; these letters are undated. In the latest letter from Vittoria Colonna to Michelangelo, we read beneath the signature: 'From the convent in Viterbo, on the 20th July.' Vittoria Colonna lived in the convent of Santa Caterina at Viterbo from the autumn of 1541 until the spring of 1544. The letter must be dated 1542, for in July 1543, the Marchesa was so ill that her life was almost despaired of, and in July 1544, she was no longer in Viterbo. As the letter mentions the frescoes in the Cappella Paolina, which were begun in 1542, we have a *terminus a quo* for the letter. The other letters were written from Rome, and may be dated between 1539 and 1541.[91]

The above-mentioned correspondence between Michelangelo and Vittoria Colonna includes the following letters:

(1) Letter written by Vittoria Colonna from Rome. She asks Michelangelo to send her the Crucifixion for a short time, even if it is not quite finished.

(2) Letter from Michelangelo to Vittoria Colonna. The Marchesa has returned the Crucifixion to Michelangelo by the hand of Tommaso de' Cavalieri. At the time of writing she was in the convent of San Silvestro al Monte, not far from Michelangelo's house in the Macel dei Corvi at Rome.

(3) Letter from Vittoria Colonna to Michelangelo. The Marchesa has received the finished drawing of the Crucifixion; she would prefer to keep this original rather than exchange it later for a painting made by an assistant; she says that she has examined the drawing

[88] Two copies are known—Windsor Castle (Cat. No. 460) and Louvre (Thode No. 495).

[89] Tolnay V, p. 173, and figs. 327–328.

[90] Tolnay believes that only parts of the drawing could be by Michelangelo; and in even those parts he can see an 'uncertainty of outlines', which would be against a judgement in favour of the drawing. Dussler considered carefully all the pros and cons, and withheld his own decision.

[91] We have proof that Vittoria Colonna was in Rome from March 1539, to March 1541 (Frey, 48, pp. 529–530, Itinerary of Vittoria Colonna; cf. *Carteggio di Vittoria Colonna*, ed. E. Ferrero and G. Müller, Turin, 1889). In June 1544, she was again in Rome, where she died on 25 February 1547, in the convent of Sant'Anna dei Funari.

with a magnifying glass and with the aid of a mirror, and found it perfectly finished.[92]

(4) Letter from Michelangelo to Vittoria Colonna. He sends this letter by the hand of his servant Francesco Urbino and acknowledges receipt of a present from Vittoria Colonna.

(5) Letter from Vittoria Colonna to Michelangelo. She mentions a painting of a Christ, and thinks that the angel on the right of the Saviour is finer than the one on the left. Frey relates this part of the letter to the following passage from Condivi's biography: 'He made, at the request of this lady [Vittoria Colonna], a nude Christ taken down from the Cross, who, as a dead body bereft of life, would have fallen at the feet of His most holy mother, had He not been supported in the arms of two little angels. And she, sitting, with a tearful and grievous countenance, at the foot of the Cross, with her arms apart, raises both her hands to heaven with this lament, which may be read, written on the trunk of the cross: "They think not how much blood it costs"—non si pensa quanto sangue costa.' The *Colonna Pietà* is probably identical with a drawing in the Isabella Stewart Gardner Museum (Plate 108). A list of the engravings (dated 1546 and 1547; cf. Appendix, Plate II–c) and painted copies is given by Thode (V, p. 493 f.). Benedetto Varchi, in his funeral oration for Michelangelo, mentions another present which the master made to Vittoria Colonna—'the statue of a nude Christ, similar to the Minerva Christ, but executed in a different manner'. This cannot have been a sculptured version of the Pietà we are discussing; on the other hand, we must remember a passage in Condivi's biography, where he is describing the Pietà in Florence Cathedral: 'Christ falls lifeless with all his limbs relapsed, but in an attitude very different from that which Michelangelo made for the Marchioness of Pescara, and from that of the 'Madonna della Febbre' (the Pietà of 1499 in St Peter's). As it is unlikely that Condivi would have compared two sculptures with one drawing, we may assume that Michelangelo executed the Colonna Pietà also in marble, probably as a relief (the replica of a relief by the hand of a pupil in the Vatican Library seems to point to this).
Thode assumes (on the basis of a letter written by the Bishop of Fano) that Vittoria Colonna presented the Pietà to Cardinal Pole in 1546.[93] Pole returned to England in 1554, and such Italian works of art as he brought with him were probably installed in Lambeth Palace, but no trace of Michelangelo's Colonna Pietà has ever been found. There is one copy in England, not mentioned by Thode, in the collection of the Earl of Pembroke, at Wilton House. The frame suggests that this copy came from France.

From the text of the letter mentioned it is not quite clear, however, whether the Marchesa di Pescara was asking for a second version or whether it was already in her possession. The text is reproduced in a study of Vittoria Colonna by Prof. A. Luzio (in *Rivista Stor. Mant.*, I, p. 51 f.) and by Karl Frey (*Michelagniolo Buonarroti, Quellen und Forschungen*, I, 1907, p. 139). In translation the text runs as follows:

'The Bishop of Fano to the Cardinal Ercole Gonzaga.

Trento, 12 May 1546.

'My lord Pole, having heard that your lordship desired a Christ by Michelangelo's hand, charged me to find out secretly if such was the case, because he happens to have one from that master which he would willingly send you; but it is in the shape of a Pietà, although the whole figure is seen. He says it will be no deprivation to him, because he can get another from the Marchesa di Pescara. Will your lordship write to me about it?'

Thus the document itself does not indicate whether it was a cartoon, a drawing, a painting or a relief, or whether two versions were available; or, lastly, which of the three persons remained in possession of the original—Vittoria Colonna, Cardinal Pole, or Cardinal Ercole Gonzaga.
Michelangelo's acquaintance with Pole is important because it enables us to interpret the deeper meaning of the Pietà (and of drawing No. 107). Pole had quarrelled with his sovereign, Henry VIII of England, over religious matters, and the King, who had not spared More and Fisher, made repeated attempts to have him eliminated by hired assassins. The family of Pole had to atone instead; his brother and cousin were executed for high treason, and on 27 May 1541, his mother, who was seventy-six years old, was beheaded in the Tower by order of the King. Thus the inscription on the Pietà—'They think not how much blood it costs'—acquires a new significance. The words are taken from Dante;[94] the lines which follow them have an obvious relationship to the ideas of the 'Spirituali' (to whom Pole, Vittoria Colonna, Contarini, Bishop Giberti, and others belonged), and to their efforts to restore the purity of the Church. 'I see thy little bark, O Peter, so laden with mire that it is in peril of sinking before the first onset of the waves', are the opening words of one of the Marchesa's sonnets.
In 1542, the year in which the Pietà was probably created, Cardinal Pole was residing in Viterbo as papal governor of the city; Vittoria Colonna was in a convent

[92] What she means by 'with the aid of a mirror' is not quite certain. Painters often use mirrors to detect errors of draughtsmanship, which show up more clearly when the picture is inverted. Apart from that, mirrors are used only in order to obtain a concentration of light. I would remind the reader of the following passage in the ninth chapter of Adalbert Stifter's *Nachsommer*: 'I fetched a magnifying glass and with the aid of a mirror we directed a shimmering light onto the spot; I looked at it through the glass and saw the fine crystals of the white marble sparkling before my eyes.'

[93] Thode, V, p. 494; Frey, *Quellen und Forschungen*, p. 139; M. Haile, *Life of Pole*, 1910, p. 323.

[94] *Paradiso*, XXIX, 91 (Thode, V, p. 494 f.). 'They think not how great the cost of blood to sow the scripture in the world, and how he pleases who humbly keeps by its side. Each one strains his wit to make a show and plies his inventions; and these are handled by the preachers and the Gospel left in silence. . . . Fables are proclaimed from the pulpit on this side and on that . . . Christ said not to his first assembly: "Go and preach trifles in the world", but gave to them the true foundation; that, and that only, sounded on their lips. . . . Now they go forth with jests and with grimaces to preach, and if loud laughter rise, the hood inflates and no more is required. But such a bird is nesting in the hood-tail that if the crowd should see it, they would see what indulgence they are trusting in.'

there, and around these two a group of adherents professing the same ideas soon gathered. Spiritually Michelangelo was a member of this group.

The Colonna Crucifixion, although drawn about 1540 and thus somewhat earlier than the Pietà, is animated by the same ideas. Here 'Justification through faith in the completeness of Christ's sacrifice on the Cross' is represented, in accordance with the formula evolved by Pole's friend, Cardinal Contarini, in April 1541, but known to the circle of the 'Spirituali' long before. In the *Beneficio di Cristo Crocifisso* (which was printed for the first time in 1542 and soon afterwards placed on the Index) we read that we shall find forgiveness for our sins so long as we faithfully cherish the sacrifice of Christ in our souls, and that only through His sinlessness can we find forgiveness for our own sins. Justification through faith 'is a work of God in us by which our old man is crucified and we become a new creature'.

The interpretation we have endeavoured to give brings us to the conclusion that the Colonna Crucifixion is not merely a representation of the Crucified Christ—slightly differentiated in that Christ is here shown with open eyes, alive, as the victory of life over death—but that it was conceived in the atmosphere of a particular religious idea and therefore has a very definite meaning. Michelangelo himself has spoken in similar terms in his poems: 'O flesh, O blood, O Cross, O agony of death, justify me and atone for my sin, in which I, like my father, was born'; or 'Dismayed, bewildered, within me my soul fears for its salvation. O Lord, in my last hour stretch out Thy merciful arms, take me out of myself and make me pleasing to Thee'; or again, 'All my travail is vain, if Thy blood help not mankind. Have mercy upon me, for I was born Thy bondsman'; and lastly: 'The soul cannot find peace in painting or sculpture; it seeks nought but the love of God, which opens its arms towards us from the Cross.'

(6) Letter from Vittoria Colonna to Michelangelo, dated 20 July (1542), from Viterbo. Vittoria asks Michelangelo to write less frequently, otherwise she will neglect her religious exercises and he his painting in the Cappella Paolina. She mentions a drawing (or perhaps a painting) which she has received from Michelangelo—'The Woman of Samaria at the Well'.[95] The original of this, too, has been lost. There is a list of engravings made from it (see Appendix, Plate II–d), and of copies in Thode (V, p. 464). The woman of Samaria who gave Jesus water to drink (St John iv. 7–9) although she knew that He belonged to a people who had no dealings with the Samaritans, symbolizes 'good works'. This reminds us of the advice given to Vittoria Colonna by Cardinal Pole, that she should order her life as if she could only be saved through deeds of mercy, but that she should think as if she could only be saved through faith.[96] Thus interpreted, 'The Woman of Samaria at the Well' is a counterpart to the 'Crucifixion'. There is, however, also a mystical interpretation possible, which would make 'The Woman of Samaria' a counterpart to the 'Pietà'. Both compositions symbolize everlasting life: the one as 'the living water', the other as 'the sacred blood' (St John iv. 13–14, and vi. 55).

(7) Letter from Vittoria Colonna to Michelangelo, undated, from Rome. Contains only a very general, appreciative mention of Michelangelo's sculptures.

No. 107 was formerly in the collections of Vittoria Colonna, the King of Naples, Brunet, Lawrence, King William II of Holland, Woodburn, Brooks (Liverpool), Malcolm.

108. 'PIETÀ' FOR VITTORIA COLONNA. Black chalk. $11\frac{1}{2} \times 7\frac{3}{4}$ in. (29·5 × 19·5 cm.) Boston, Isabella Stewart Gardner Museum.

See the note on No. 107.

The drawing is accepted as authentic by Tolnay (Vol. V, p. 194 f.), who points out that it is 'badly damaged, cut, mounted, frayed around the edges, and three toes of Christ's left foot are patched'. The whole background, top and bottom has also been reworked. Dussler thinks that it is only a copy; one of his arguments is that the crown of thorns is missing—but it is only invisible in Tolnay's reproduction (Vol. V, fig. 159), not in the original.

For a list of copies see Tolnay, *Record of the Art Museum, Princeton University*, 1953, p. 44 f. For a reproduction of Bonasone's engraving see Appendix, Plate II–c.

From the collections of Brunet, Lawrence, Woodburn, Palgrave, Charles Robinson.

109. THE HOLY FAMILY ('MADONNA DEL SILENZIO'). Red chalk. $14 \times 11\frac{1}{4}$ in. (38·2 × 28·5 cm.) London, The Duke of Portland.

Regarded as authentic by Popham, Wilde, Cecil Gould,[97] Tolnay, and by Dussler, who suggested that it was possibly a presentation drawing for Vittoria Colonna.[98]

A famous composition, which, even in Michelangelo's lifetime, was often reproduced in etchings and oil-paintings.[99]

Formerly in the Casa Buonarroti, and in the collections of Wicar, Lawrence, Woodburn, and King William II of Holland.

110. THE VIRGIN BENEATH THE CROSS. Black chalk. 9 × 4 in. (23 × 10 cm.) Paris, Louvre (No. 720 *recto*).

This study and the following one were used for an elaborated version of the 'Colonna Crucifixion', painted by Marcello Venusti for Tommaso de' Cavalieri (Thode V, p. 469). A copy of this kind is now in the Galleria Borghese, Rome (No. 422) and there is another one in the Uffizi (see Appendix, Plate II–b).

On the *verso* of the sheet is a sketch for the same figure, but drawn from a male model.

Drawings Nos. 110 and 111 are much cut on all four sides.

Formerly in the Coypel collection.

[95] There is a sonnet on the Woman of Samaria by Vittoria Colonna. (D. Tordi, *Sonetti inediti di Vittoria Colonna*, Rome 1891). Michelangelo certainly knew this poem.

[96] *Estratto del Processo di Pietro Carnesecchi*, ed. G. Manzoni, in *Miscellanea di Storia Italiana*, Vol. X, 1870, p. 269.

[97] In the Burlington Magazine, September 1951, p. 279 f.

[98] I reproduced this sheet as Plate 137 in the first edition of my *Michelangelo Drawings*, in Spring 1951, and called it 'doubtful'. I saw it again in the British Museum Exhibition of 1953, and have no doubts any longer—it is an autograph drawing.

[99] For a list of those etchings, see Thode V, p. 435; for a list of painted copies and versions, see C. Gould, *National Gallery Catalogue*, 1962, *The Sixteenth Century Italian Schools*, p. 102.

111. ST JOHN BENEATH THE CROSS. Black chalk. 10 × 3¼ in. (25·5 × 8·4 cm.) Paris, Louvre (No. 698).

See note to No. 110.

112. FRAGMENT OF A CARTOON FOR THE 'CRUCIFIXION OF ST PETER'. Charcoal, black chalk and washes. 103½ × 61½ in. (263 × 156 cm.) Naples, Museo Nazionale di Capodimonte (No. 398).

The cartoon shows the figures in the left bottom corner of the fresco 'Crucifixion of St Peter' (in the Cappella Paolina in Rome) which was begun in 1545. (See Baumgart & Biagetti, 8, pl. XXXVII.)
The outlines in No. 112 are pricked for transfer. This is the only extant cartoon for a fresco by Michelangelo. Berenson's vaguely indicated doubts as to its authenticity are not justified. It is, however, true that the cartoon has been repaired and in parts restored; but it is unlikely that this restoration was done by Daniele da Volterra.
(See E. Steinmann, *Cartoni di Michelangelo in* 'Bollettino d'Arte', ser. 2a, *anno* V, 1925–26, p. 11 f.)
Formerly in the collections of Fulvio Orsini, the Farnese family, the King of Naples (1759), the National Gallery of Naples. In June 1957 the cartoon was transferred to the *Pinacoteca Reggia di Capodimonte*, together with all the pictures belonging to the Museo nazionale, Naples.

113. THE VIRGIN OF THE ANNUNCIATION. Black chalk. 13⅞ × 9¼ in. (34·8 × 22·4 cm.) London, British Museum (Cat. No. 71 *recto*).

Nos. 113 and 114 are fragments of the same large sheet as has been noticed by Professor Wilde. The sheet was folded in half and cut (probably by Michelangelo himself). The Angel of the Annunciation is now on No. 114 *verso*, whereas his right hand can be seen on No. 113 *recto*, above the left arm of the Virgin.
Vasari[100] relates that Tommaso de' Cavalieri commissioned Marcello Venusti to paint an 'Annunciation', from Michelangelo's designs, for the Cesi Chapel[101] in the church S. Maria della Pace in Rome, and that Venusti painted also another version of the 'Annunciation' for the church San Giovanni in Laterano.
'The cartoon [for this second version], by Michelangelo's own hand, was presented to Duke Cosimo by Leonardo Buonarroti [nephew of Michelangelo], together with other designs', adds Vasari.
This cartoon, for the painting in San Giovanni in Laterano, is perhaps identical with the one in the Uffizi, attributed there to Marcello Venusti (see Paola Barocchi, 66, 1962, Cat. No. 197, p. 245). Delacre (1938) and Wilde (1959) are agreed that the cartoon in the Uffizi is by 'Michelangelo's own hand'; but this judgment was not acclaimed by Dussler, Tolnay, and Barocchi.
The cartoon for the first version of the 'Annunciation' in S. Maria della Pace is by most critics also regarded as a work by Marcello Venusti, in spite of Delacre and Wilde who described it as an original by Michelangelo.[102]
Pietro d'Achiardi (*Sebastiano del Piombo*, Rome 1908, p. 319) attributed No. 113 to Sebastiano del Piombo. F. Baumgart (in 'Bolletino d'Arte', XXVIII, 1934, p. 346 f.) attributed No. 114 to Daniele da Volterra. None of the later writers on Sebastiano or on Daniele da Volterra has consented to those views. No. 113 was formerly in the Casa Buonarroti, and in the collections of Wicar, Lawrence, Woodburn, and Miss K. Radford (who presented the drawing in 1900 to the British Museum).

114. THE ANNUNCIATION. Black chalk. 11⅞ × 7½ in. (28·3 × 19·6 cm.) London, British Museum (Cat. No. 72 *recto*).

Fragment of a large sheet (see note on No. 113).
No. 114 was formerly in the Casa Buonarroti, and in the collections of Wicar, Lawrence, Woodburn, and Malcolm.

115. APOSTLE, HOLDING A BOOK. Black chalk. 7 × 5¼ in. (18 × 13·6 cm.) Haarlem, Teyler Museum (No. 18 *recto*).

The figure of the Apostle is drawn over various architectural sketches. Marcuard, Thode, and Berenson thought that these architectural designs had some connection with Michelangelo's work for the building of St Peter's and that the figure on this sheet was intended for the decorations on the inside of the cupola. (This idea has since been given up, but may be well worth to be reconsidered.)
The broad band across the page is the sketch for a cornice. At the top, in the left corner, is a faint sketch for the upper part of the Apostle. Below (upside down) are two outlines of a figure hastening forward.
The present reproduction is in actual size but not quite complete—omitting parts on the left and at the top. (The reproduction in Dussler's book is larger than the original.)
No. 116 on the *verso* of the sheet.
Formerly in the collections of Queen Christina of Sweden, Cardinal Azzolino, Prince Odeschalchi, and the Duke of Bracciano.

116. AENEAS AND DIDO. (*Verso* of No. 115.)

The figures are drawn over various architectural sketches. Daniele da Volterra made use of No. 116 when he painted this scene for Giovanni della Casa. H. Voss (in *Kunstchronik*, new series, 34, 1923, p. 375 f.) published a picture in a Swedish private collection, claiming that this was the rediscovered painting by Daniele da Volterra.[103] J. Wilde (in *Belvedere*, 1927, p. 142 f.) connected Daniele da Volterra's *Aeneas and Dido* with the present Michelangelo drawing.
The scene represented in No. 116 is based on Virgil's *Aeneid* (IV, 259 f.): Jupiter sends Mercury to Carthage to bid Aeneas to leave Dido and sail to Italy.
The herculean figure in the foreground of the drawing is

[100] Vasari-Milanesi VII, p. 272 and p. 575.
[101] The chapel was commissioned by Agnolo Cesi and completed by his brother Federigo, who was appointed cardinal in 1544. (This date is the *terminus a quo* for the drawings 113 and 114. The *terminus ad quem* is probably 1549 when Venusti became very busy, copying Michelangelo's 'Last Judgement' and preparing cartoons for frescoes.)

[102] See Delacre (8, p. 197), fig. 93 (which is reproduced after plate 65 in: A. Woodburn, *The Lawrence Gallery: A series of facsimiles of original drawings by Michelangelo*). Johannes Wilde identified this cartoon with a black chalk drawing in the Pierpont Morgan Library, New York, and published it as fig. 1 in his article 'Cartonetti by Michelangelo' in Burlington Magazine, November 1959, pp. 370–381.
[103] S. H. Levie (*Der Maler Daniele da Volterra*, Cologne, 1962, p. 133 f.) has demonstrated that the picture in Sweden is only a copy. The original was painted in 1555–56.

FIG. 20.—Hans Sebald Beham: Cain murdering Abel. Woodcut, 1533.

FIG. 21.—Michelangelo: Battle scene. Detail of No. 118, about 1550.

Aeneas, taking off his tunic and handing it over to the servant boy; Dido is waiting in the background. Mercury has delivered his message and 'vanished into thin air . . . Aeneas aghast at the sight, was struck dumb . . . he turns to flee away and quit that pleasant land, awed by that warning and divine commandment' (Virgil).

Tolnay dates this drawing (*recto* and *verso*) about 1547; Berenson, about 1550; Wilde and Dussler, about 1556.

117. CARTOON FOR A 'HOLY FAMILY' (also called 'Epifania'). Charcoal and black chalk. 92 × 65 in. (233 × 165·5 cm.) London, British Museum (Cat. No. 75).

Vasari says of Condivi: 'He spent several years over a picture for which Michelangelo had given him the cartoon, and, at a word, the hopes conceived of him vanished in smoke. I remember that Michelangelo, having compassion on Condivi's hard labours, would sometimes help him with his own hands, but it was all to little purpose.'[104]

Daniele da Volterra, in a letter, dated 17 March 1564, calls the cartoon an 'Epiphany' and mentions Condivi's copy (now in the Casa Buonarroti; Thode III, 703, illustrated).

The figure of the 'speaker' (on the left[105]) is reminiscent of the *Baptist* in the 'Last Judgement' (22A, pl. XXXVII); but there are much stronger resemblances to figures in the Paolina frescoes.[106].

Tolnay believes that only the five figures in the foreground are drawn by Michelangelo, but the two weak heads in the upper left corner and the two heads in the background between the Madonna and St Joseph were added by Condivi. Wilde thinks 'there is no basis for this suggestion'.

[104] Vasari stayed in Rome from 1542 to 1544, and from 1550 to 1553 (W. Kallab, *Vasaristudien*, 1908, p. 87 f.). Daniele da Volterra, in a letter dated 17 March 1564, calls the cartoon 'Epifania' and mentions Condivi's painted copy (now in the Casa Buonarroti; illustrated in Thode III, p. 703). The cartoon was handed over to the notary who, after Michelangelo's death, wound up the estate; later on the cartoon was in the following collections: Fulvio Orsini, Cardinal Odoardo Farnese, Cardinal Silvio Valenti, Lucien Buonaparte, Lawrence, Woodburn, Malcolm.

[105] In an inventory, drawn up in 1600, the 'speaker' was identified with Giuliano. St Julian the Hospitaller was probably meant, but cannot be represented here, as this saint is usually depicted as a warrior holding a sword or as a knight with a hunting-horn in his hand. Berenson, who identified the figure with the Baptist, was probably right.

[106] *Ph. M.*, Plate 244.

118. STUDIES FOR A BATTLE SCENE (and Studies for 'Christ expelling the Money-changers'). Black chalk. $8\frac{1}{4} \times 9\frac{3}{4}$ in. (21 × 24·6 cm.) Oxford, Ashmolean Museum (Cat. No. 328 *recto*).

The battle group has been called, probably erroneously, 'Hercules and Cacus', and 'Samson battling with a Philistine'. This composition is related to the 'Last Judgement'; a similar figure with raised right arm appears, for example, in the London design (No. 98) in the group of the mortal sins. As Thode was the first to remark, the figure of the victor is identical with the one in the background of the 'Dream' (No. 97; in the 'Ira' group, at the top on the right).

According to E. Panofsky,[107] the battle scene in No. 118 is derived from a scene in Hell by Signorelli (Orvieto Cathedral, about 1504). Signorelli's group, however, is not much different from Van Eyck's 'Cain slaying Abel' in the lunette above Eve on the Ghent Altar-piece. The prototype of both representations was probably a Bible illustration, and Michelangelo's immediate model may have been a woodcut by Hans Sebald Beham (1533)—Cain murdering Abel (see Fig. 20).[108] These relationships seem to point, not to a scene from the lives of Hercules or Samson, but to the representation of a sin—not of a heroic feat, but of murder.

No. 118 has been variously dated—between 1525 and 1556. A date near to 1550 appears to me now the most probable.

The upper right corner was cut out and a sketch for the 'Expulsion of the Moneychangers' inserted. (The motive appears connected with early studies for 'Hercules and Cacus', e.g. Casa Buonarroti, Cat. No. 10; Dussler fig. 216.)

On the *verso*: sketch of a leg and writing; not by Michelangelo. Formerly in the Casa Buonarroti, and in the Wicar, and the Lawrence collections.

119. DAVID AND GOLIATH. Two studies, reproduced in the actual size. Black chalk. New York, Pierpont Morgan Library (I, 32D and 32A).

[107] *Die Michelangelo-Literatur seit* 1914, in the 'Jahrbuch für Kunstgeschichte', 1923, figs. 1–2.

[108] Cain, here undistinguishable from Samson, swings an ass's jawbone on which a few teeth can be seen.

The Morgan Library possesses altogether four such sketches; the two reproduced here are the best. It is possible that the four small sketches are fragments from a large sheet (cut into parts, as were Nos. 118 and 123).
According to Vasari, Daniele da Volterra was commissioned by Giovanni della Casa[109] 'to make a clay model of *David* and then a painting from it, so as to show it from every side.'[110] Tolnay dates the sketches No. 119 'around 1542–45'; Daniele da Volterra's picture was painted 1555–56.
No. 119 was formerly in the Reynolds, Breadalbane, Leighton, and Fairfax Murray collections.

120. CHRIST DRIVING THE MONEY-CHANGERS FROM THE TEMPLE. Black chalk. $5\frac{1}{2} \times 6\frac{1}{2}$ in. (13·9 × 16·7 cm.) London, British Museum (Cat. No. 77 *recto*).

There are three sketches for this composition in the British Museum (Cat. Nos. 76–78; with sketches for the same composition on the backs of the sheets); and there is another small sketch in the Ashmolean Museum (see Plate 118). A painting in the National Gallery, London, 'The Purification of the Temple',[111] rightly attributed to Marcello Venusti, is based on Michelangelo's drawings (see Fig 22).
From the time of Savonarola to the Council of Trent and the Counter-reformation, the purification of the church was an urgent request of orthodox Catholics in Italy, passionately discussed in the circle of the 'Spirituali' (see a paragraph in the note to No. 107, p. 60).
Nos. 120–122 went through the collections of the Casa Buonarroti, Wicar, Lawrence, King William II of Holland, and Woodburn.

121. CHRIST DRIVING THE MONEY-CHANGERS FROM THE TEMPLE. Black chalk. $5\frac{3}{4} \times 10\frac{7}{8}$ in. (14·8 × 27·6 cm.) London, British Museum (Cat. No. 76 *recto*).

See note on No. 120.
The page contains two sketches for the same composition. The smaller sketch, on the right, shows only Christ, three or four other figures, and one table.
On the *verso*—sketches for the same composition, and for the architectural background belonging to it.

122. CHRIST DRIVING THE MONEY-CHANGERS FROM THE TEMPLE. Black chalk. $6\frac{3}{4} \times 14\frac{5}{8}$ in. (17·8 × 37·2 cm.) London, British Museum (Cat. No. 78 *recto*).

See note on No. 120.
This sheet, consisting of six pieces of paper pasted together, represents the final version of the composition, and was used by Venusti for the figures in his painting in the National Gallery (see Fig. 22).

123. STUDIES FOR A PIETÀ, AND FOR AN ENTOMBMENT. Black chalk. $3\frac{1}{4} \times 11\frac{1}{16}$ in. (10·8 × 28·1 cm.) Oxford, Ashmolean Museum (Cat. No. 339).

FIGS. 22–23.—Paintings by Marcello Venusti, after drawings by Michelangelo.—(22) 'The Purification of the Temple' (Detail). London, National Gallery (Cat. No. 1194).—(23) 'Christ in Gethsemane', Vienna Museum.

The sketch on the extreme left shows the dead Christ held upright by the Virgin Mary. This sketch may have been used for the 'Rondanini Pietà'.[112] The sketch next to it is for a similar composition, but here the head of Christ is resting on his right shoulder, the right arm hanging down vertically, and the legs turned in the opposite direction. This sketch agrees with the 'Palestrina Pietà'.[113] The sketch on the extreme right is a version of the first one, as Dr Parker has noticed.[114]
The two sketches for a 'Deposition' (in the centre of the drawing) show the body of Christ carried to the tomb by two disciples. Whether this composition was drawn with a sculpture in mind, or a cartoon, is not known.
As Dr Parker has demonstrated (65, p. 177), the sheet containing No. 123 was originally about twice as large as it is now; a composition of 'Christ in Gethsemane' has been cut off.[115] Marcello Venusti made a painting of this composition. Copies of Venusti's painting can be seen in the Galleria Doria in Rome, and in the Vienna Museum (Fig. 23).
No. 123 was formerly in the collections of Ottley, Lawrence, and Woodburn.

---

109 About Daniele da Volterra's painting 'Aeneas and Dido', also commissioned by Giovanni della Casa, see note Plate 116.
110 Vasari-Milanesi VII, p. 61. It was Thode (VI, p. 163) who claimed that Daniele da Volterra used sketches by Michelangelo for the painting 'David vanquishing Goliath' (painted, 1555–56, on both sides of a slate slab. Formerly in the Louvre, No. 1462; now in the Château de Fontainebleau).
111 See Matthew xxi, 12–13; Mark xi, 15–17; John ii, 13–16.

112 First version, about 1553; second version, about 1555–56; third version in the last months before Michelangelo's death. (It was, during those ten or eleven years, one and the same block of marble that was used for all the alterations from the first to the third version.—*Ph. M.*, Plate 267.)
113 *Ph. M.*, Plate 268.
114 Over the left arm of Christ appear *two* heads. The second head is either a sketch for an alternative position of the head of the Madonna, or else it could be the head of Mary Magdalen (as it appears in the Palestrina Pietà).
115 Ashmolean Museum, Cat. No. 340.

124. CHRIST ON THE CROSS. Black chalk; with corrections in white chalk (oxydized). 11 × 9¼ in. (27·8 × 23·4 cm.) Oxford, Ashmolean Museum (Cat. No. 343 *recto*).

This drawing belongs to a group of compositions which show the *dead* Christ (not the Saviour alive, as in No. 108).
The body of Christ is about one quarter larger than the assistant figures and looks much heavier than in the later Crucifixion drawings (Nos. 126, 127).
There is no consensus about the interpretation of the assistant figures. The figure on the right[116] was explained by Robinson as the Virgin Mary, the figure on the left as St John. But according to tradition, St John ought to be represented on the right. Neither can the figure on the left be meant as a sketch of the Virgin, although Michelangelo often used male models for female figures. The figure on the left is of a herculean type, looking similar to the Apostle in No. 115 and even like Michelangelo himself.
Thode's interpretation of the figure on the left as the Holy Virgin was rejected by Dr Parker, who in his Catalogue of the Oxford drawings (65, p. 181) called this interpretation 'surely completely incredible.'[117]

[116] *Right* and *left* are referring to the *spectator's* right and left.
[117] In spite of Parker, Dussler accepts Thode's view. (Dussler, 70, pp. 128–129, No. 204.)

In 1951 I ventured the suggestion that the figure on the right was St John, and the other figure St Peter denying Christ as he hastens away. This suggestion found no favour with Dussler (1959); he called it 'absurd and not even worthy to be refuted.'
Tolnay's explanation is indeed much more plausible: 'In our opinion, the figure on the right which has a long mantle corresponding to the garments of the soldiers in the 'Crucifixion of St Peter' [of the Cappella Paolina fresco] could be Stephaton the centurion, and the figure on the left would be Longinus[118] (Tolnay 69, 1960, V. p. 224).
The difficulty of interpretation of the two assistant figures does not detract anything from the great impact of the drawing.
The *verso* study, also by Michelangelo, was first uncovered by Parker in 1953. It shows essentially the same figure as the one of Christ on the *recto*.
No. 124 was formerly in the Casa Buonarroti, and afterwards in the collections of Wicar, Lawrence, and Woodburn.

125. THE ANNUNCIATION. Black chalk. 8½ × 7½ in. (22·1 × 20 cm.) Oxford, Ashmolean Museum (Cat. No. 345).

[118] Alexander Perrig (71, 1960, p. 125) had the same idea and called the two flanking figures *Longinus and Stephaton.*

FIG. 24.—Crucifixion. Windsor (BB. 1622).

FIG. 25.—Crucifixion. Louvre (BB. 1583).

The note in the upper left corner, transcribed by Thode and containing the words 'Pasquino' and 'Casteldurante', provides a *terminus a quo* for the dating of this drawing. From 1556 on the widow of Michelangelo's servant Urbino lived in Casteldurante and Michelangelo used to send her messages by a muleteer whose name was Pasquino. The correspondence between Michelangelo lasted until 1561, and was particularly frequent about 1559 (cf. Frey, *Sammlung ausgewählter Briefe an Michelagniolo Buonarroti*, 1899, Nos. 351 f.).
The angel is of huge dimensions and is hovering just above the ground, as if he had tried to alight but was unable to do so—a *pentimento* of one leg resting on the ground is visible.
The visionary spirit of this drawing and the dissolution of forms are reminiscent of the Rondanini Pietà on which Michelangelo was working again at the same time.
Formerly in the Casa Buonarroti, and the Wicar, Lawrence, and Woodburn collections.

126. CHRIST ON THE CROSS BETWEEN THE VIRGIN AND ST JOHN. Black chalk; corrections in white wash (oxidized). $15\frac{3}{4} \times 8\frac{1}{2}$ in. ($40 \times 21{\cdot}6$ cm.) Windsor Castle, Royal Library (Cat. No. 437 *recto*).

According to Brinckmann the chronology of the Crucifixion drawings of the late period is as follows: (1) The present drawing; (2) Windsor Castle, Cat. No. 436; see Fig. 24; (3) Louvre, BB. 1583; see Fig. 25; (4) British Museum, Cat. No. 82; see Plate 127. The other version in the British Museum, Cat. No. 81, our No. 129, is evidently, in the opinion of Brinckmann, who does not mention it, only a variant of (1). In this connexion he remarks: 'Concerning the chronology of those drawings, there will doubtless be much discussion, which will lead to no results'. (Compare R. Wittkower, in *Burlington Magazine*, Vol. LXXVIII, 1941, p. 159 f.).
On the back of No. 126 is a leg study in black chalk, and the outline of a marble block.[119]

127. CHRIST ON THE CROSS BETWEEN THE VIRGIN AND ST JOHN. Black chalk. $16\frac{1}{8} \times 11\frac{1}{4}$ in. ($41{\cdot}2 \times 28$ cm.) London, British Museum (Cat. No. 82).

See the note on No. 126.
Numerous *pentimenti* and some re-touchings in white (oxydized).
Formerly in the Casa Buonarroti, and the Wicar, Lawrence, Woodburn, and Malcolm Collection.

128. VIRGIN AND THE INFANT CHRIST. Black chalk. $10\frac{1}{4} \times 4\frac{3}{4}$ in. ($26{\cdot}6 \times 11{\cdot}7$ cm.) London, British Museum (Cat. No. 83).

The figure is, according to Thode, derived from the Virgin in No. 127; he assigned the same date to both drawings.
This is probably the latest of all extant Michelangelo drawings.
Formerly in the Casa Buonarroti.

129. CHRIST ON THE CROSS BETWEEN THE VIRGIN AND ST JOHN. Black chalk. $16\frac{1}{8} \times 11\frac{1}{4}$ in. ($41{\cdot}3 \times 28{\cdot}6$ cm.) London, British Museum (Cat. No. 81).

Reproduced as Frontispiece.

See the note on No. 126.
Both the flanking figures reveal numerous *pentimenti* and vigorous retouchings over white washes (oxydized).
No. 129 is closest to the Louvre version (reproduced here as Fig. 25), but in No. 129 the Cross is Y-shaped, as in No. 126 which is earlier.
Formerly in the Casa Buonarroti, and in the collections of Wicar, Lawrence, King William II of Holland, Woodburn, and Malcolm.

---

119 'The shape of it exactly fits the silhouette of Christ on the *recto* and was drawn against the light by Michelangelo. It is probably the shape of the marble block from which he intended to make this crucifix. This observation explains the whole series of Crucifixion drawings as projects for a marble group' (Tolnay V, p. 230).
On the other hand, Wilde says (64, p. 120): 'We do not know whether the drawings were made with a painting in view', and connects one of the Crucifixion drawings with Venusti's picture (see Appendix, Plate II–b).
It seems that Michelangelo, while he made the series of Crucifixion drawings, had at one time a sculpture in mind, and at another time a cartoon; but the evidence for either assumption is insufficient.

BIBLIOGRAPHY
OF MICHELANGELO DRAWINGS

The following list of books and articles is intentionally kept concise, in order to help the student to find the most important titles first. Some further articles are quoted in the Catalogue of the present volume. There is a complete Michelangelo Bibliography in Vols. I and VIII of the *Römische Forschungen* of the Biblioteca Hertziana in Rome—*Michelangelo-Bibliographie* by E. Steinmann and R. Wittkower (1927), and a continuation by H. W. Schmidt in E. Steinmann's *Michelangelo im Spiegel seiner Zeit* (1930). For publications after 1930, see *Art Index*, New York, 1929 f.; and Cherubelli, *Supplemento alla bibliografia michelangiolesca*, 1931–1942. Florence, 1942. Bibliography from 1942 to the present in *Zeitschrift für Kunstgeschichte*, Munich; for literature after 1952 the *Annuario bibliografico* (Bibl. dell'Istituto nazionale d'archeologia e storia dell'arte, Rome).

I. COMPLETE CATALOGUES · REPRODUCTIONS

1. Karl Frey, *Die Handzeichnungen Michelagniolos Buonarroti*, 3 vols. Berlin, 1909–11. (Publication of 300 drawings in two volumes with one volume of critical text).

2. Fritz Knapp, *Erster Nachtragsband* (zu Frey's Corpus). Berlin, 1925. (First supplement, containing the Haarlem drawings.)

2A. *Zweiter Nachtragsband*. Berlin, n.d. (This second supplementary volume contains 45 plates without text.)

3. Henry Thode, *Michelangelo und das Ende der Renaissance*, 3 vols. (Vol. I, 1902; II, 1903; III, 1912). *Michelangelo, Kritische Untersuchungen*, 3 vols. (Vol. I, 1908; II, 1908; III, 1913). The last three are referred to as Thode IV-VI. Volume VI, the most important one for our purposes, is listed separately as the following item.

3A. Henry Thode, *Michelangelo, Kritische Untersuchungen über seine Werke*, Vol. III: *Verzeichnis der Zeichnungen, Kartons und Modelle*. Berlin, 1913. (A very full list with short notes, often contradicting Frey. This volume is identical with Vol. VI of the complete work—see No. 3.)

4. Bernard Berenson, *The Drawings of the Fiorentine Painters*, Amplified Edition, 3 vols. Chicago, 1938.

4A. Bernard Berenson, *I Disegni dei Pittori Fiorentini.* (Revised edition, edited by Nicky Mariano and Luisa Vertova-Nicolson.) 3 vols. Milan, 1961.

5. Michelangelo, *Disegni*. Istituto di edizioni artistiche, Fratelli Alinari. Florence, n.d. (1920 f.).

6. Erwin Panofsky, *Handzeichnungen Michelangelos*. Leipzig, 1922. (Twenty drawings with an excellent introduction.)

7. A. E. Brinckmann, *Michelangelo-Zeichnungen*. Munich, 1925. (Reproduces and discusses 83 drawings of which 15 are not by Michelangelo. The appendix contains 14 drawings which the author calls copies and imitations; but J. Wilde claims six of them for Michelangelo.)

7A. Anny E. Popp, *Review of Brinckmann's book*, in *Belvedere* (Forum), VIII, p. 72 f. Vienna, 1925.

8. Maurice Delacre, *Le Dessin de Michel-Ange*. Brussels, 1938. (With 324 illustrations.)

9. Charles Rogers, *A Collection of Prints in Imitation of Drawings*. London, 1778.

10. William Young Ottley, *The Italian School of Design*. London, 1823.

There are quite a number of *Selections from Michelangelo Drawings*, including those by O. Zoff, H. Leporini, etc.; of these only the volume by A. E. Popham (London, 1930) is of value for his charming descriptions of twelve drawings.

II. SINGLE PERIODS

11. Friedrich von Portheim, *Beiträge zu den Werken Michelangelos*, in *Repertorium für Kunstwissenschaft*, Vol. XII (1889), p. 140 f. (Contains, *inter alia*, the first attributions of the pen and ink drawings after Giotto and Masaccio to Michelangelo.)

12. Giovanni Morelli, *Handzeichnungen italienischer Meister . . .*, in *Kunstchronik*, new series III (1891–92) and IV (1892–93). (Contradicts von Portheim with regard to the attribution of the early pen and ink drawings to Michelangelo. Discusses the presentation drawings for Perini, etc.)

13. Heinrich Wölfflin, *Die Jugendwerke des Michelangelo.* Munich, 1891. (Discusses on pp. 61 and 85 f. a number of drawings.)

14. Wilhelm Köhler, *Michelangelos Schlachtkarton*, in *Kunsthistorisches Jahrbuch der Zentralkommission*, Vienna, 1907, pp. 115 f. (Discusses the drawings connected with Michelangelo's Battle Cartoon.)

14A. Carl Justi, *Der Carton* (a chapter on the lost 'Battle Cartoon', in his *Michelangelo, Neue Beiträge zur Erklärung seiner Werke*, pp. 151–172). Berlin, 1909.

15. Aldo Bertini, *Michelangelo fino alla Sistina*, 2nd edition, Turin, 1945.

16. Fritz Baumgart, *Die Jugendzeichnungen Michelangelos bis 1506* in *Marburger Jahrbuch für Kunstwissenschaft*, Vol. X (1937), p. 209 f. Also Separatum of 54 pp., Marburg, 1939.

17. Charles de Tolnay, *The Youth of Michelangelo*. Princeton, 1947. (With a Catalogue Raisonné of the drawings, of which he himself has published many for the first time.)

18. Ernst Steinmann, *Die Sixtinische Kapelle*, Vol. II. Munich, 1905. (A part also separately printed in folio under the title *Die Handzeichnungen Michelangelos*. Munich, n.d.)

19. Charles de Tolnay, *The Sistine Ceiling*. Princeton, 1945. (With a Catalogue of the drawings.)

20. Anny E. Popp, *Die Medicikapelle Michelangelos*. Munich, 1922.

21. Charles de Tolnay, *The Medici Chapel*. Princeton, 1948. (With a Catalogue of the drawings of about 1519–33, including the presentation drawings for Tommaso de' Cavalieri.)

22. F. Baumgart & B. Biagetti, *Gli Affreschi di Michelangelo . . . nella Cappella Paolina*. Città del Vaticano, 1934.

22A. A. D. Redig de Campos e B. Biagetti, *Il Giudizio universale di Michelangelo*, 2 vols., Rome, 1943.

III. MICHELANGELO DRAWINGS IN PUBLIC COLLECTIONS

FLORENCE, UFFIZI AND CASA BUONARROTI

23. *Album Michelangiolesco dei disegni originali; riprodotti in fotolitografia.* Florence, 1875.

FLORENCE, UFFIZI

23A. Emil Jacobsen & Nerino Ferri, *Dessins inconnus de Michel-Ange, récemment découverts aux Offices de Florence.* Leipzig, 1905.

FLORENCE, ARCHIVIO BUONARROTI

24. Charles de Tolnay, *Die Handzeichnungen Michelangelos im Archivio Buonarroti*, in *Münchner Jahrbuch der bildender Kunst*, Vol. V (1928), p. 450 f.

HAARLEM, TEYLER MUSEUM

25. F. van Marcuard, *Die Zeichnungen Michelangelos im Museum Teyler zu Haarlem.* Munich, 1901. (Valuable only for the plates printed by Bruckmann; the notes by van Marcuard are of little use.)

26. Erwin Panofsky, *Bemerkungen zu der Neuherausgabe der Haarlemer Michelangelo-Zeichnungen durch Fr. Knapp* in *Repertorium für Kunstwissenschaft*, Vol. XLVIII, p. 25 f. Berlin, 1927.

26A. Johannes Wilde, *Zur Kritik der Haarlemer Michelangelo-Zeichnungen*, in *Belvedere* XI (1927), Heft 59, p. 142–147.

LONDON, BRITISH MUSEUM

27. Louis Fagan, *The Art of Michael Angelo Buonarroti in the British Museum.* London, 1883. (This volume is out of date. For the drawings in the British Museum one can only use Frey's text volume, Thode VI, and Berenson II, pp. 78–193, 230–232, 322–323. A complete catalogue of the Michelangelo drawings in the B.M. by J. Wilde and A. E. Popham, is in preparation.) See No. 64.

LONDON, BRITISH MUSEUM

28. *Descriptive Catalogue of the Drawings by the Old Masters, forming the Collection of John Malcolm*, by J. C. Robinson. London, 1869.

LONDON, BRITISH MUSEUM

29. *Drawings in the Collection . . . of T. Fitzroy Phillips Fenwick*, by A. E. Popham, London, 1935.

LONDON, BRITISH MUSEUM

30. Wolf Maurenbrecher, *Die Aufzeichnungen des Michelangelo Buonarroti im Britischen Museum*, etc., in *Römische Forschungen der Biblioteca Hertziana*, Vol. XIV. Leipzig, 1938.

LONDON, LAWRENCE COLLECTION

31. *A series of facsimiles of original drawings by M. Angelo Buonarroti selected from the matchless Collection formed by Sir Thomas Lawrence.* London, 1853. (Published by S. and A. Woodburn. The drawings are now in the Ashmolean Museum, the British Museum, the Louvre, and in Haarlem.)

OXFORD

32. *The Drawings by Michel Angelo and Raffaello in the University Galleries, Oxford*, by J. C. Robinson.Oxford, 1870. (With a very good introduction about the history of the drawings, a note on Battista Franco, and reproductions of 84 papermarks.)

OXFORD (*continued*)

32A. Joseph Fisher, *Drawings and Studies in the University Galleries, Oxford.* London, 1879.

33. *Drawings of the Old Masters in the University Galleries and in the Library of Christ Church, Oxford*, by Sidney Colvin. Oxford, 1903–07.

34. *Drawings by the Old Masters in the Library of Christ Church, Oxford*, by C. F. Bell, Oxford, 1914.

PARIS, LOUVRE

35. *Notice des dessins, cartons, pastels . . . au Musée National du Louvre; première partie: Ecole d'Italie*, etc., par Reiset. Paris, 1878.

35A. *Deuxième notice supplémentaire: Dessins, cartons . . . exposés depuis 1879 au Musée National du Louvre*, par Both de Tauzia, Paris, 1888.

36. Louis Demonts, *Les dessins de Michel-Ange* (au Musée du Louvre). Paris, n.d. (1922). (Demonts reproduces eleven drawings which he thinks genuine and five as doubtful. The publication is neither critical nor complete. See No. 50.)
There are two attractive old publications, the one also containing reproductions of a few Michelangelo drawings: '*Recueil de 283 estampes . . . d'apres les dessins de grands Maîtres, que possedoit autrefois Mr. Jabach.* Paris, Joullein, 1754.' This is actually a reprint of 286 engravings from drawings, issued in six folders between *c.* 1660 and 1670. The other publication on drawings, some by Michelangelo, which are now at the Louvre, is 'P. J. Mariette, *Description sommaire des dessins des grands maîtres d'Italie . . . du cabinet de feu M. Crozat.* Paris, 1741'.

VIENNA, ALBERTINA

37. Franz Wickhoff, *Die italienischen Handzeichnungen der Albertina*, in *Jahrbuch der Kunsthistorischen Sammlungen* XII and XIII (Vienna, 1891 and 1892).

38. *Albertina Catalogue III:* Alfred Stix and L. Fröhlich-Bum, *Beschreibender Katalog der Handzeichnungen in der Albertina: Die toskanischen, umbrischen und römischen Schulen.* Vienna, 1932.

39. *An Exhibition of Old Master Drawings from the Albertina.* (Catalogue by A. E. Popham.) London, 1948.

VIENNA, ALBERTINA

40. Facsimiles: (*a*) *Schönbrunner-Meder*, 12 portfolios, Vienna, 1896–1908; (*b*) *Joseph Meder, new series I.*, Vienna, 1922 (English edition, 1930); (*c*) *Alfred Stix, new series II.*, Vienna, 1925.

WINDSOR CASTLE, ROYAL LIBRARY

41. Johannes Wilde, *The Drawings of Michelangelo and his School, Sebastiano del Piombo, Daniele da Volterra, Baccio Bandinelli and Raffaello da Montelupo* (in A. E. Popham's 'The Italian Drawings of the XV and XVI centuries in the Collection of His Majesty the King at Windsor Castle'). London, 1949. (The most important contribution towards a critical understanding of Michelangelo's drawings as a whole.)

IV. CRITICAL NOTES · ICONOLOGY CHRONOLOGY

42. Otto Hettner, *Zeichnerische Gepflogenheiten bei Michelangelo* in *Monatshefte für Kunstwissenschaft*, Berlin, 1909.

43. (*a*) Franz Wickhoff, *Die Antike im Bildungsgange Michelangelos*, in *Mitteilungen des Instituts für österreichische Geschichtsforschung*. Vienna, 1882.
(*b*) Alois Grünwald, *Über einige Werke Michelangelos und ihr Verhältnis zur Antike*, in *Vienna Yearbook* (Jahrbuch der Kunsthistorischen Sammlungen des Allerhöchsten Kaiserhauses), Vol. 27, part 4, 1908.
(*c*) Anton Hekler, *Michelangelo und die Antike*, in *Wiener Jahrbuch für Kunstgeschichte*, VII, 1930, pp. 201–23.

44. Franz Wickhoff, *Abhandlungen Vorträge und Anzeigen* (herausgegeben von Max Dvořák). Berlin, 1913.

45. Anny E. Popp, *Bemerkungen zu einigen Zeichnungen Michelangelos*, in *Zeitschrift für bildende Kunst*, Vol. LIX (1925–26), p. 134 f. and 169 f.; also in Vol. LXI (1927–28) and Vol. LXII (1928–29).

46. Johannes Wilde, *Eine Studie Michelangelos nach der Antike*, in *Mitteilungen des Kunsthistorischen Instituts in Florenz*, Vol. IV, pp. 41–64. Augsburg, 1932.

47. Erwin Panofsky, *Studies in Iconology*. New York, 1939. (Discusses *inter alia* the presentation drawings for Tommaso de' Cavalieri.)

48. Karl Frey, *Die Dichtungen des Michelagniolo Buonarroti*. Berlin, 1897. (A large number of drawings are described, dated and discussed in the commentary, pp. 281–501. The 'register' at the end of the book contains several documents which can be taken as a basis for the chronology of the drawings.)

49. Henry Thode, *Michelangelos Gedichte* (German translation). Berlin, 1914. (The commentary, pp. 259–279, dealing mainly with the chronology of the poems, also proposes dates for some of the drawings. Thode argues in many cases against the chronology of Frey.)

50. Erwin Panofsky, *Die Michelangelo-Literatur seit* 1914, in *Jahrbuch für Kunstgeschichte*, Vol. I (1921–22), Vienna, 1923. (On col. 23 a review of Demonts' little volume of the Louvre drawings; discusses *passim* several other drawings.)

51. Pietro Toesca, *Michelangelo Buonarroti*, in Enciclopedia Italiana, Vol. XXIII, pp. 165–91. Rome, 1934.

52. Charles de Tolnay, *Michelangelo*, in Thieme-Becker's Künstlerlexikon, Vol. XXIV, Leipzig, 1930.

V. FOLLOWERS OF MICHELANGELO

53. L. Dorez, *Nouvelles Recherches sur Michel-Ange et son entourage*, in *Bibliothèque de l'Ecole des Chartes*, Vols. LXXVII and LXXVIII (1916–17).

54. Hermann Voss, *Die Malerei der Spätrenaissance in Rom and Florenz*, Vol. I, Berlin, 1920. (Chapter V, pp. 111–48, *Das plastische Ideal im Kreise Michelangelos*, with valuable notes on Sebastiano del Piombo, Marcello Venusti, Battista Franco, Daniele da Volterra and Jacopino del Conte.)

55. Anny E. Popp, *Garzoni Michelangelos*, in *Belvedere*, Vol. VIII, p. 6 f. Vienna, 1925.

56. Bernard Berenson, *Andrea di Michelangelo e Antonio Mini*, in *L'Arte*, 1935.

57. Carlo Gamba, *Silvio Cosini* in *Dedalo*, X, pp. 228–54, Milan, 1930.

58. Erwin Panofsky, *Kopie oder Fälschung? Ein Beitrag zur Kritik einiger Zeichnungen aus der Werkstatt Michelangelos*, in *Zeitschrift für bildende Kunst*, LXI (1927–28), pp. 221–44; LXII (1928–29), pp. 179–83; and A. E. Popp's remarks in Vol. LXII (1928), pp. 54–67.

59. Oskar Fischel, *A new approach to Sebastiano del Piombo as a draughtsman*, in *Old Master Drawings*, 1939–40.

60. Rodolfo Pallucchini, *Sebastian Viniziano* (Fra Sebastiano del Piombo). Milan, 1944. (The Catalogue discusses also the previous attributions of Michelangelo drawings to Sebastiano del Piombo by Wickhoff, d'Achiardi, Berenson, Dussler, etc.)

61. A. Bertolotti, *Don Giulio Clovio*, Modena, 1882. (Recording the Michelangelo drawings in the collection of Giulio Clovio, and his copies after them.)

62. Kurt Kusenberg, *Le Rosso*. Paris, 1931. (Proves that several drawings which Berenson attributed to Michelangelo are by Rosso Fiorentino.)

63. F. Baumgart, *Daniele da Volterra e Michelangelo* in *Bollettino d'Arte*, XXVIII, 1934. (Other attributions of drawings to Daniele da Volterra by E. Panofsky in *Festschrift für J. Schlosser*, Vienna, 1927.)

The revised, Italian edition of Berenson's Drawings of the Florentine Painters (1961) has been listed in the present Bibliography as No. 4A.

For other books published during the last fifteen years see the next page.

SUPPLEMENT TO THE BIBLIOGRAPHY

Since Spring 1951 (when the first edition of this book was published) a large number of books, catalogues, and articles on Michelangelo and his drawings have been issued. Only the most important books are listed below.

64. Johannes Wilde, *Italian Drawings in . . . the British Museum : Michelangelo and his Studio*, London, 1953.

65. K. T. Parker, *Catalogue of the collection of Drawings in the Ashmolean Museum*, Oxford, 1956.

66. Paola Barocchi, *Michelangelo e la sua scuola : I disegni di Casa Buonarroti e degli Uffizi*, 2 vols. Florence, 1962.

67. Paola Barocchi, *Michelangelo e la sua scuola : I disegni dell'Archivio Buonarroti*. Florence, 1964.

68. Charles de Tolnay, *The tomb of Julius II*. (*Michelangelo*, vol. IV.) Princeton, 1954.

69. Charles de Tolnay, *The final Period*. (*Michelangelo*, vol. V.) Princeton, 1960.

70. Luitpold Dussler, *Die Zeichnungen des Michelangelo : Kritischer Katalog*. Berlin, 1959.

71. Alexander Perrig, *Michelangelo Buonarrotis letzte Pietà-Idee*. Bern, 1960. (Discussing also a number of Michelangelo drawings, p. 84 f., and *passim*.)

72. Vasari, *La Vita di Michelangelo, curata e commentata da Paola Barocchi*, 5 vols., Milan, 1962.

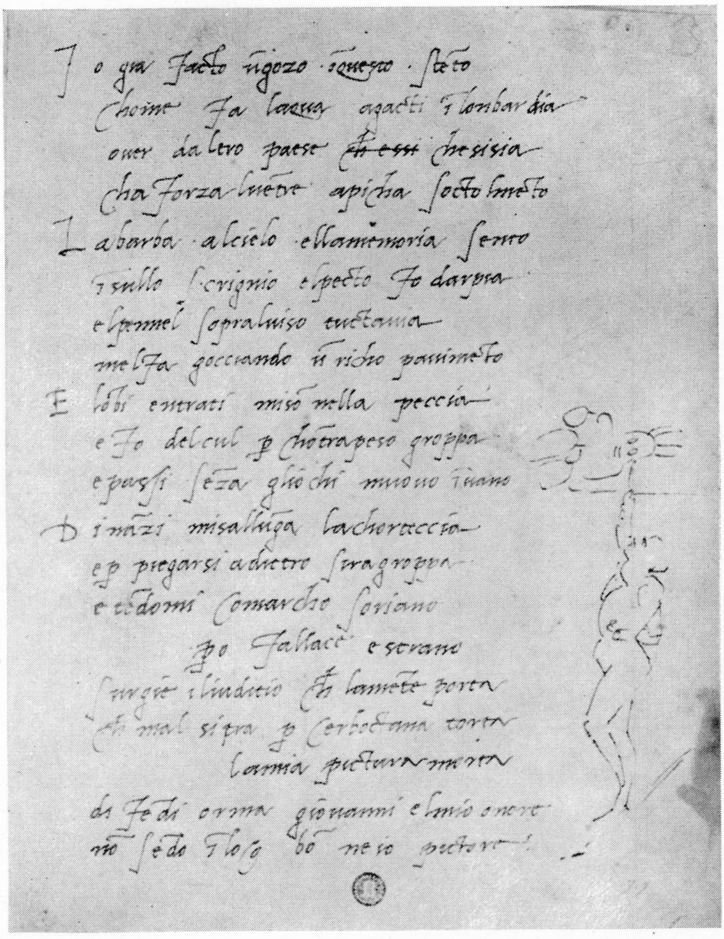

Michelangelo: A sonnet, and a self-portrait, showing the artist at work on the Sistine Ceiling frescoes, c. 1510. Florence, Archivio Buonarroti.

THE PLATES

AN ASTERISK (*) IN FRONT OF THE NUMBER INDICATES THAT
THE REPRODUCTION IS IN THE SAME SIZE AS THE ORIGINAL

The descriptive titles of the drawings and the names of the collections are given in abbreviated form in the captions
For fuller descriptions see the corresponding numbers in the Catalogue.

1. *Michelangelo's copy of two Figures from a fresco by Giotto*. About 1489–90. Louvre

2. *Copy of three Figures from a fresco by Masaccio.* About 1491. Vienna

3. *Copy of a Figure from a fresco by Masaccio* (?) About 1491. Vienna

4. *Copy of a Figure from a fresco by Masaccio*. About 1493. Munich

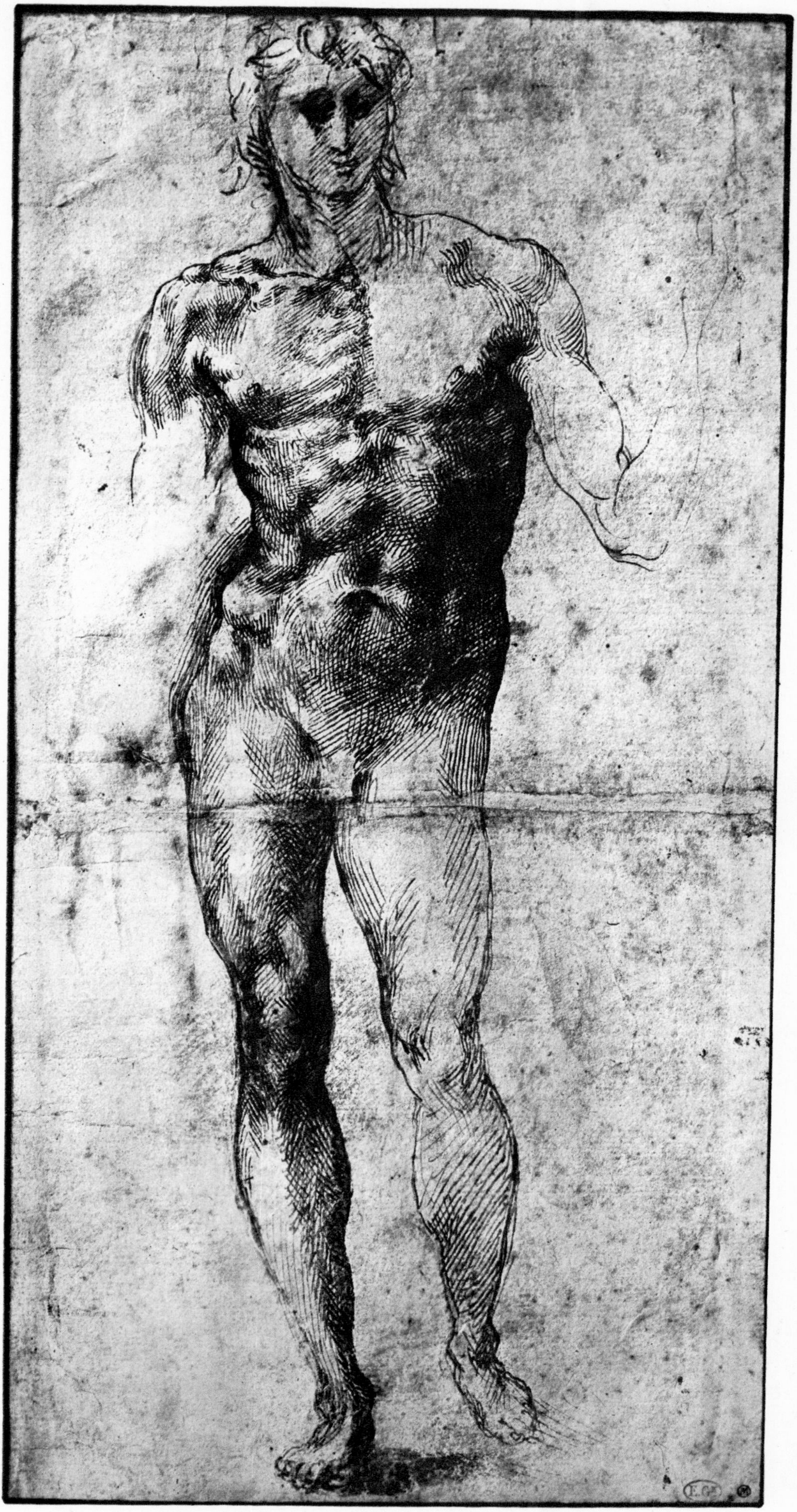

5. *Figure in antique style*. Between 1496 and 1500. Louvre

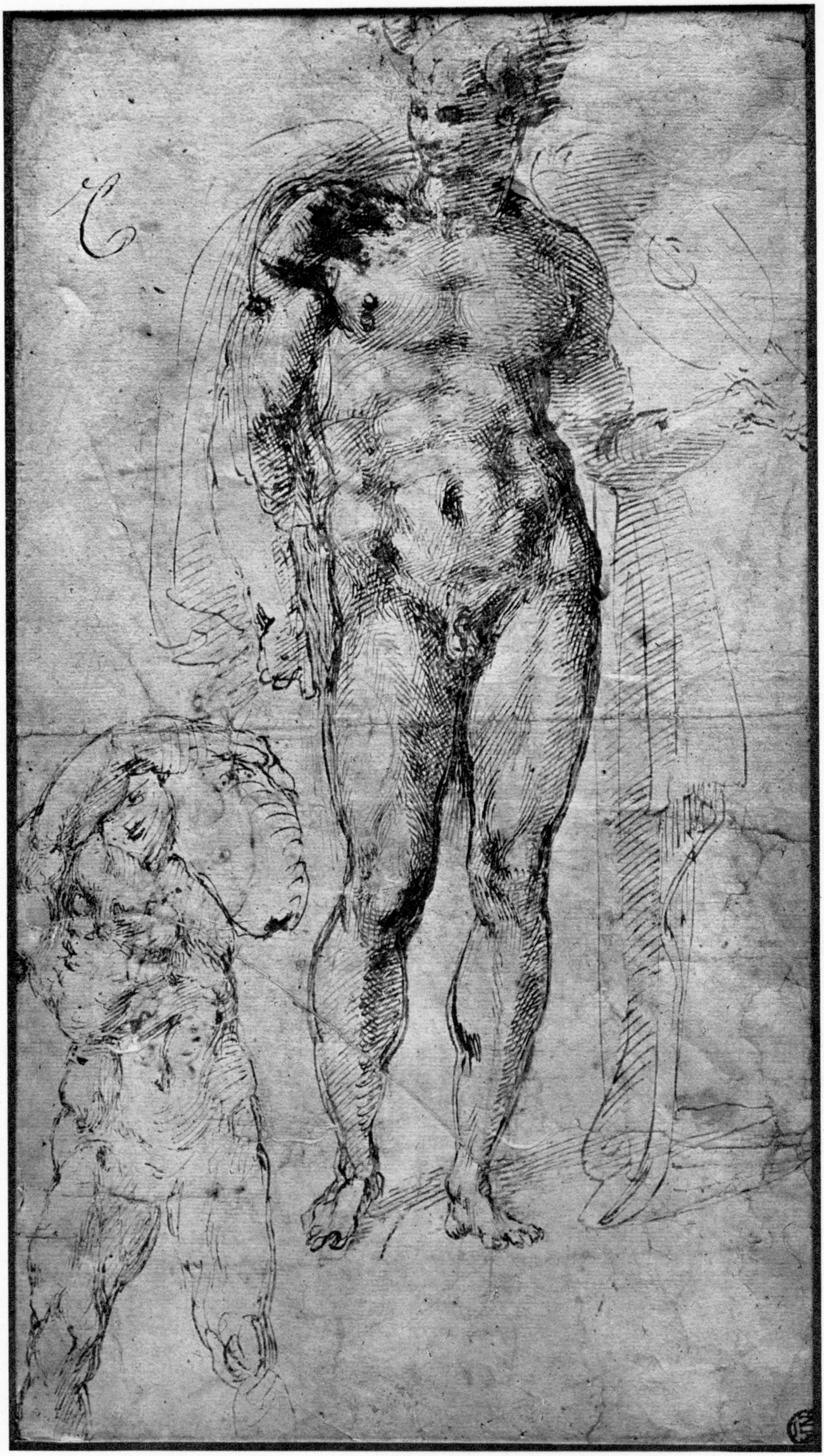

6. *Studies from antique Sculptures*. About 1501. Louvre

*7. *Back view of a male Torso, and five Heads*. About 1501. Oxford

*8. *St Anne, the Virgin and the Infant Christ.* About 1501. Oxford

*9. *Man digging, and other Studies from the Nude*. About 1501. Louvre

*10. *Sketch for the Bronze David, and Study for a right Arm*. 1501–02. Louvre

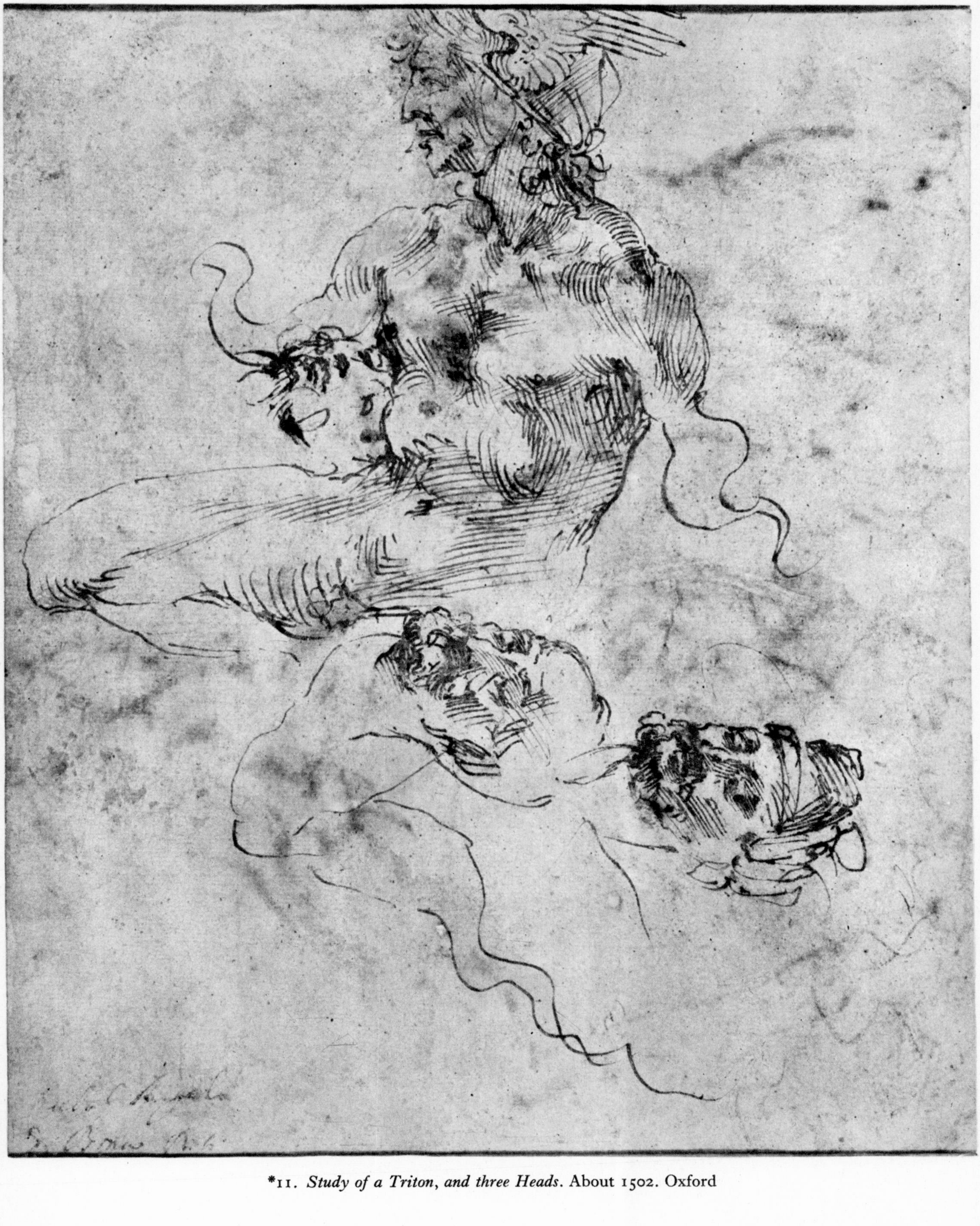

*11. *Study of a Triton, and three Heads*. About 1502. Oxford

*12. Studies from the Nude. About [illegible]. Oxford

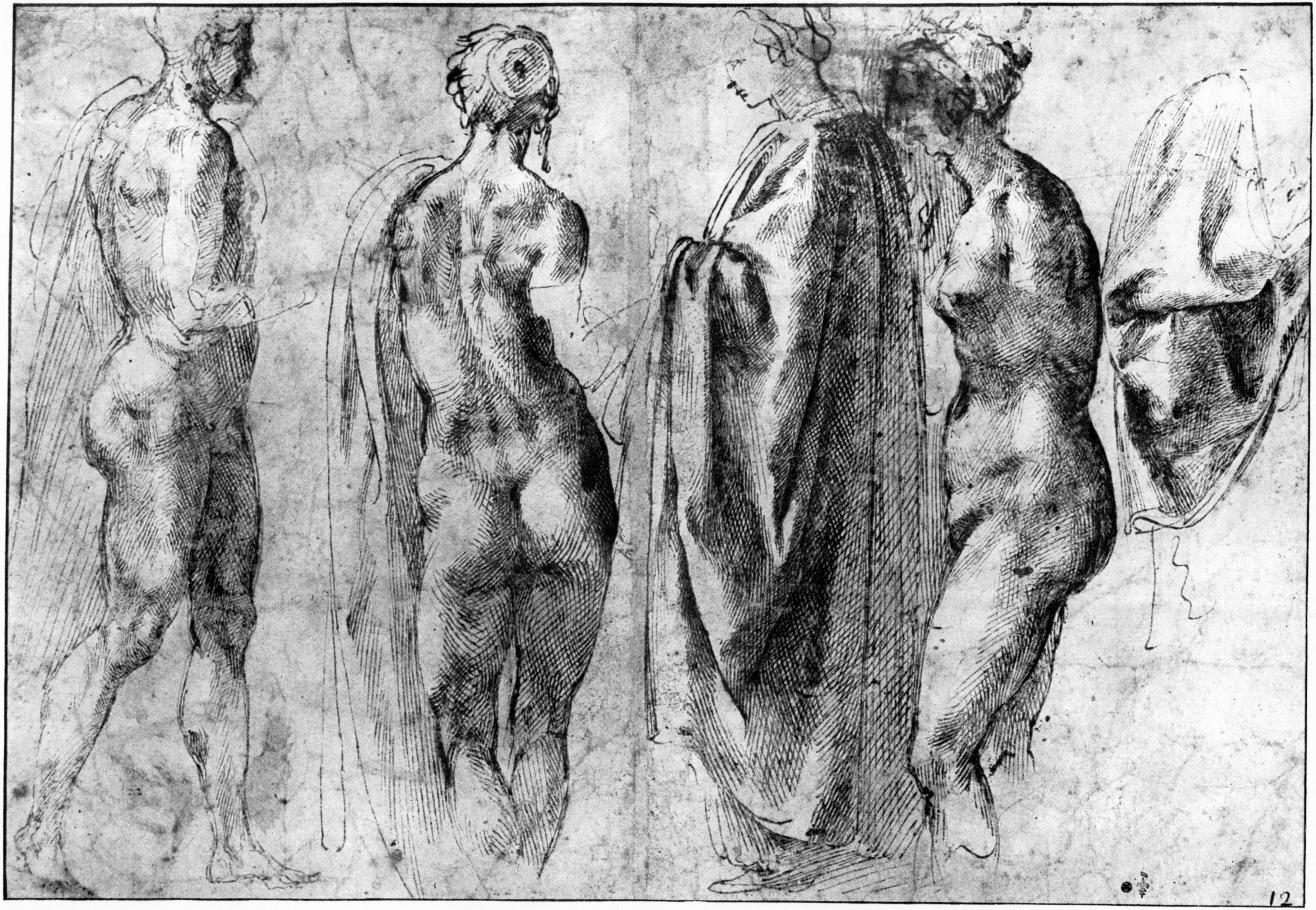

13. *Studies of Draperies and from antique Statues*. About 1503. Chantilly

14. *A 'Philosopher'*. About 1503. British Museum

*15. *Head of a Satyr*. About 1503. British Museum

16. *Nude Youth with left arm extended*. About 1504. British Museum

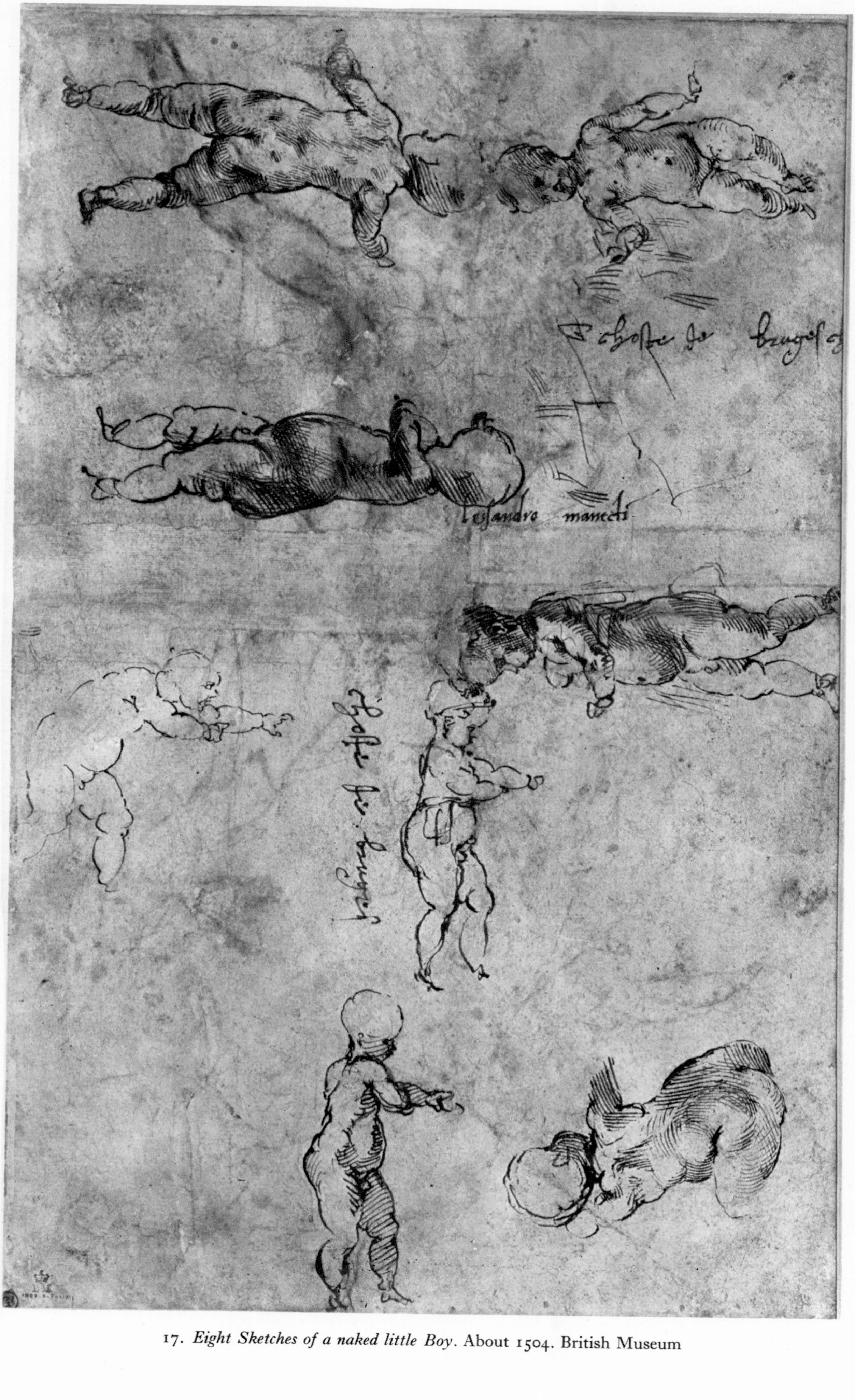

17. *Eight Sketches of a naked little Boy*. About 1504. British Museum

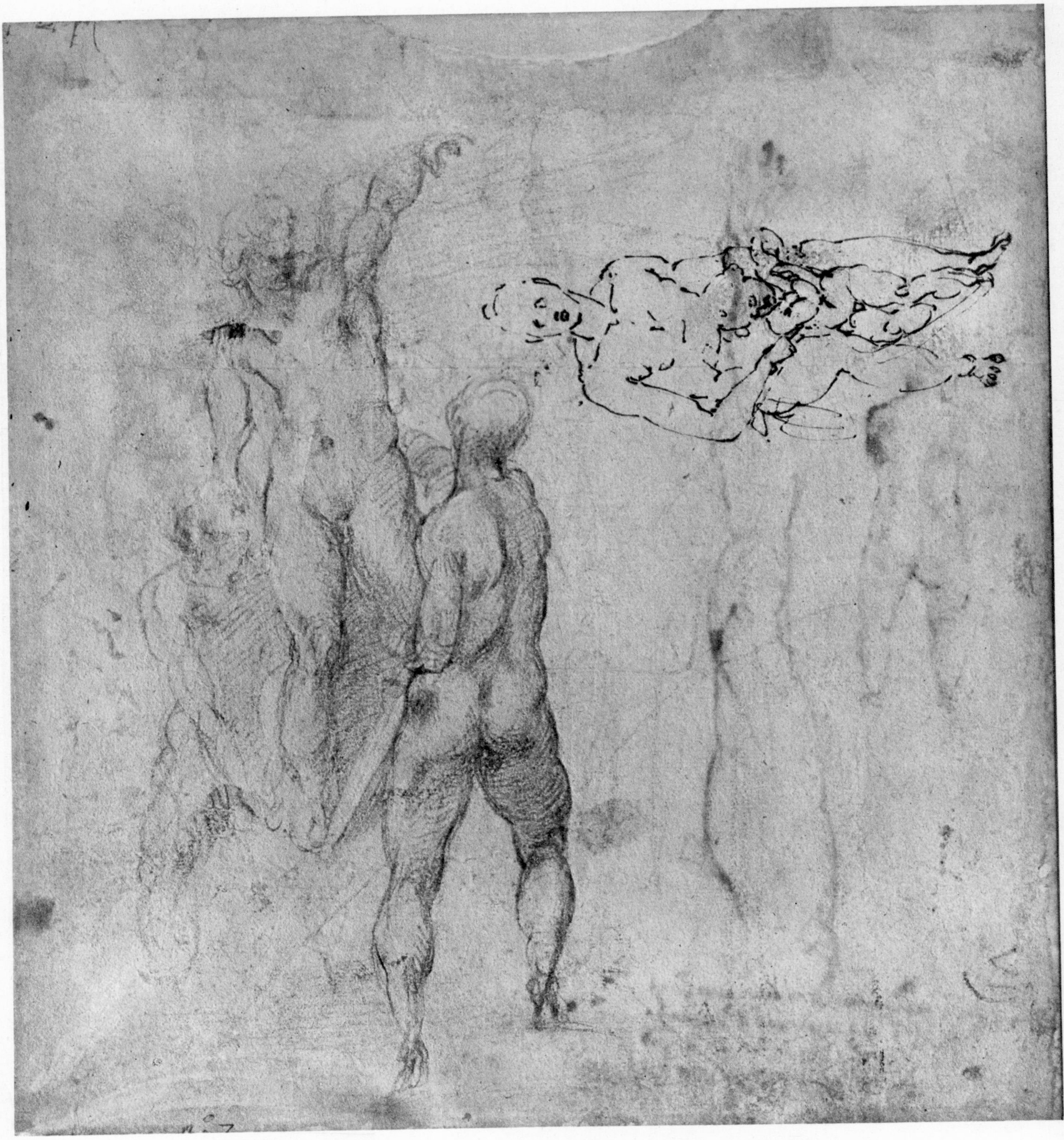

18. *Studies for the 'Bruges Madonna' and for the 'Battle Cartoon'*. About 1504. British Museum

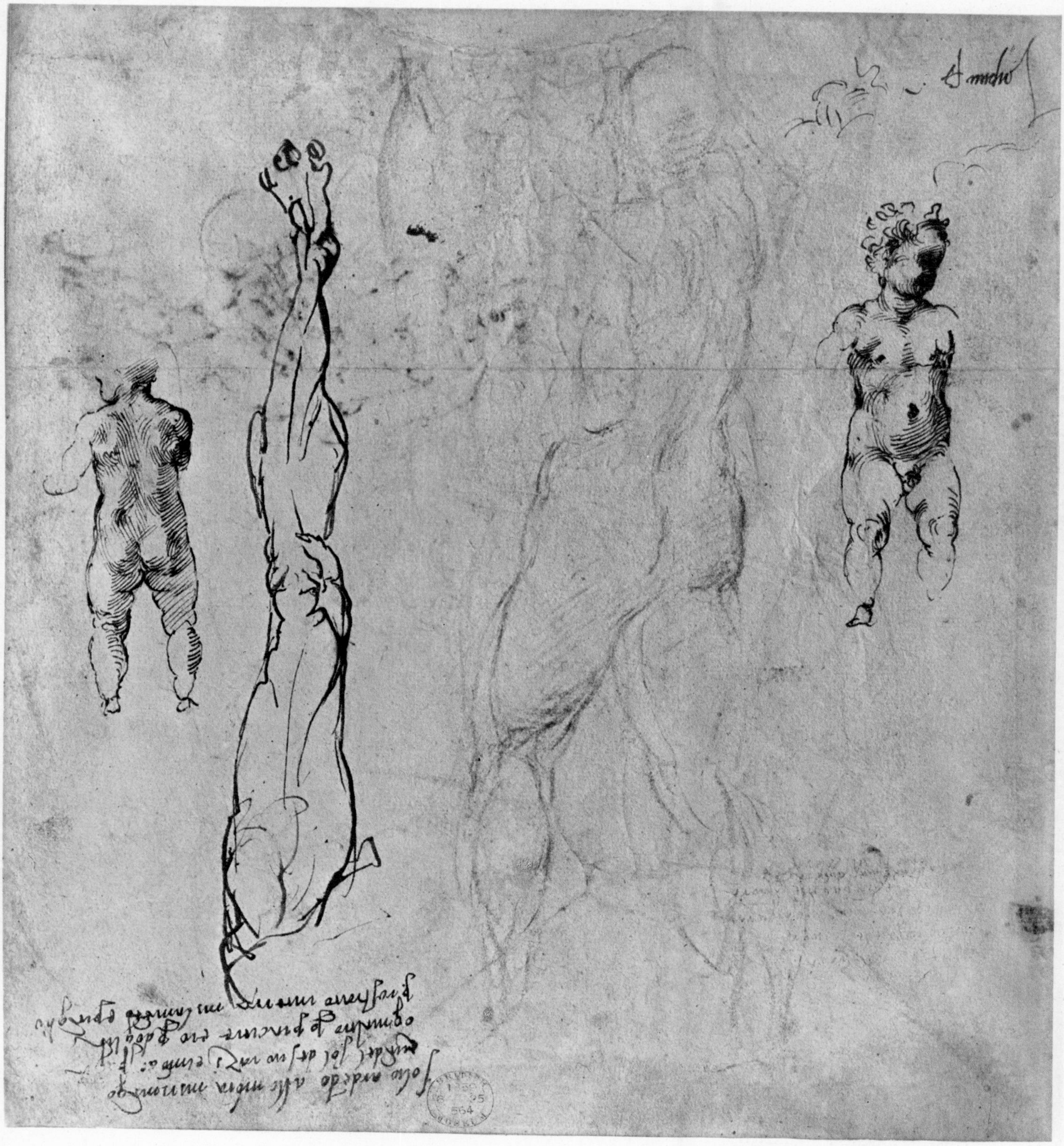

19. *Back and Front view of a Putto; Nude Man, seen from the rear; Sketch of a Leg.* About 1504. British Museum

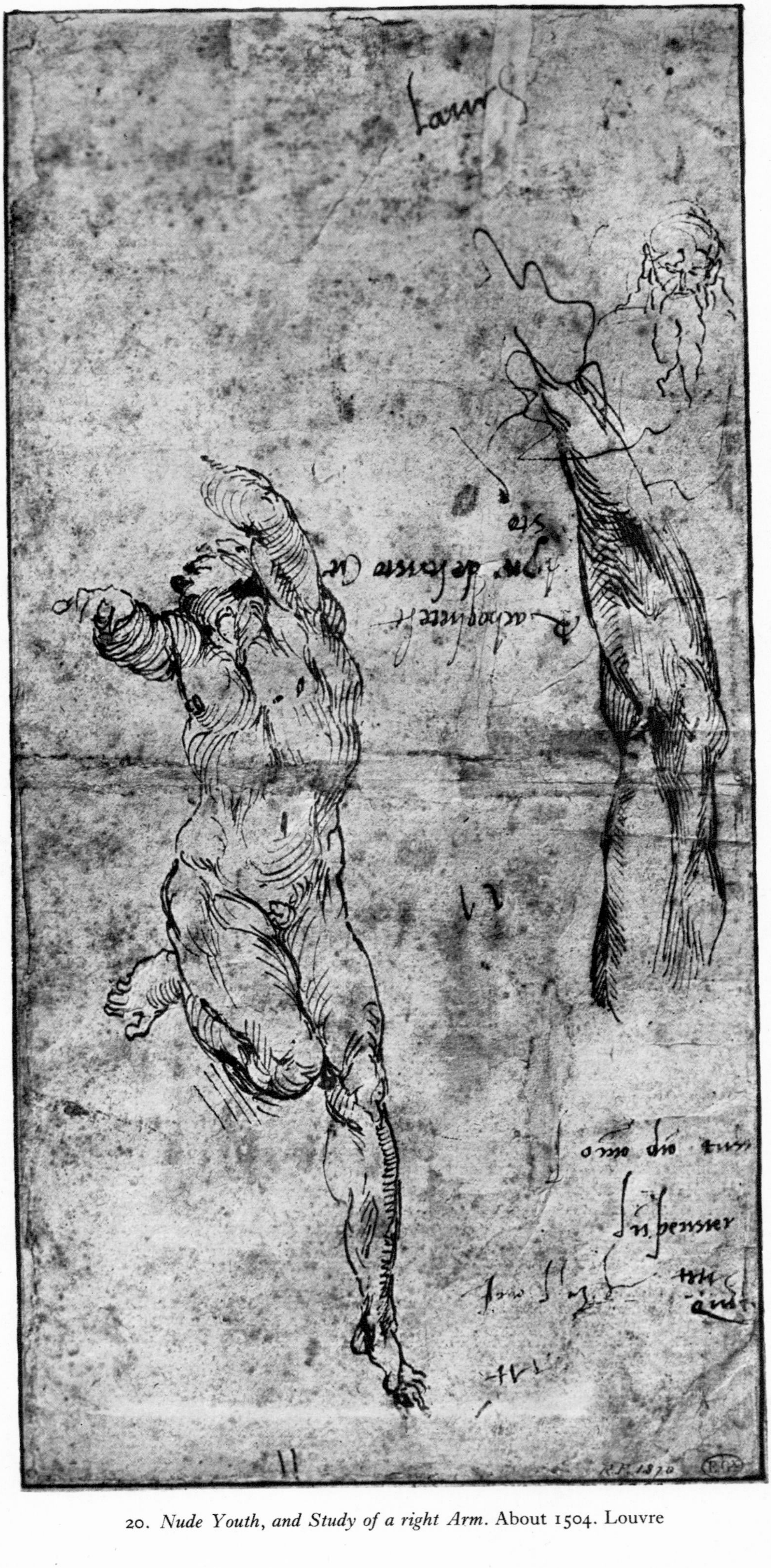

20. *Nude Youth, and Study of a right Arm*. About 1504. Louvre

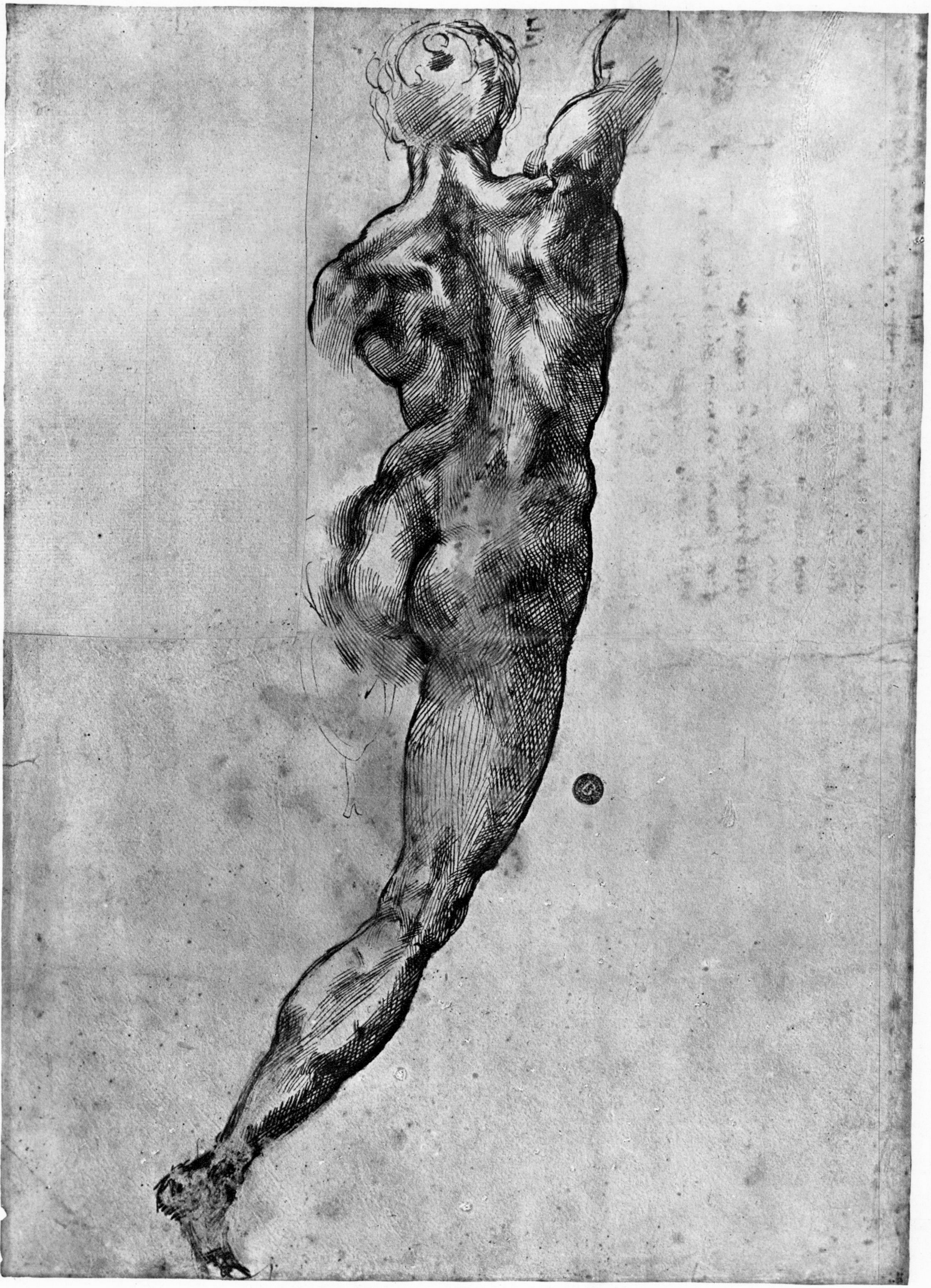

21. *Male Nude, seen from the back*. (Study for the 'Battle Cartoon'.) About 1504. Casa Buonarroti

22. *Male Torso, seen from the back*. (Study for the 'Battle Cartoon'.) About 1504. Casa Buonarroti

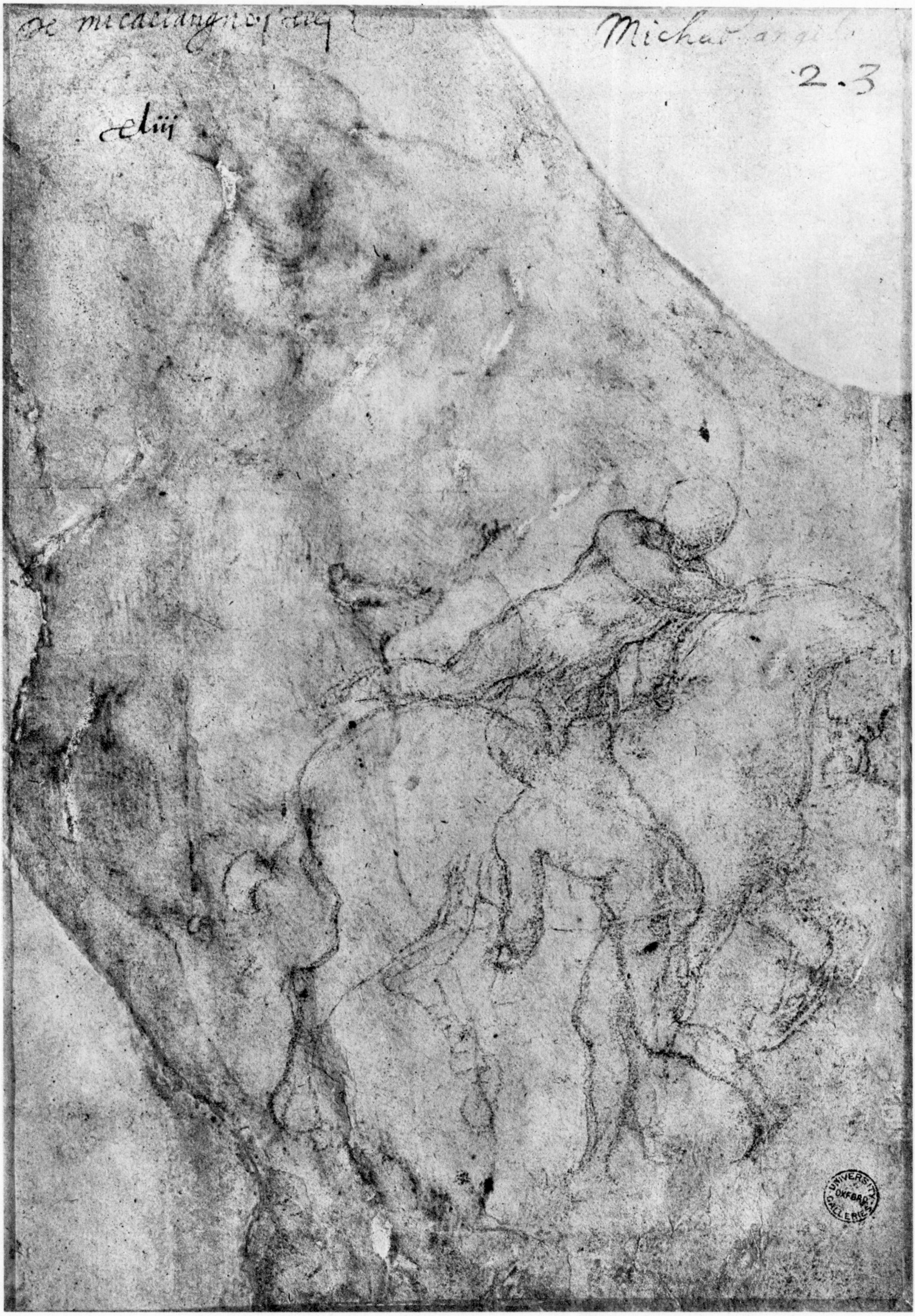

*23. *Nude Man mounting a Horse, and another Man holding the Stirrup*. (Study for the 'Battle Cartoon'.) About 1504. Oxford

24. *Male Torso, seen from the back*. (Study for the 'Battle Cartoon'.) About 1504. Vienna

25. *Nude Man, seated*. (Study for the 'Battle Cartoon'.) About 1504. British Museum

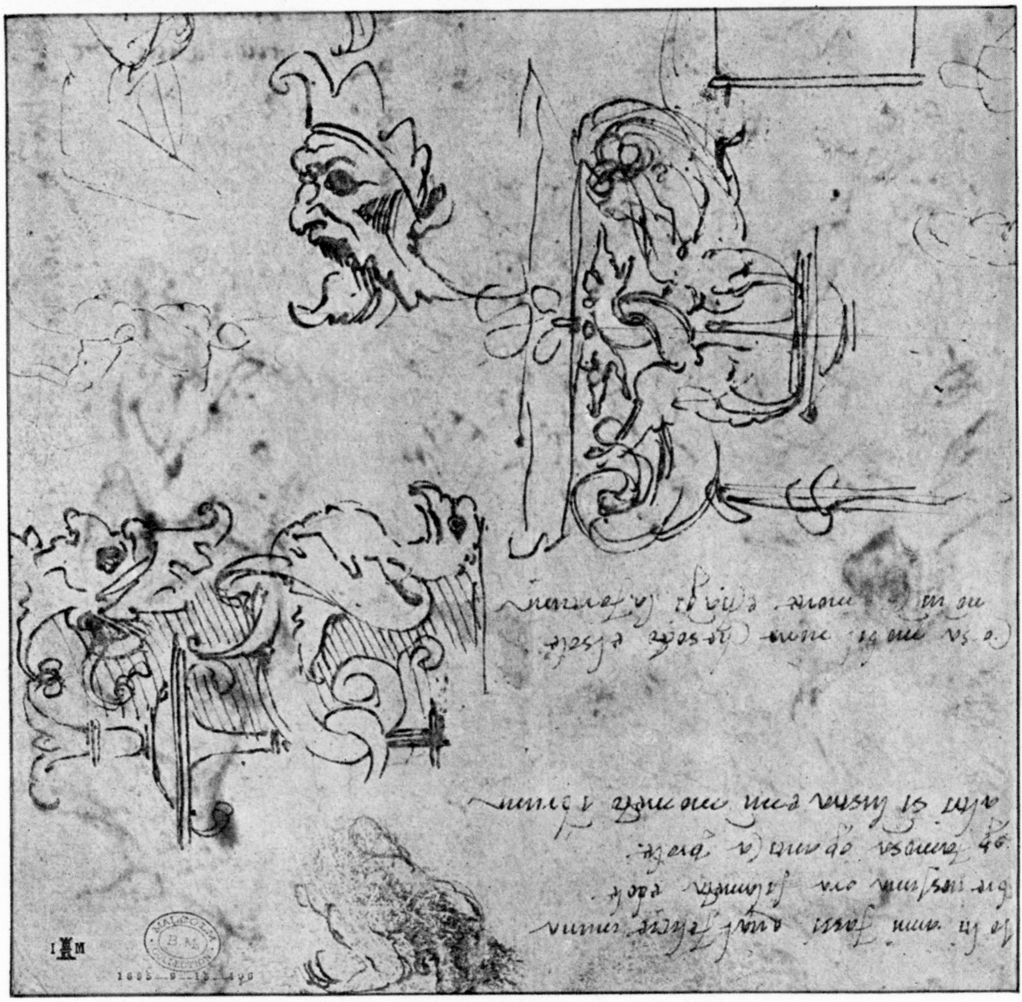

26–27. *Cavalry Battle; Study for an Apostle – Ornament Sketches.* About 1504. British Museum

28. *Salome with the Head of the Baptist* (?) About 1504–05. Louvre

29. *St Anne, the Virgin and the Infant Christ*. About 1504–05. Louvre

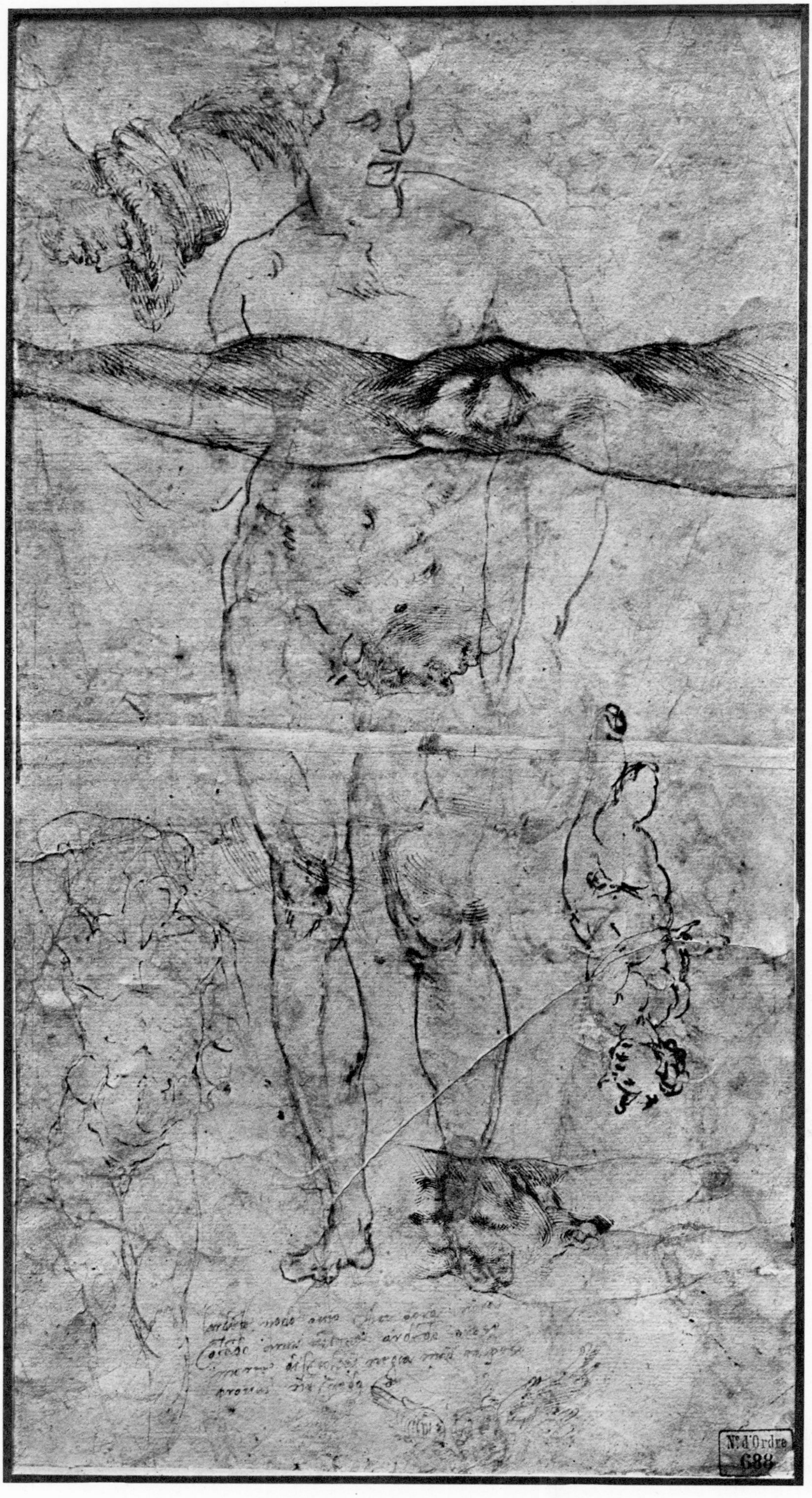

30. *Sketches for a Captive; a Putto, and other Studies*. About 1504–05. Louvre

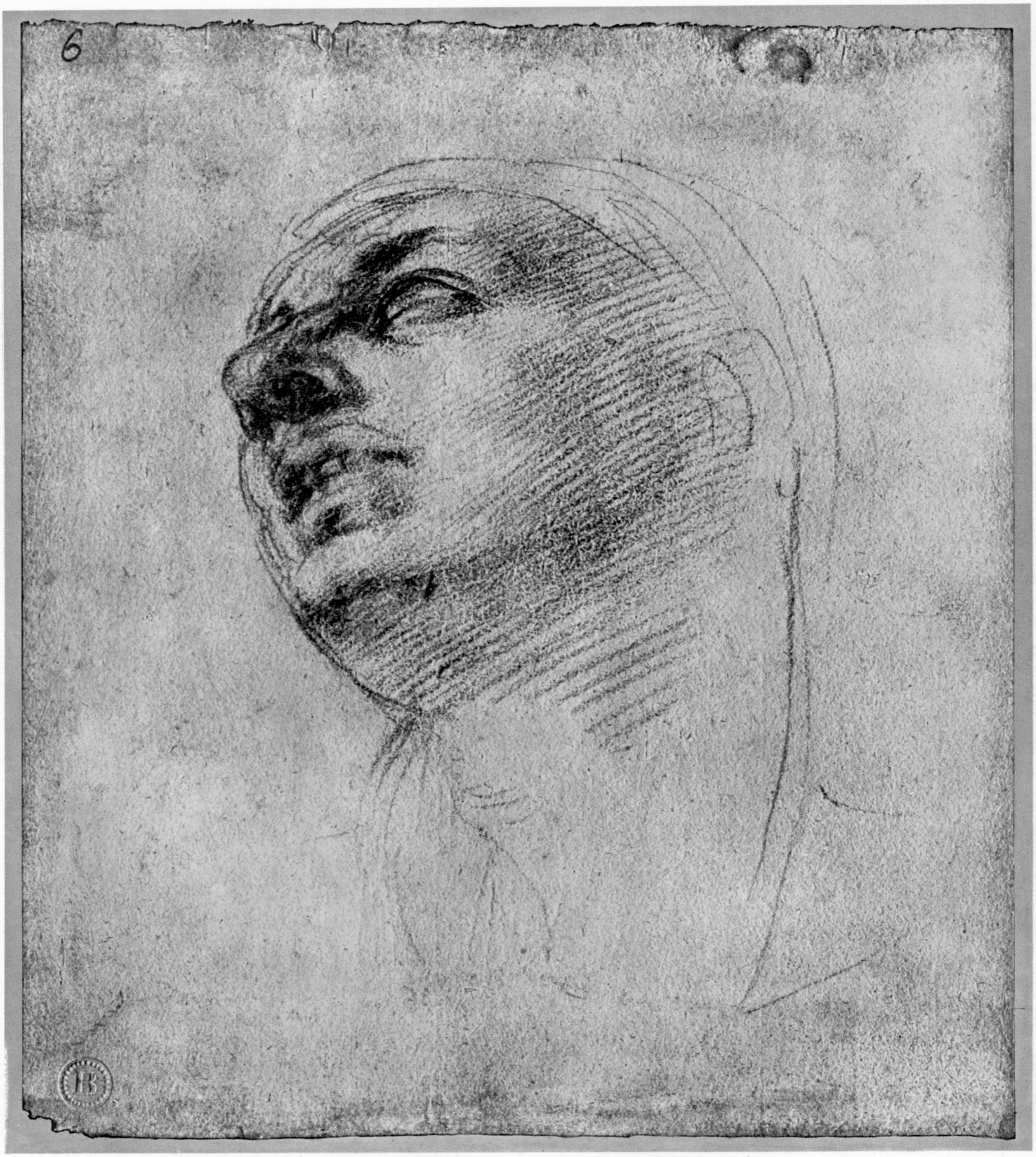

*31. *Study of a Head*. Between 1503 and 1505. Casa Buonarroti

32. *Head of a young Man*. Between 1505 and 1508. British Museum

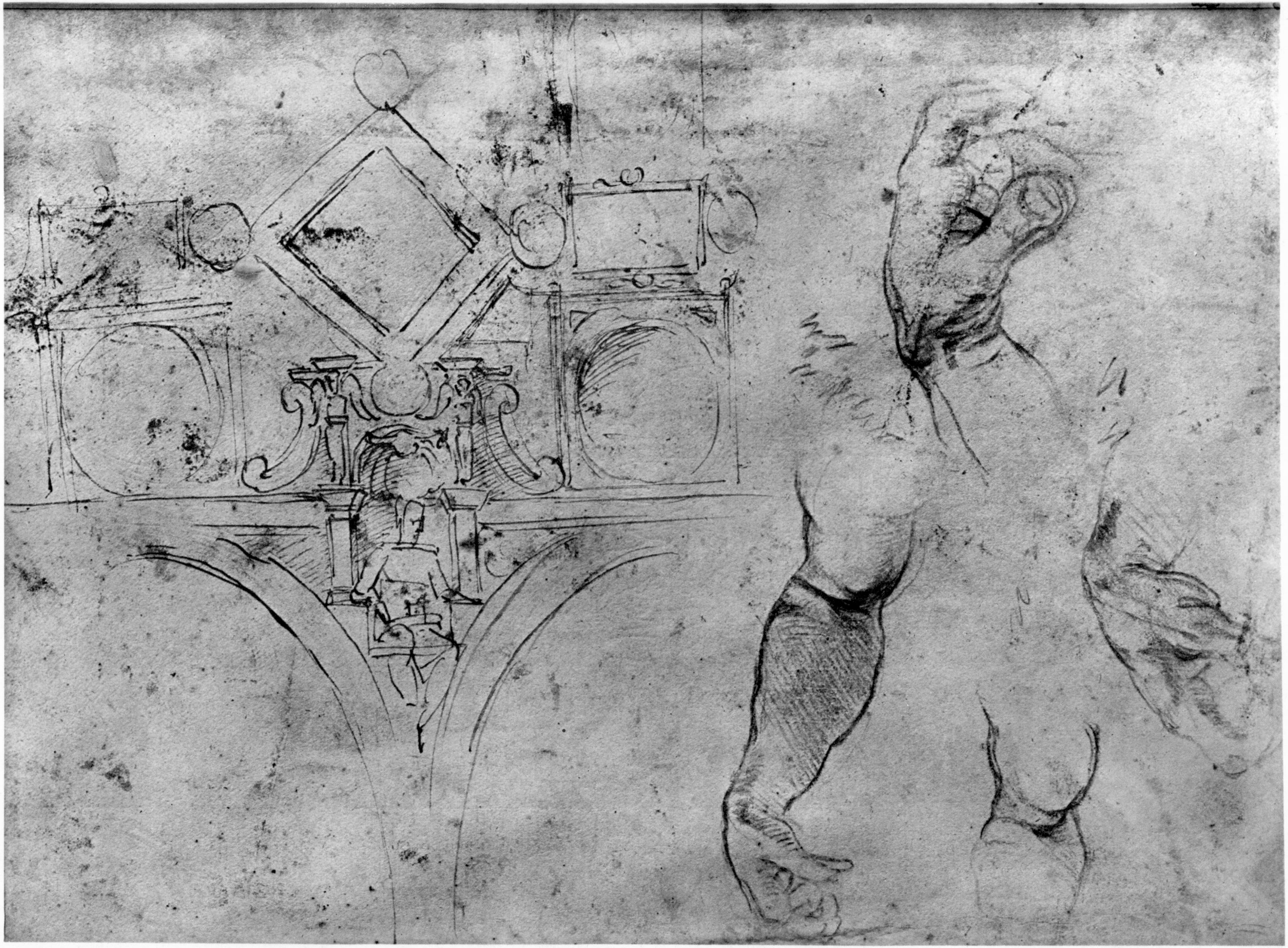

33. *Studies for the Sistine Ceiling Fresco*. About 1508. British Museum

34. *Adam.* (Study for the Sistine Ceiling Fresco.) About 1511. British Museum

35. *Head Study for the Ignudo at the left over Isaiah*. About 1509. Louvre

36. *Head Study for Zechariah of the Sistine Ceiling Fresco*. About 1509. Uffizi

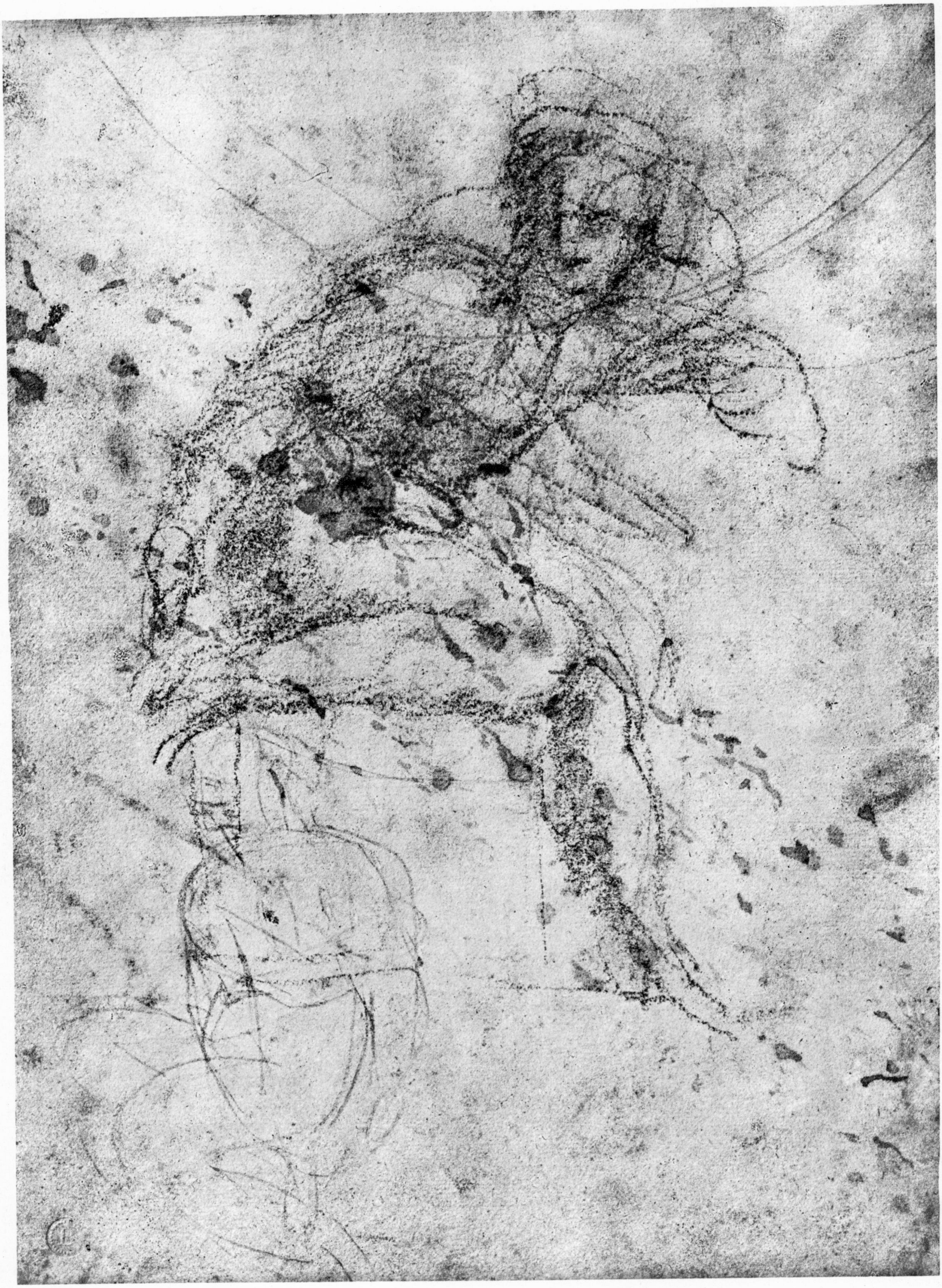

37. *First Sketch for the Ignudo at the left over Joel.* About 1509. Casa Buonarroti

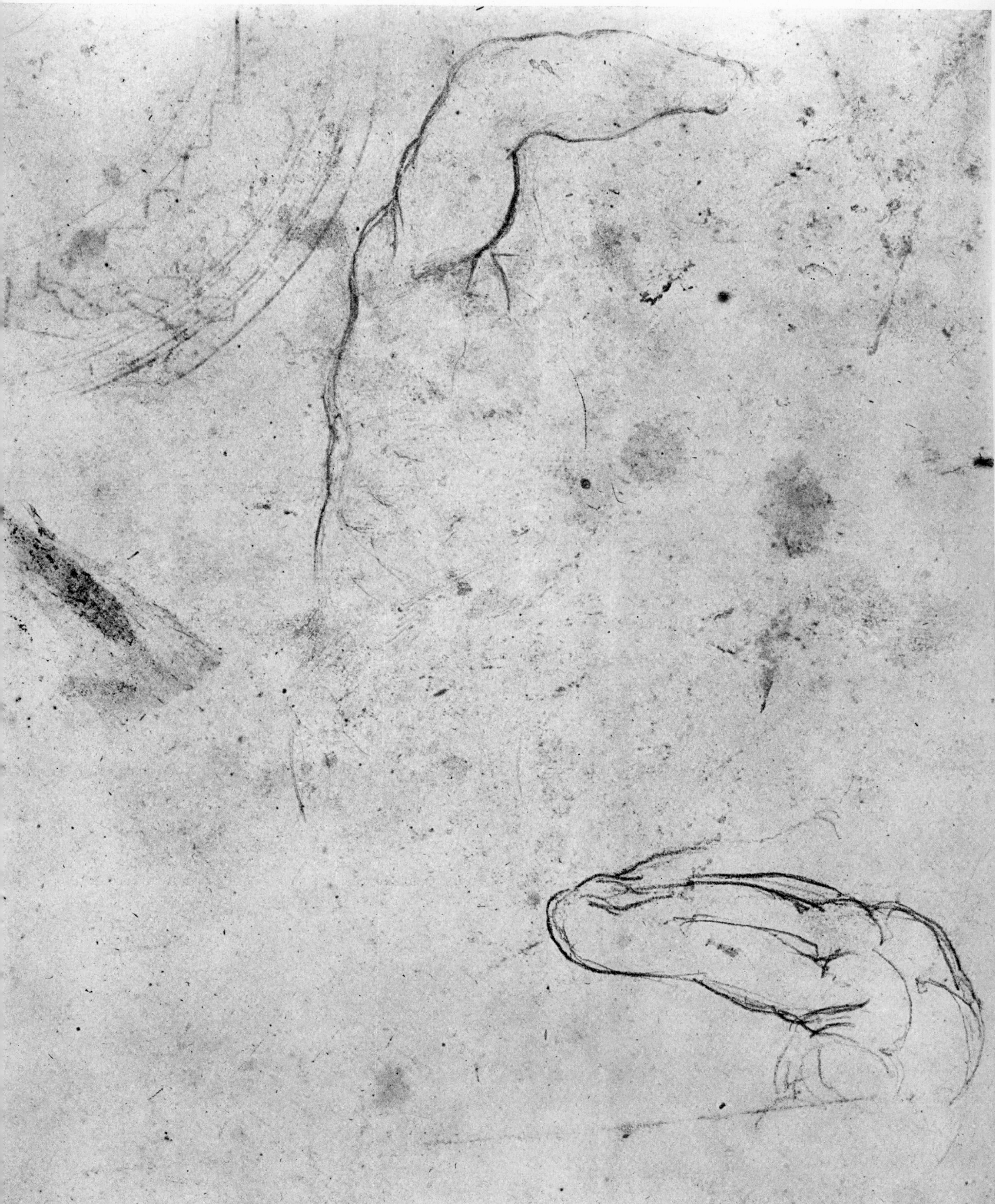

38. *First Sketch for the Ignudo at the right over Isaiah*. About 1509. Casa Buonarroti

39. *Studies for the Libyan Sibyl*. About 1511. New York

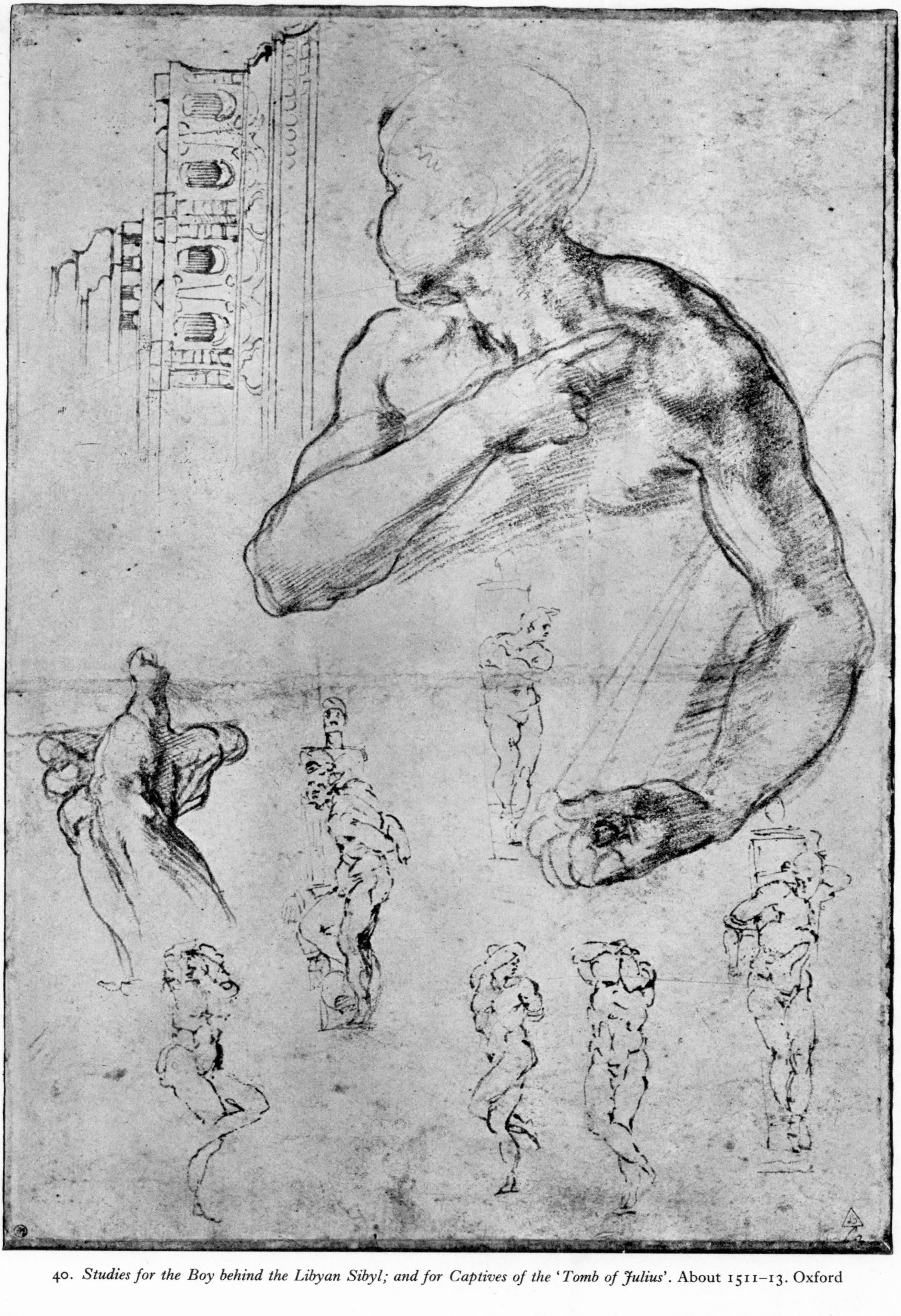

40. *Studies for the Boy behind the Libyan Sibyl; and for Captives of the 'Tomb of Julius'*. About 1511–13. Oxford

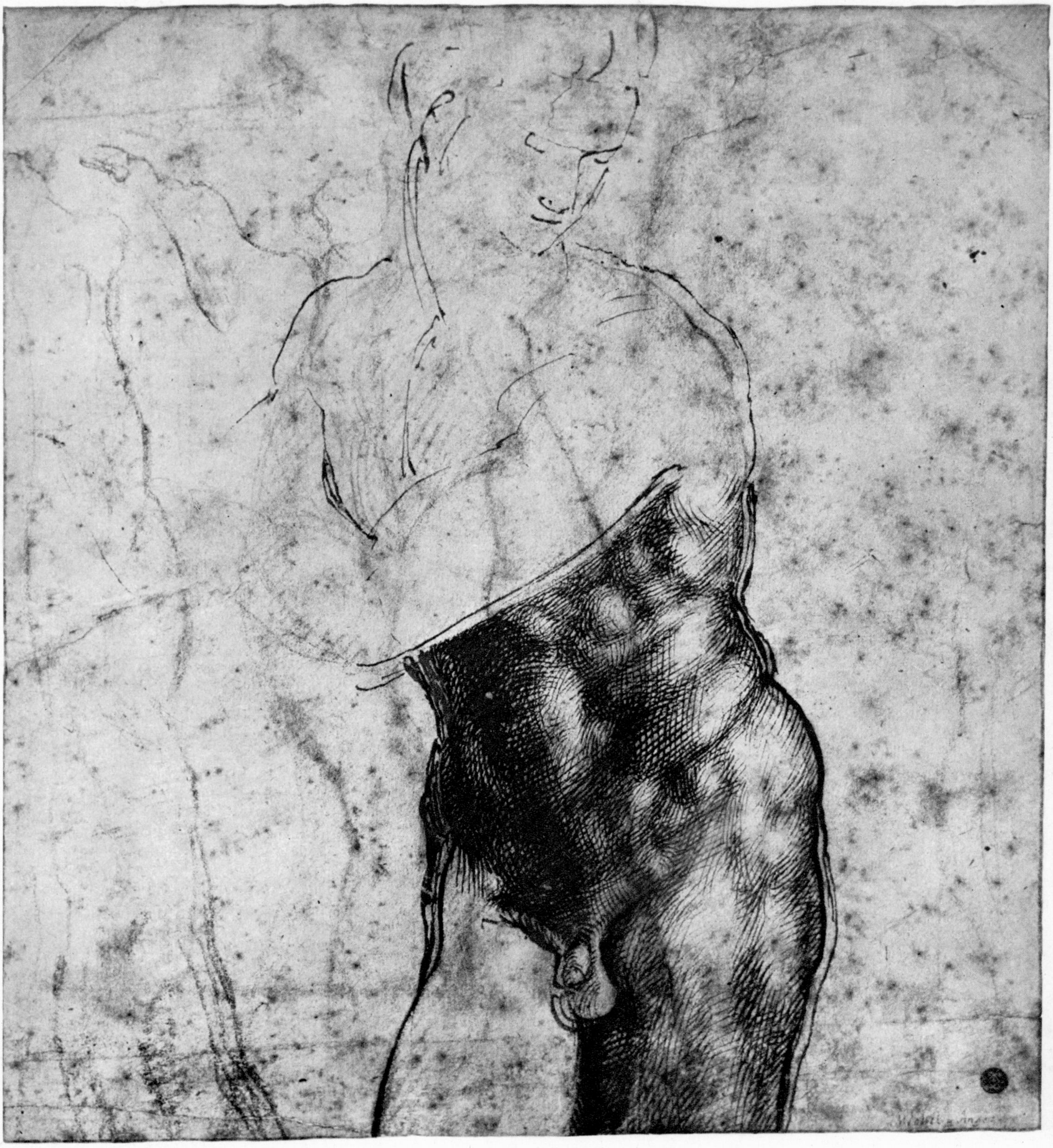

41. *Study for the first version of the statue of Christ in S. Maria sopra Minerva, Rome*. 1514. London, Brinsley Ford Collection

*42. *Study for the 'Raising of Lazarus'*. 1516. British Museum

*43. *Study of a Horse*. (Upper half of a sheet.) About 1520. Oxford

*44. *Two Studies of a Horse, and a Battle Scene*. (Lower half of a sheet.) About 1520. Oxford

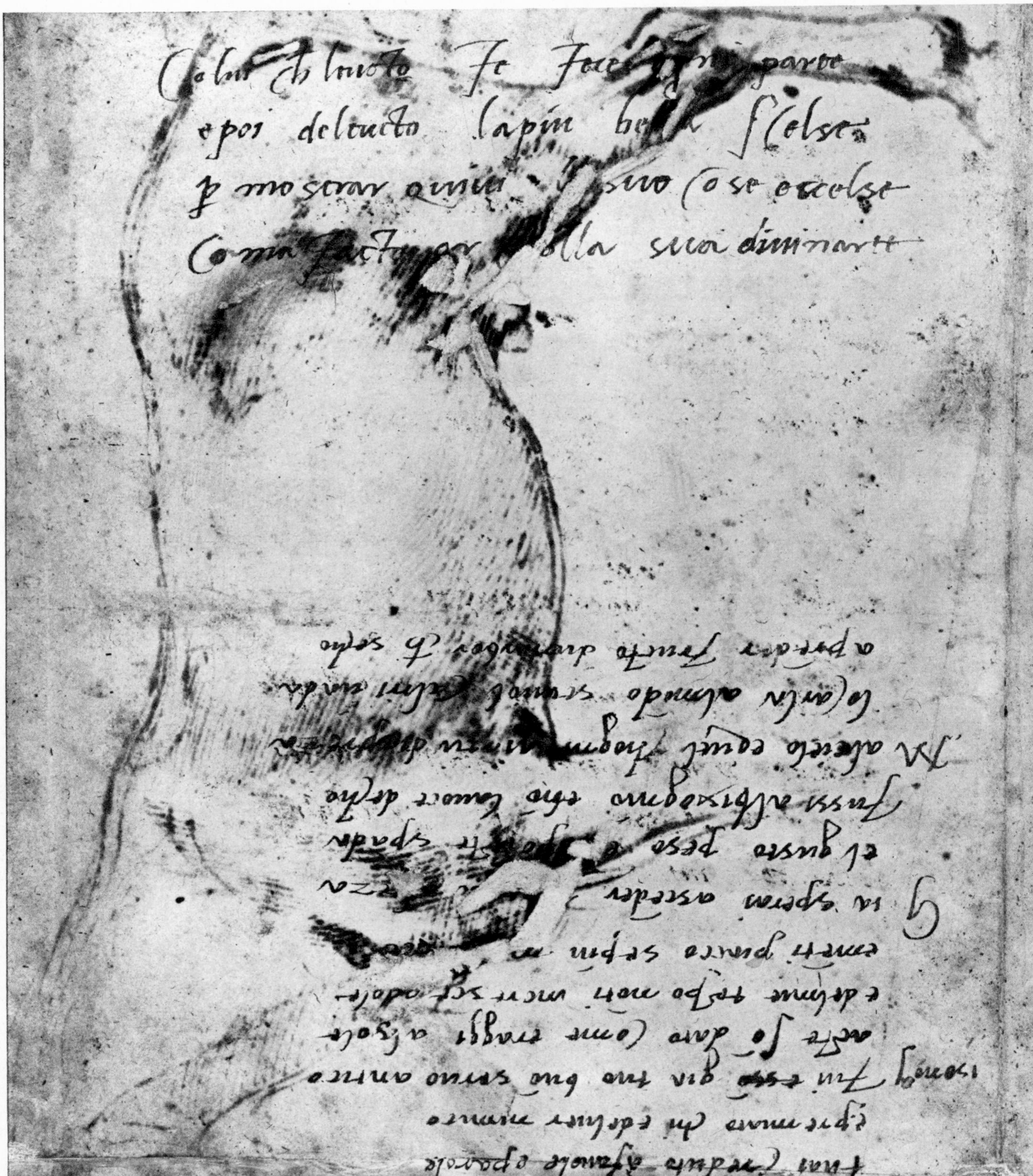

45. *A Sonnet.* (Verso of No. 43.) Oxford

*46. *A Horseman attacking Foot-soldiers*. About 1520. Oxford

47. *Triton*. About 1520–22. Villa Michelangelo, Settignano

48. *Dragon*. About 1522. Oxford

*49. *Profile with oriental Head-dress*. (Presentation drawing?) About 1522. Oxford

50. '*Damned Soul*'. (Presentation drawing for Gherardo Perini.) 1522. Uffizi

51. *Three female Profiles*. (Presentation drawing for Gherardo Perini.) 1522. Uffizi

52. *Venus, Mars, and Cupid*. (Presentation drawing for Gherardo Perini.) 1522. Uffizi

53. *Girl, holding a Distaff*. About 1524. British Museum

54. *Sibylline half-length Figure*. About 1524. British Museum

55. *Two Sketches for a Madonna and Child*. 1524. British Museum

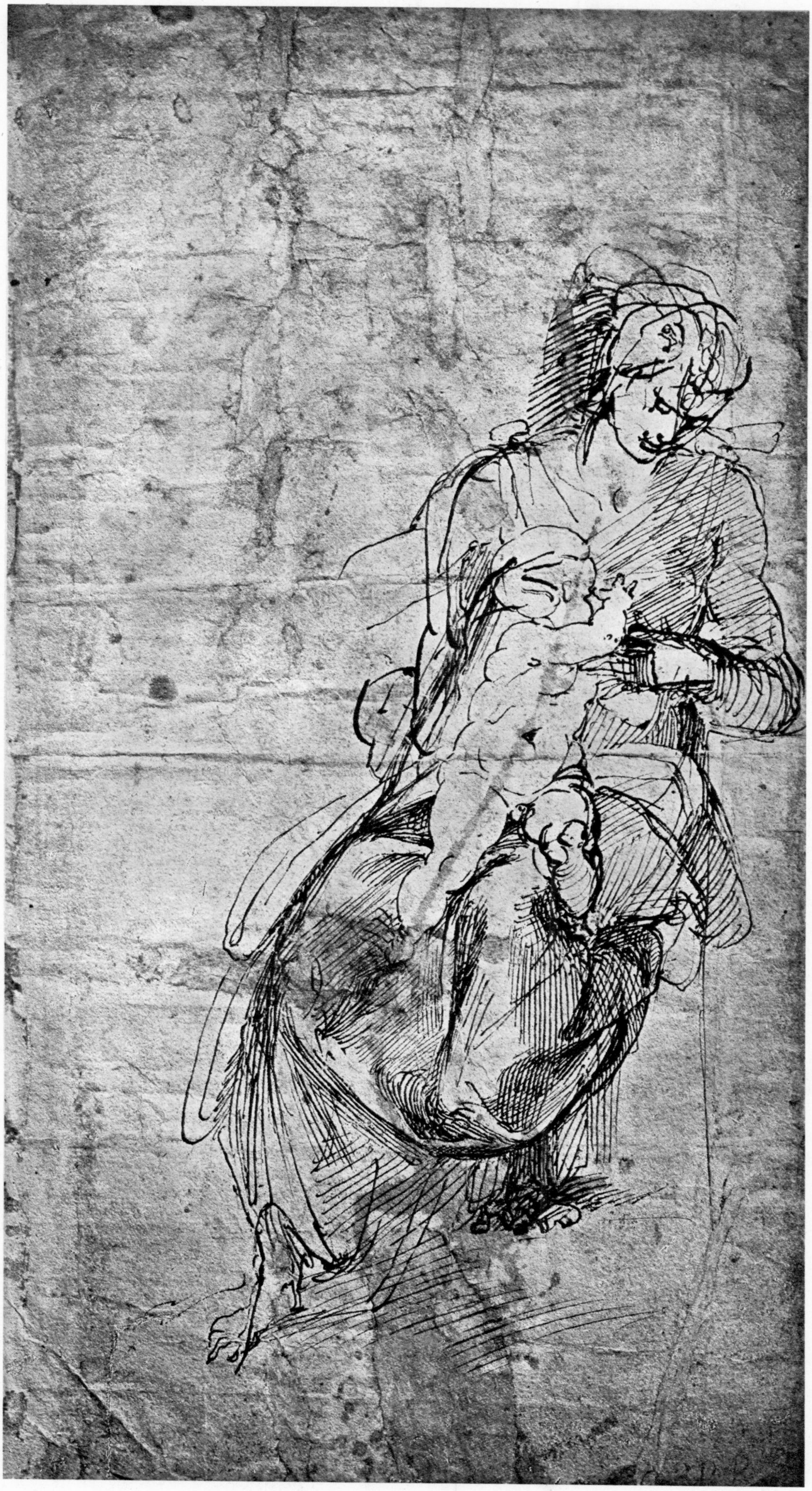

56. *Madonna and Child*. About 1524. Vienna

*57. *Two rapid Sketches of Crucified Men*. About 1524. British Museum

*58. *Two Studies for a Madonna and Child*. About 1524. Louvre

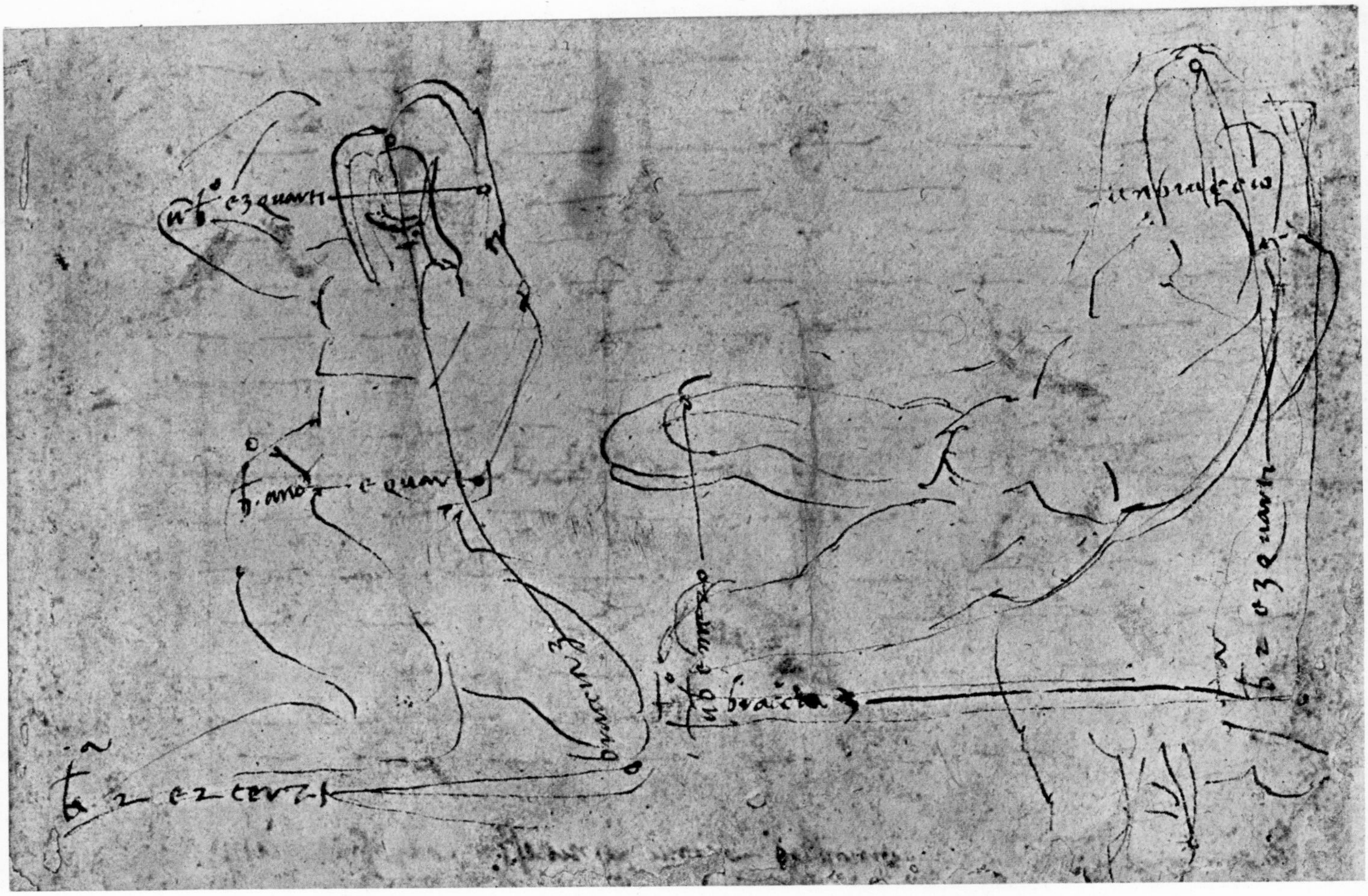

59. *Sketches for a River-God* (intended for the Medici Tombs). 1525. British Museum

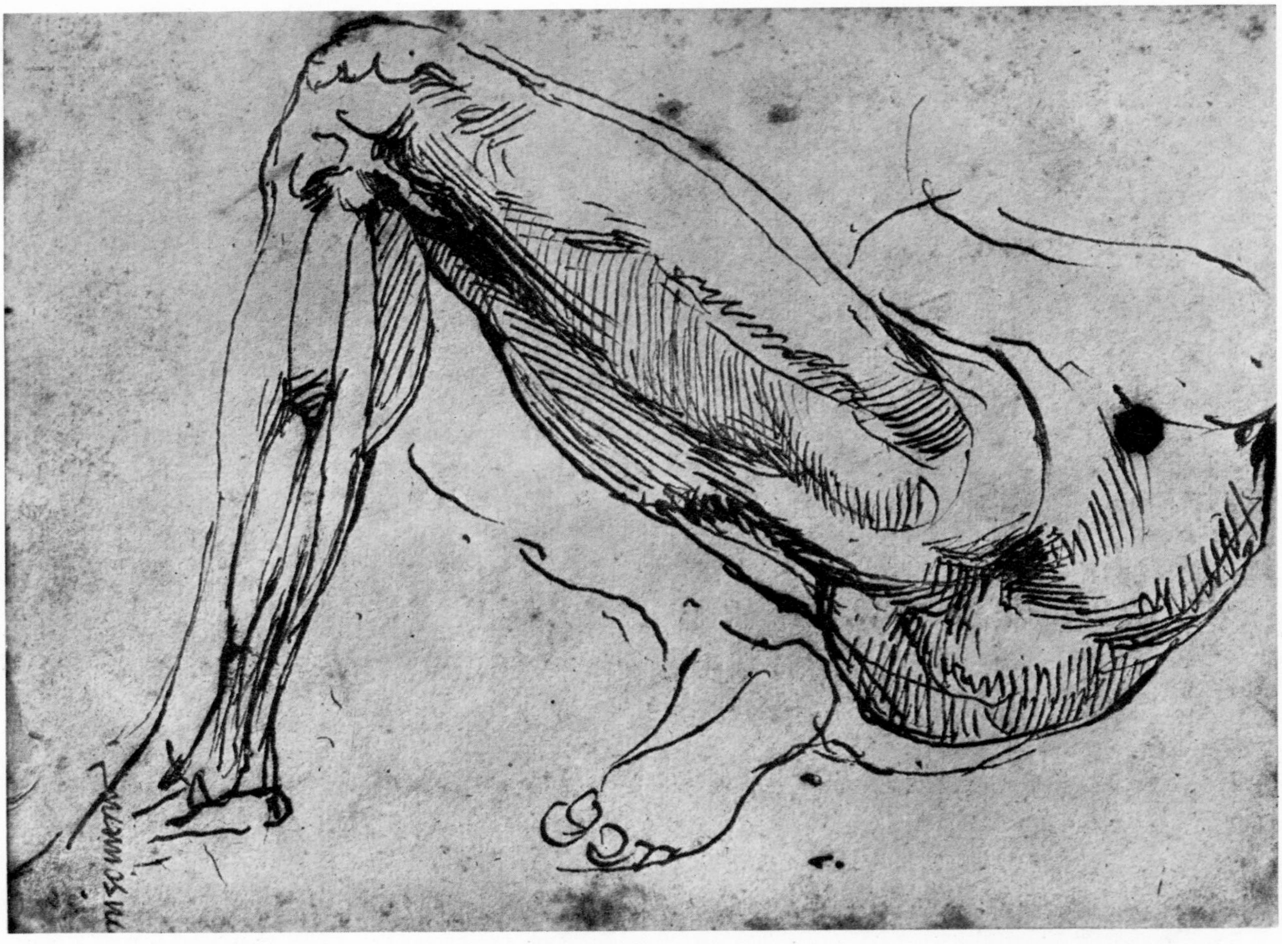

60. *Study of Torso and Legs* (probably for a River-God). About 1525–30. Casa Buonarroti

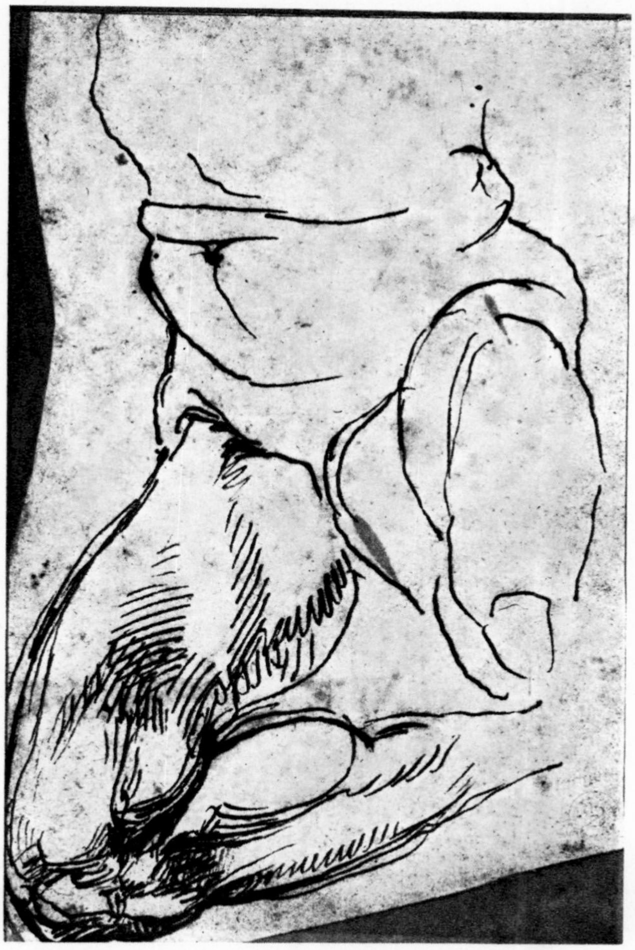

61. *Study of Torso and Legs* (probably for a River-God). About 1525–30. Casa Buonarroti

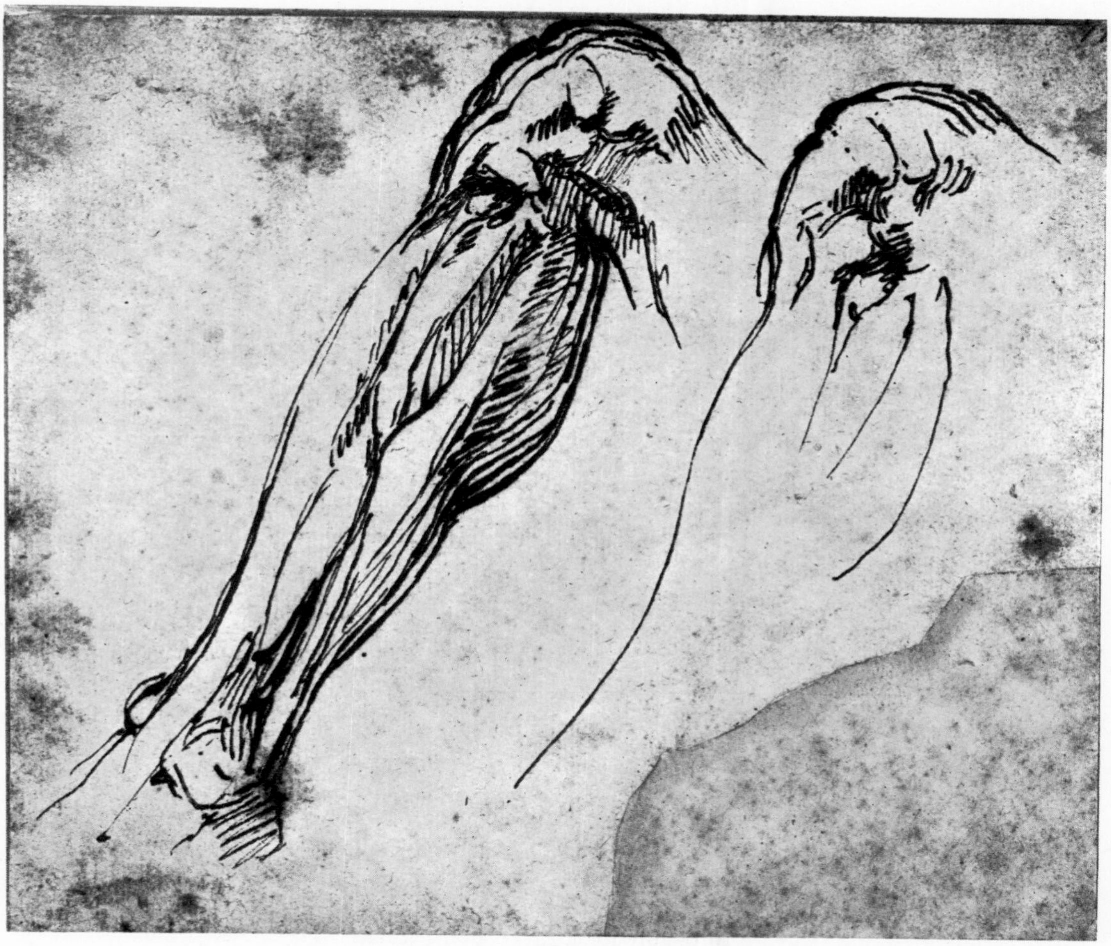

62. *Study of Legs, for a reclining Figure.* About 1525–30. Casa Buonarroti

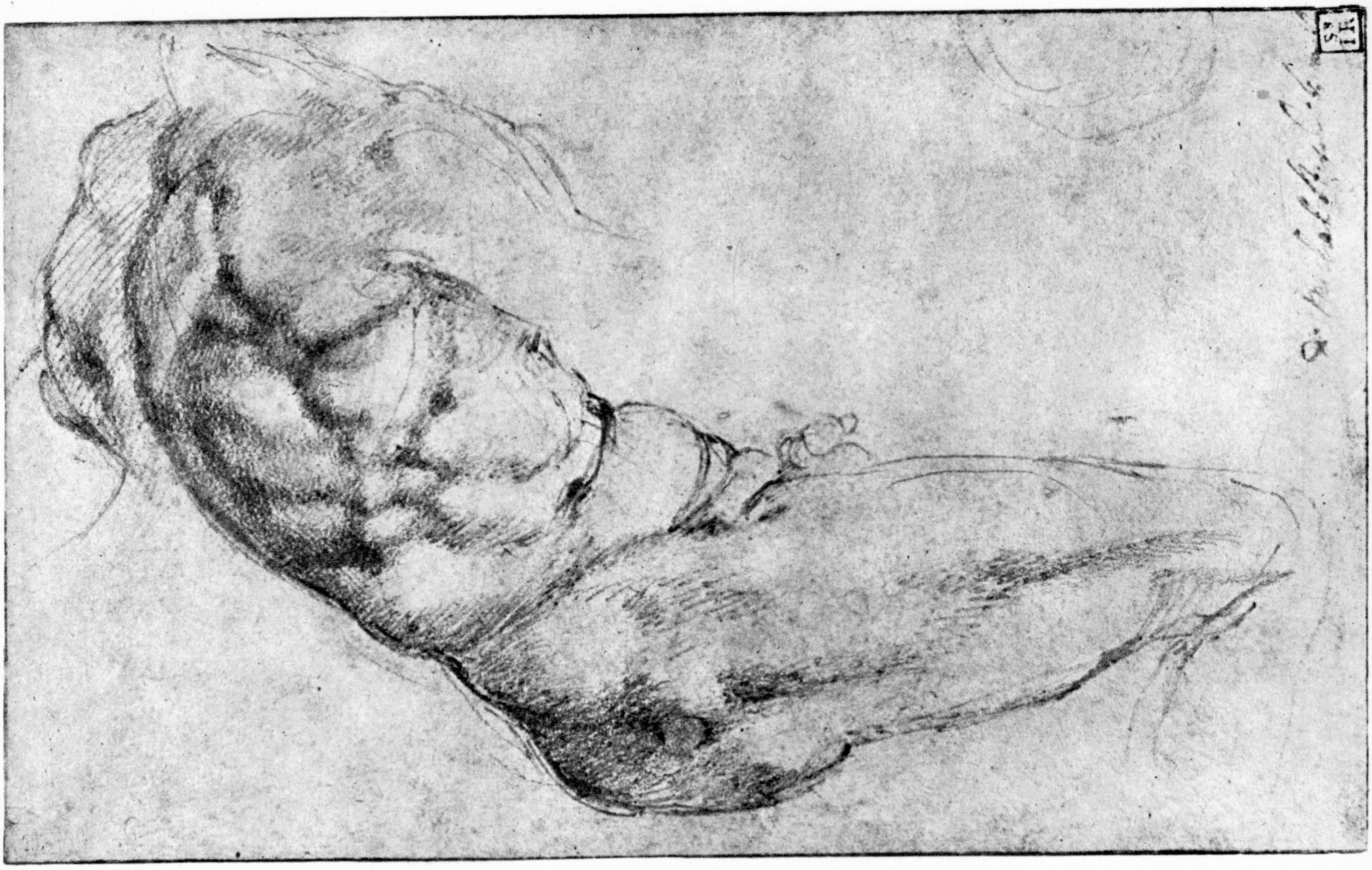

63. *Study for the 'Day' in the Medici Chapel*. 1525–30. Oxford

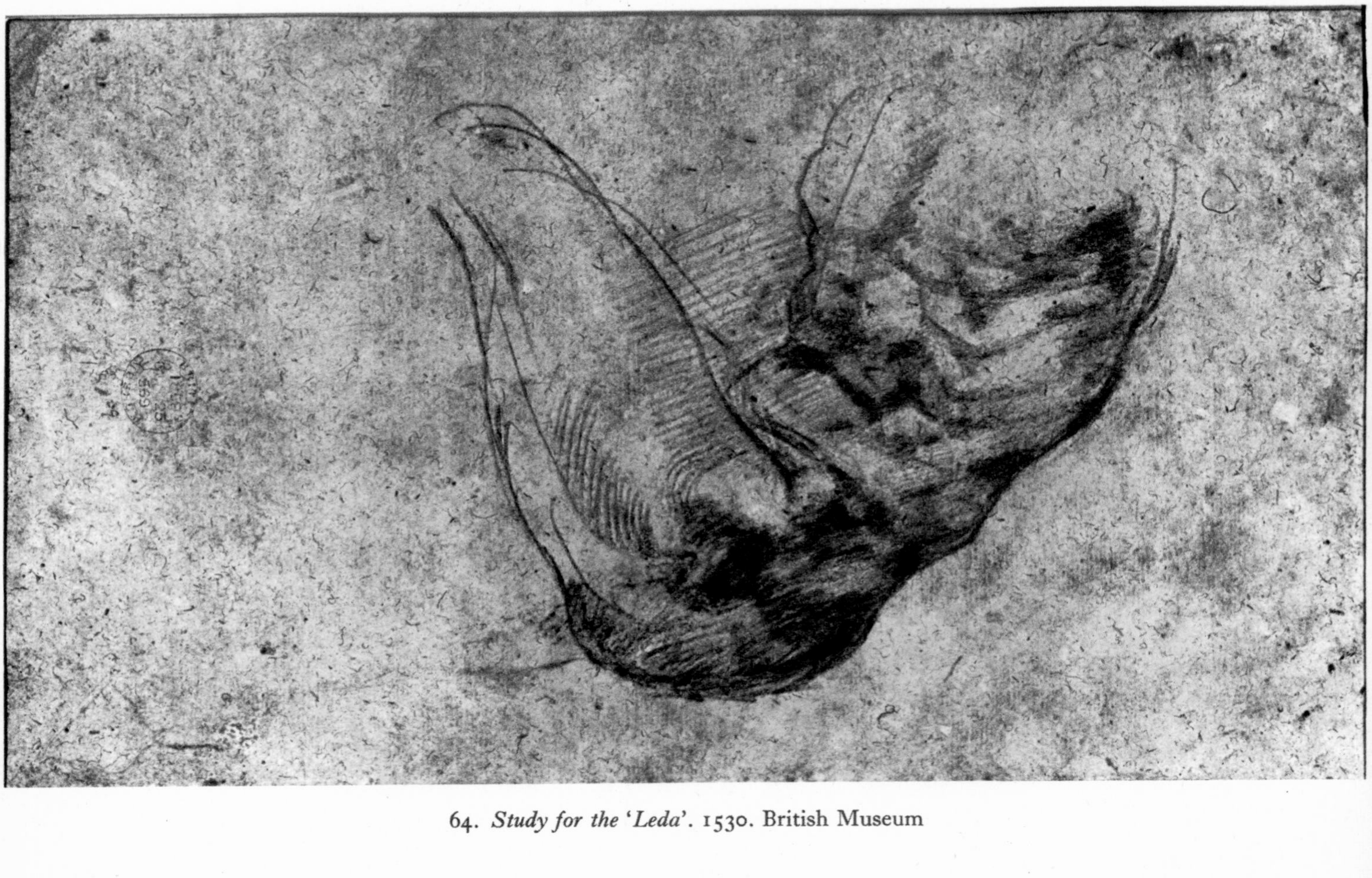

64. *Study for the 'Leda'*. 1530. British Museum

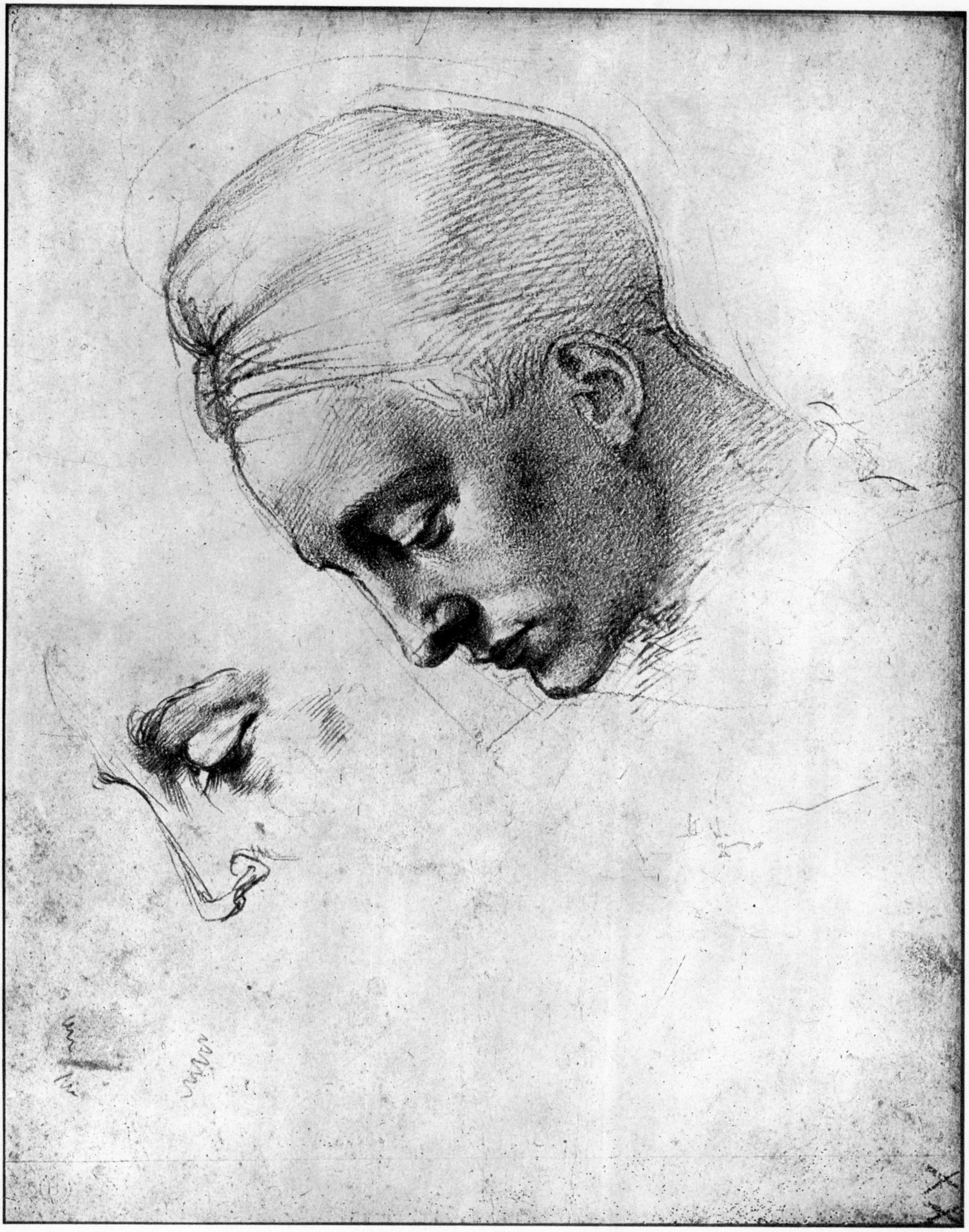

65. *Study for the Head of 'Leda'*. 1530. Casa Buonarroti

66. *Four Masks, and a Sketch for 'Hercules and Antaeus'*. About 1525. British Museum

67. *Two Figures struggling.* (*Abduction of a Woman.*) About 1530. Haarlem

68. *Three male Figures in violent movement*. About 1531. Casa Buonarroti

69. *Design for small plastic works*. About 1530. Fogg Museum

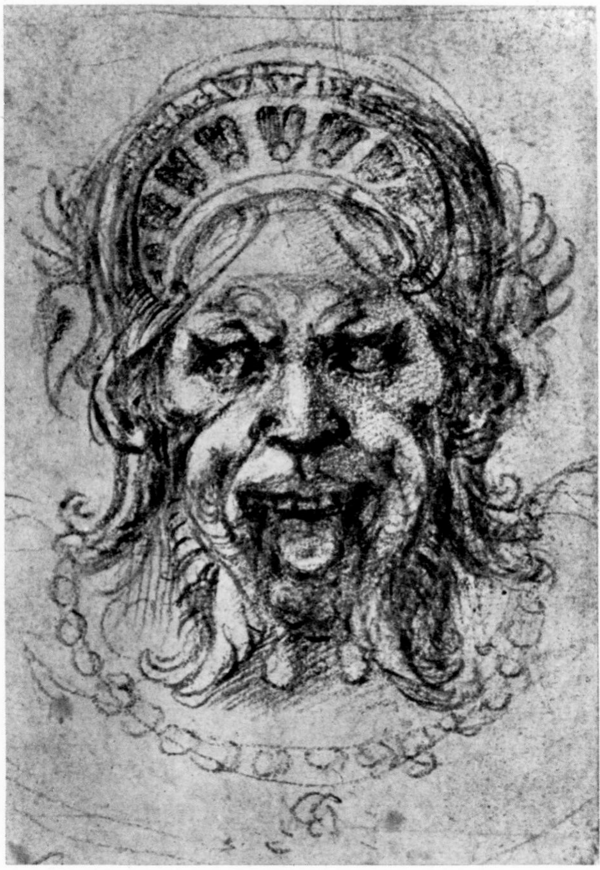

70. *Decorative Mask*. About 1530. Windsor

71. *Design for a Salt-cellar*. About 1537. British Museum

72. *Samson and Delilah*. About 1530. Oxford

73. *Three Labours of Hercules.* (Presentation drawing.) About 1530. Windsor

74. *Archers shooting at a Herm.* (Presentation drawing.) About 1530. Windsor

75. *Tityus.* (Presentation drawing for Tommaso de' Cavalieri.) 1532. Windsor

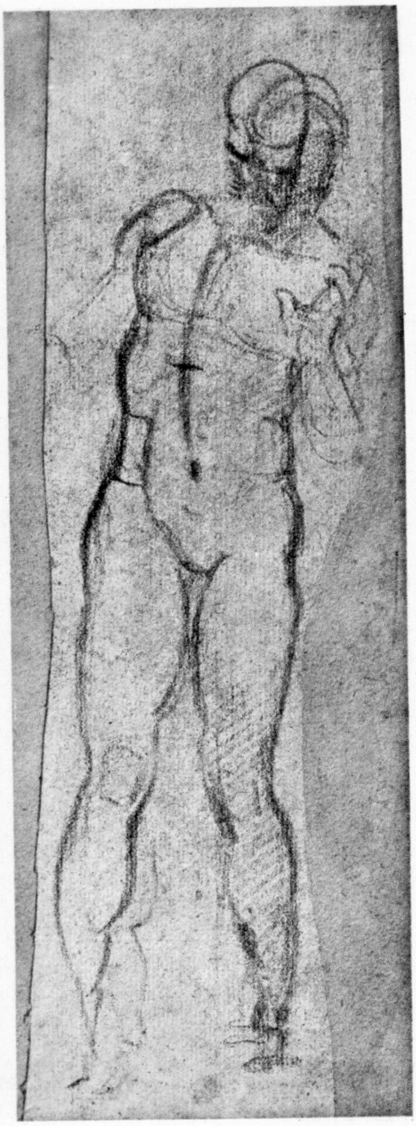

76–78. *Three Studies for the 'Resurrection of Christ'*. About 1532–33. Windsor (76), and Casa Buonarroti (77 and 78)

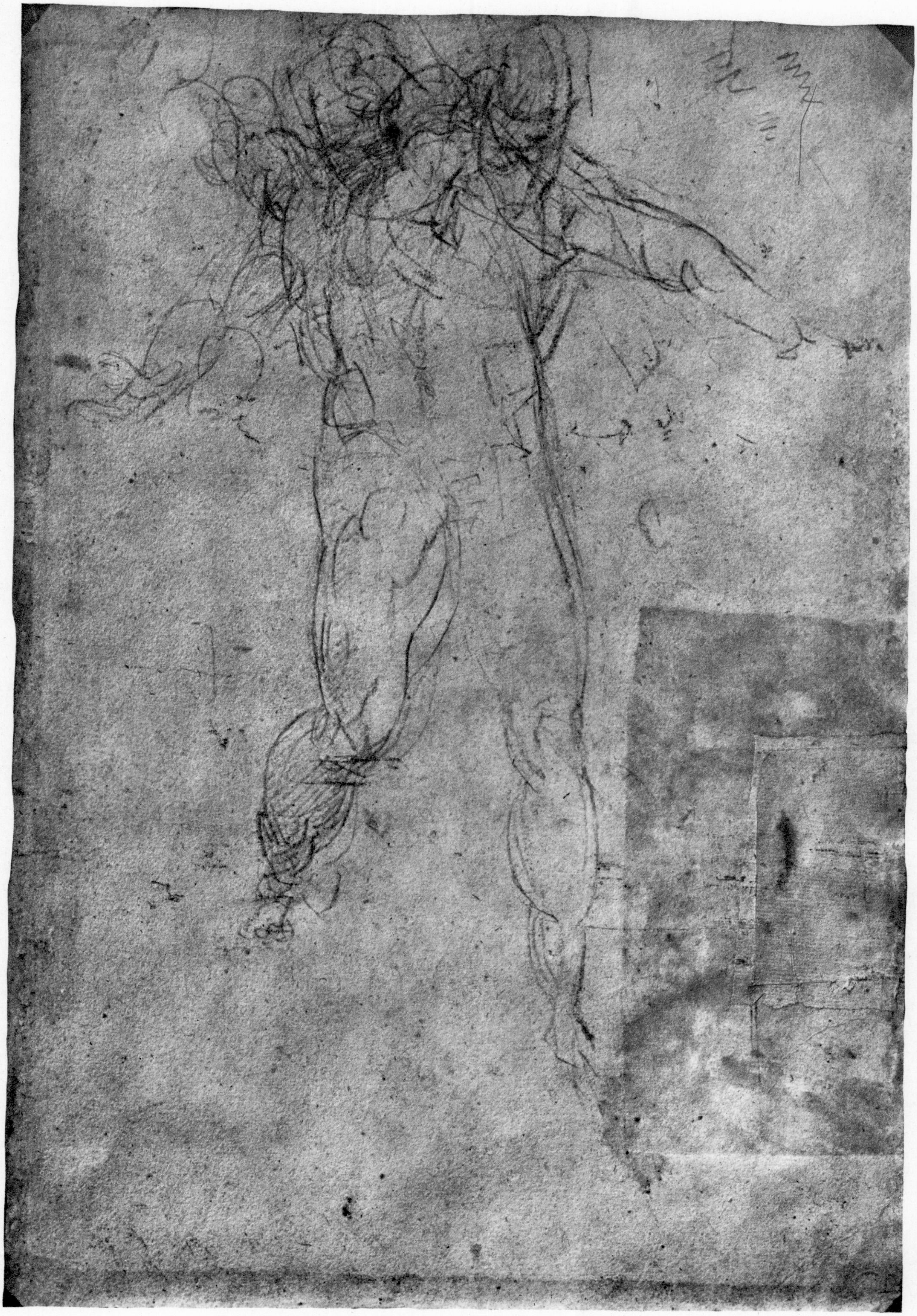

79. *Study for the 'Resurrection of Christ'*. About 1532. Casa Buonarroti

*80. *The Resurrection of Christ*. About 1532. Louvre

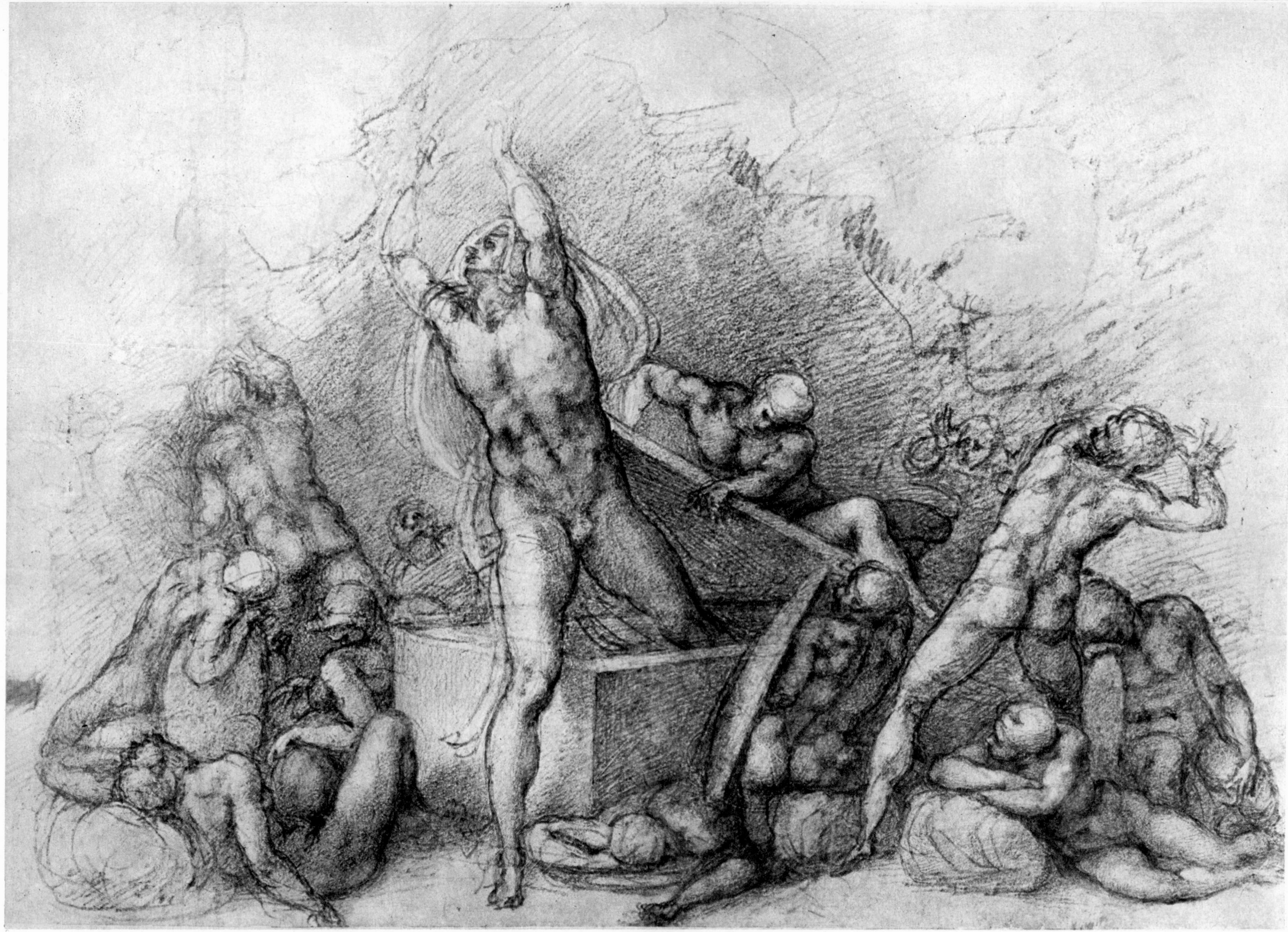

81. *The Resurrection of Christ*. About 1532–33. Windsor

82. *The Resurrection of Christ*. About 1532–33. British Museum

83. *The Risen Christ*. About 1533. British Museum

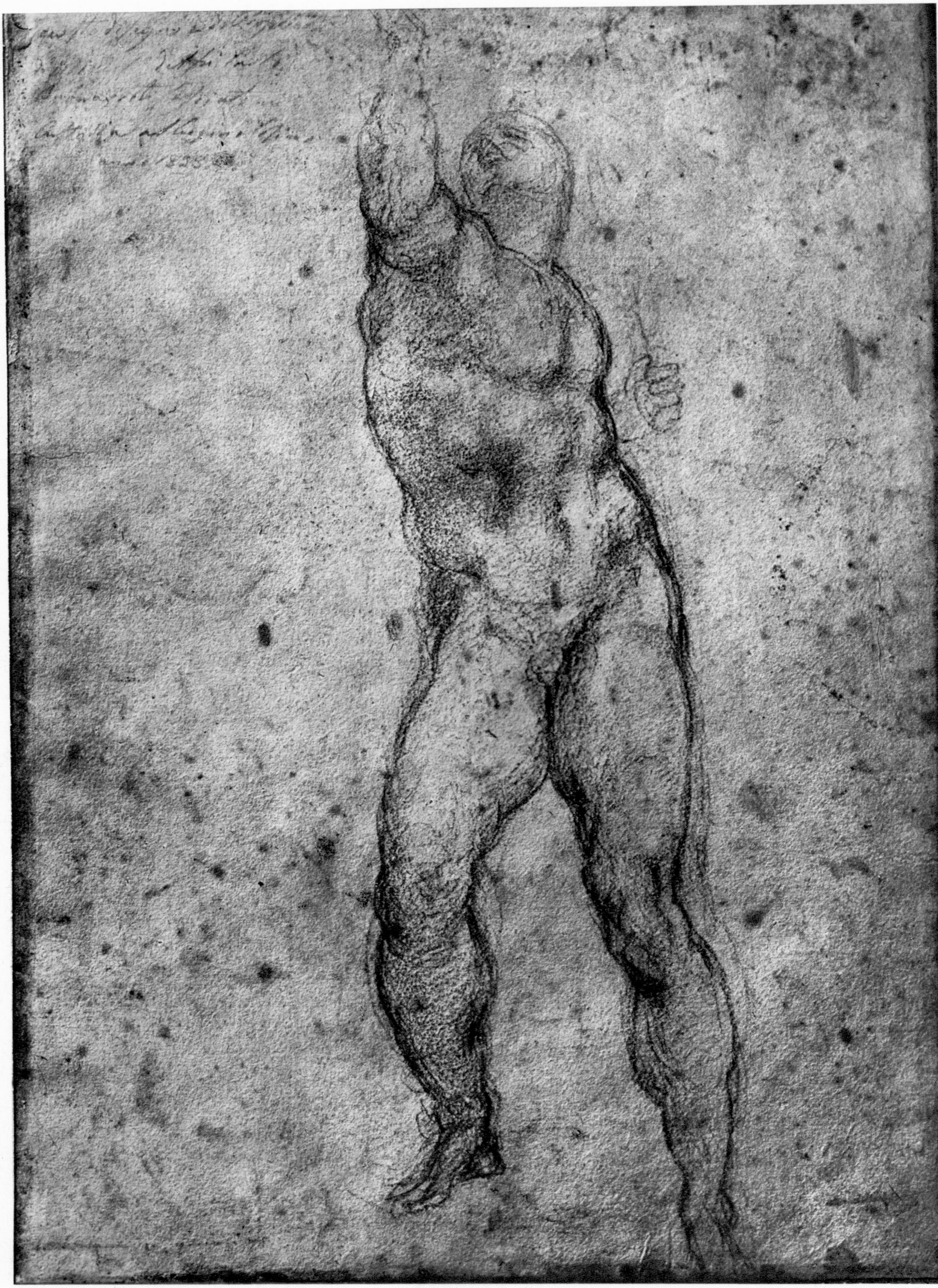

84. *The Risen Christ*. About 1533. Casa Buonarroti

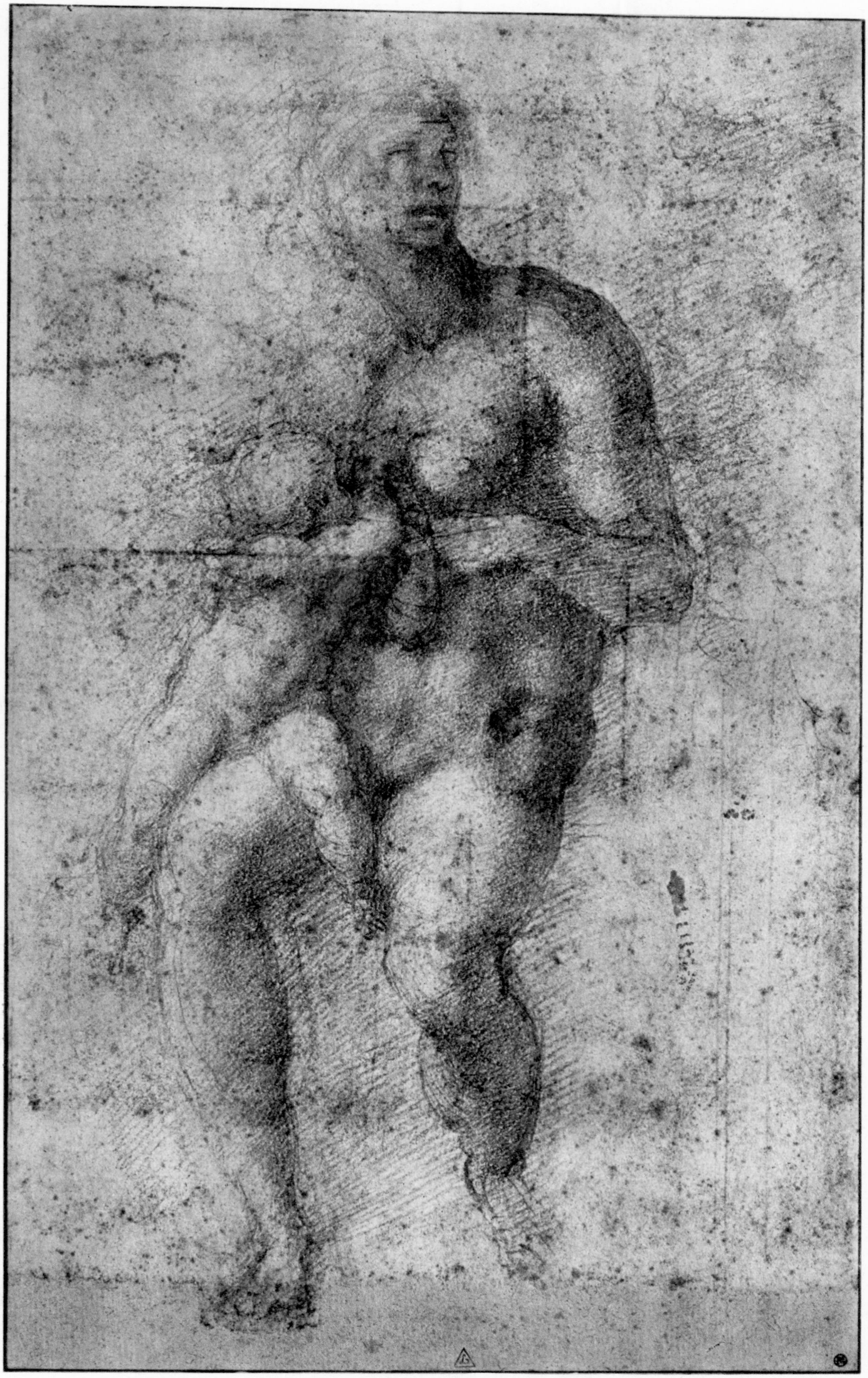

85. *Study for a 'Holy Family'*. About 1533. British Museum

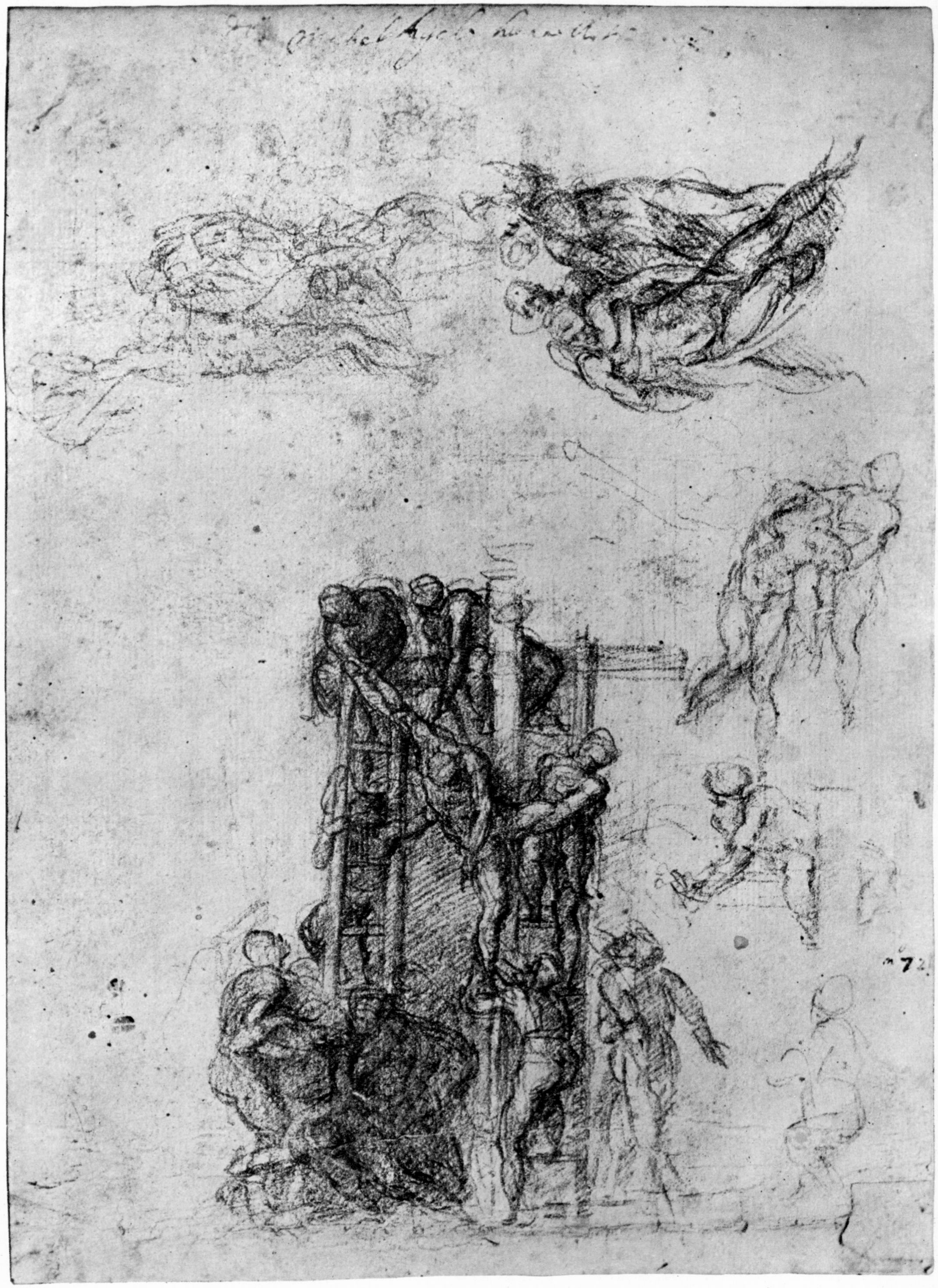

*86. *The Descent from the Cross.* About 1533. Haarlem

87. *The Three Crosses*. About 1533. British Museum

88. '*The Brazen Serpent*'. About 1533. Oxford

89. *A Bacchanal of Children.* (Presentation drawing for Tommaso de' Cavalieri.) About 1533. Windsor

*90. *Unfinished Study of a Head*. About 1533. Windsor

91. *The Fall of Phaethon*. (Presentation drawing for Tommaso de' Cavalieri. First version.) 1533. British Museum

92. *The Fall of Phaethon*. (Presentation drawing for Tommaso de' Cavalieri. Second version.) 1533. Venice

93. *The Fall of Phaethon.* (Presentation drawing for Tommaso de' Cavalieri. Third version.) 1533. Windsor

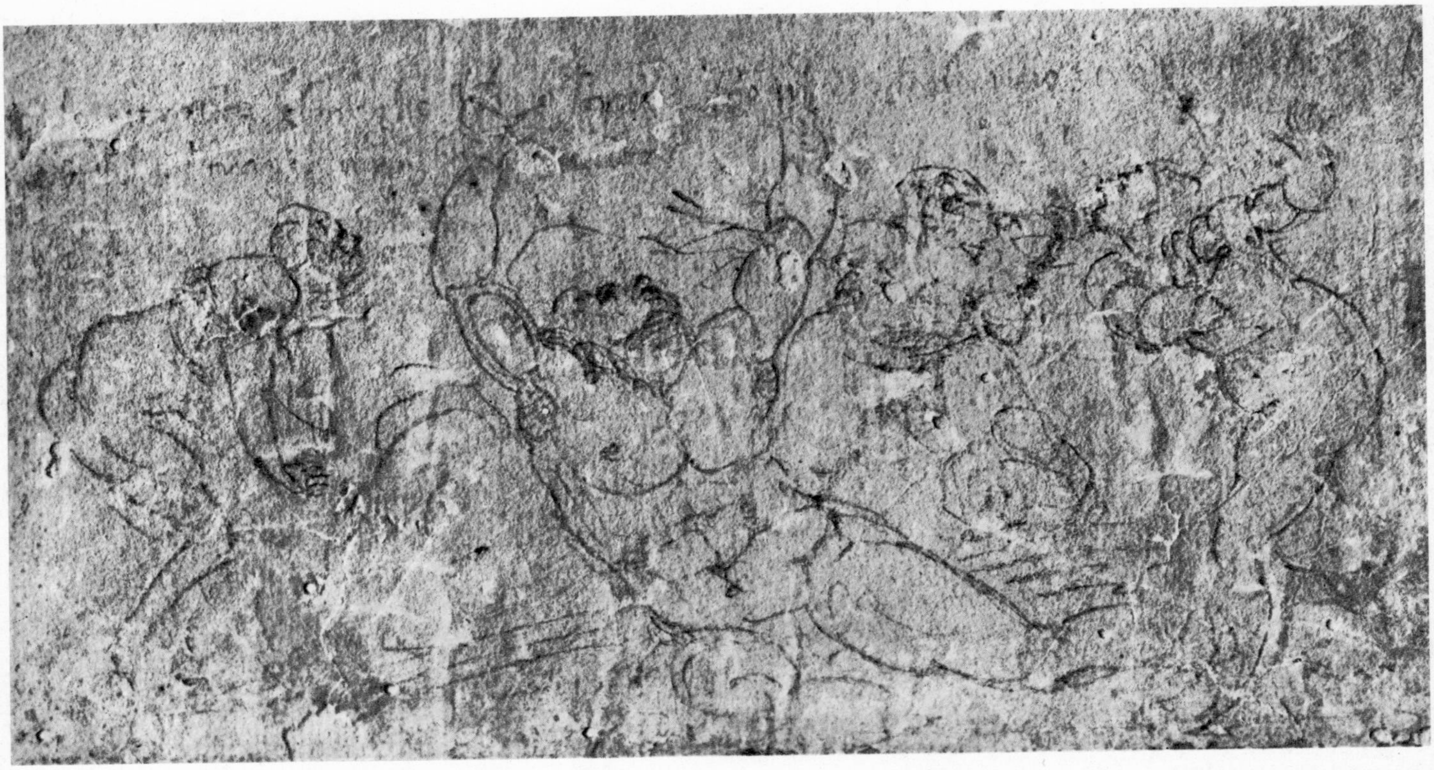

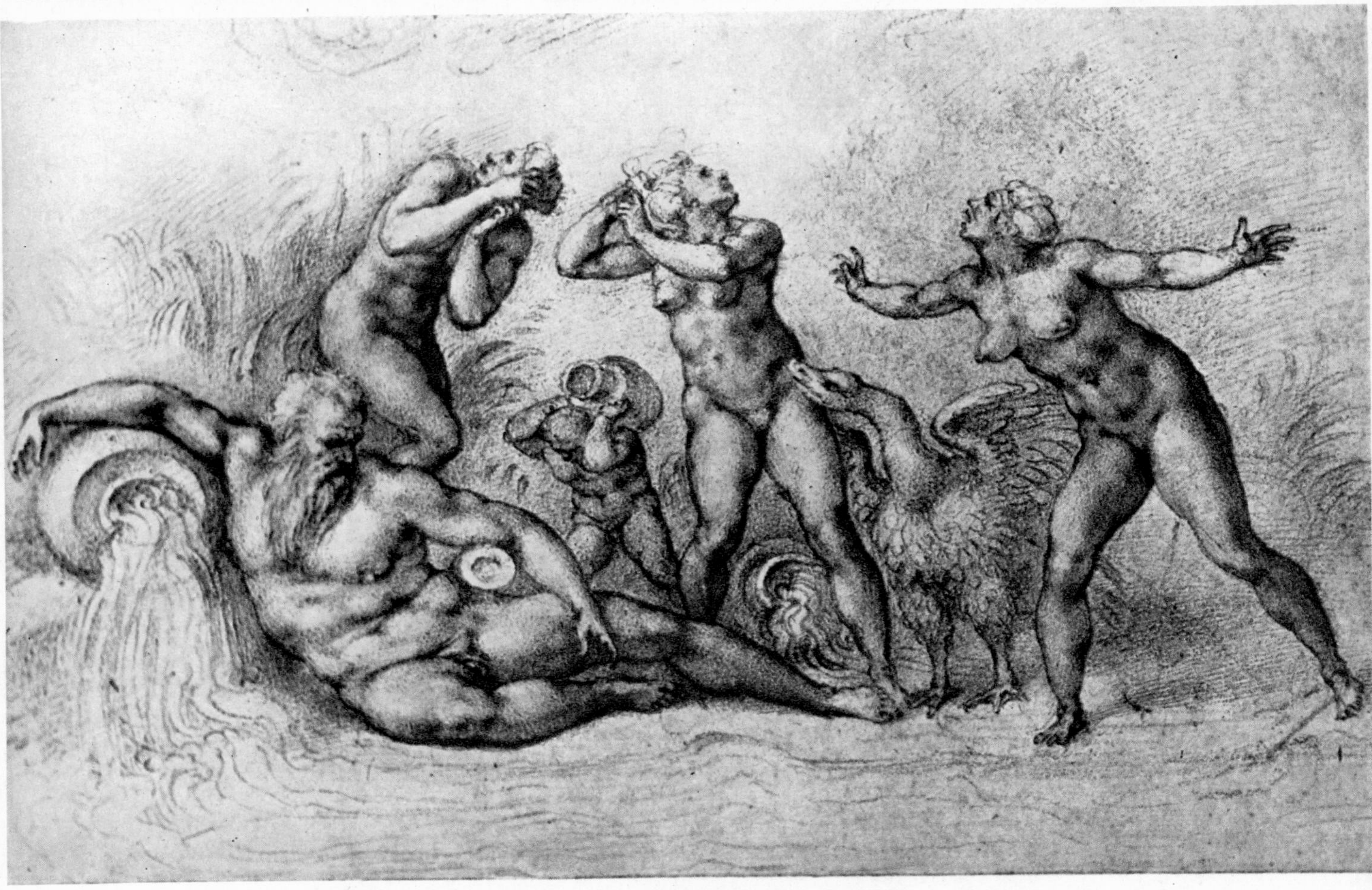

94–95. *Eridanus and the Heliades*. 1533. Details from Plates 92 and 93

*96. *Cleopatra*. (Presentation drawing.) About 1533. Casa Buonarroti

97. '*The Dream*'. (Presentation drawing.) About 1534. London, Count Antoine Seilern

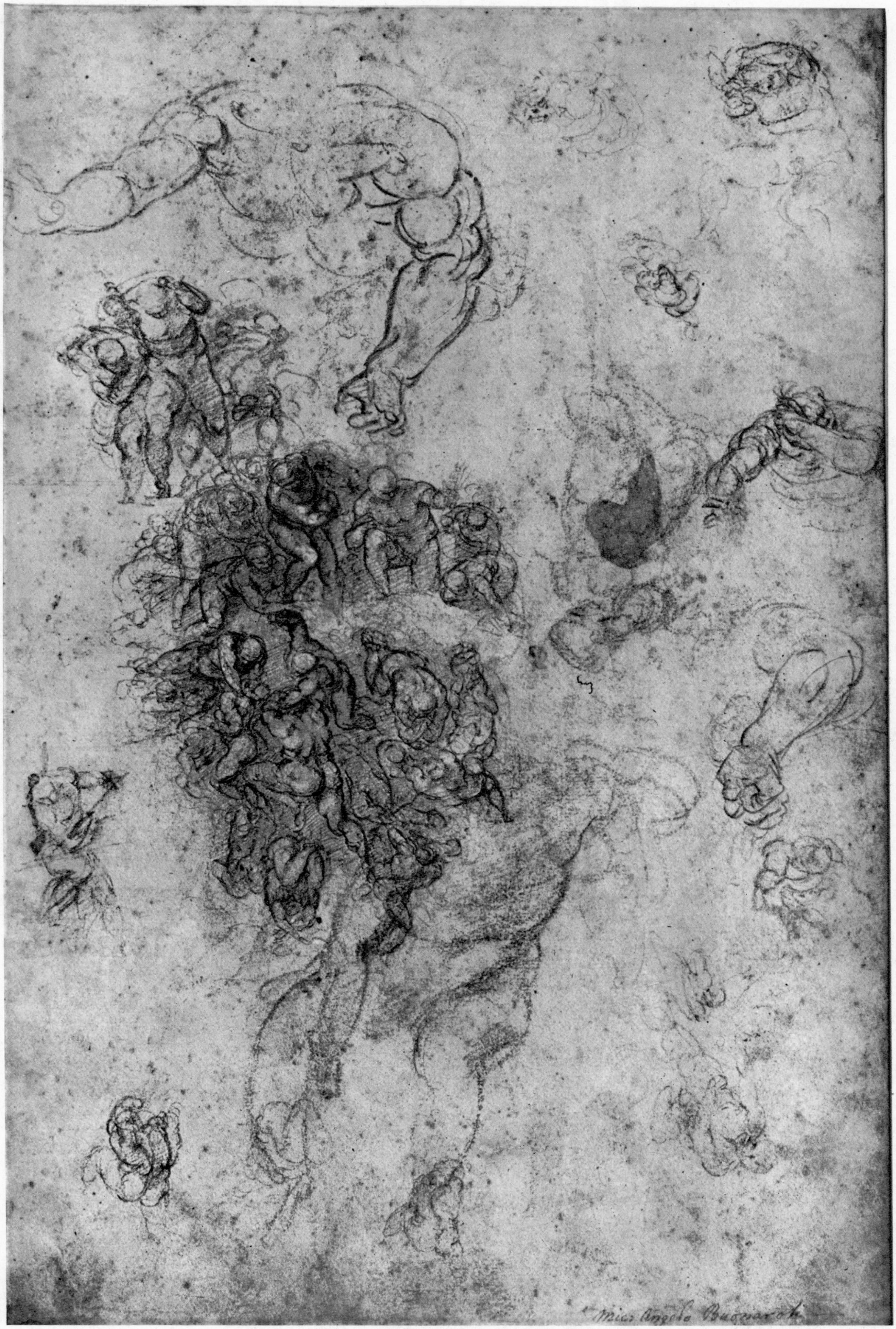

98. *Study for the 'Last Judgement'*. About 1534. British Museum

99. *Study for the 'Last Judgement'*. About 1533–34. Bayonne

100. *Study for the 'Last Judgement'*. About 1534. Casa Buonarroti

101. *Study for the St Lawrence of the 'Last Judgement'*. About 1534. Haarlem

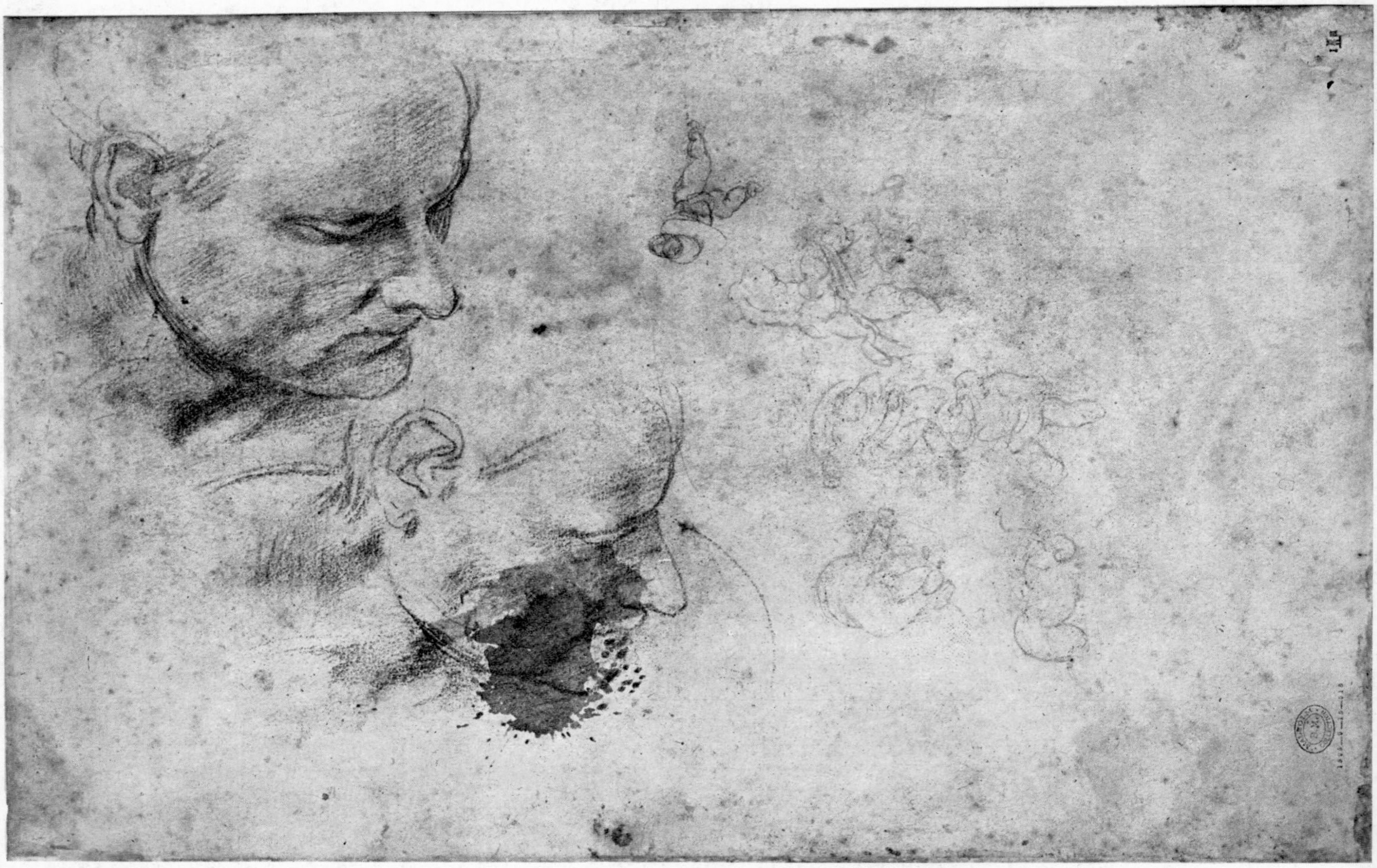

102. *Studies of Heads for the 'Last Judgement'*. About 1534. British Museum

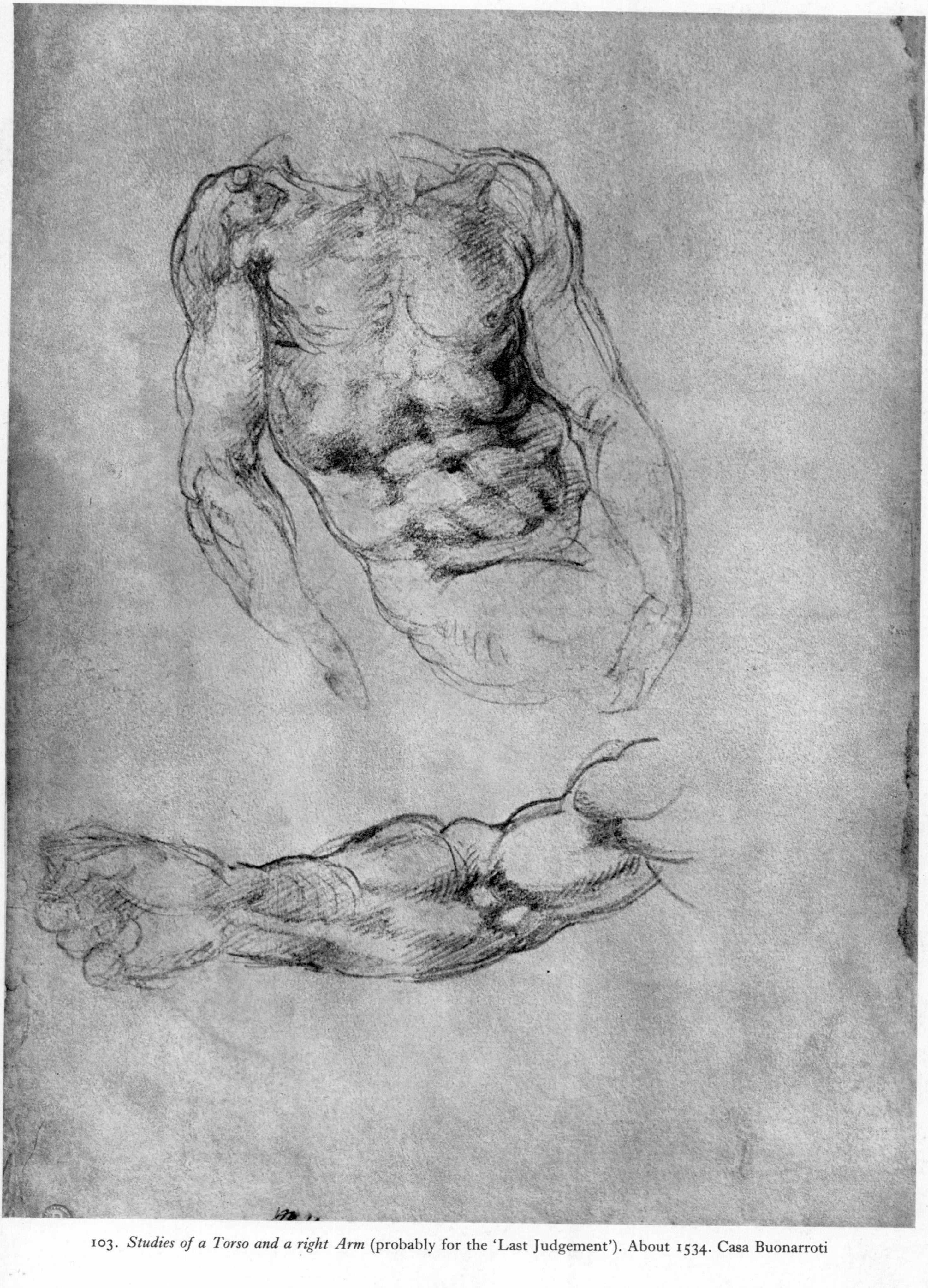

103. *Studies of a Torso and a right Arm* (probably for the 'Last Judgement'). About 1534. Casa Buonarroti

104. *The Sacrifice of Isaac*. About 1535–38. Casa Buonarroti

*105. *Mourning Women at the Foot of the Cross*. About 1535–38. British Museum

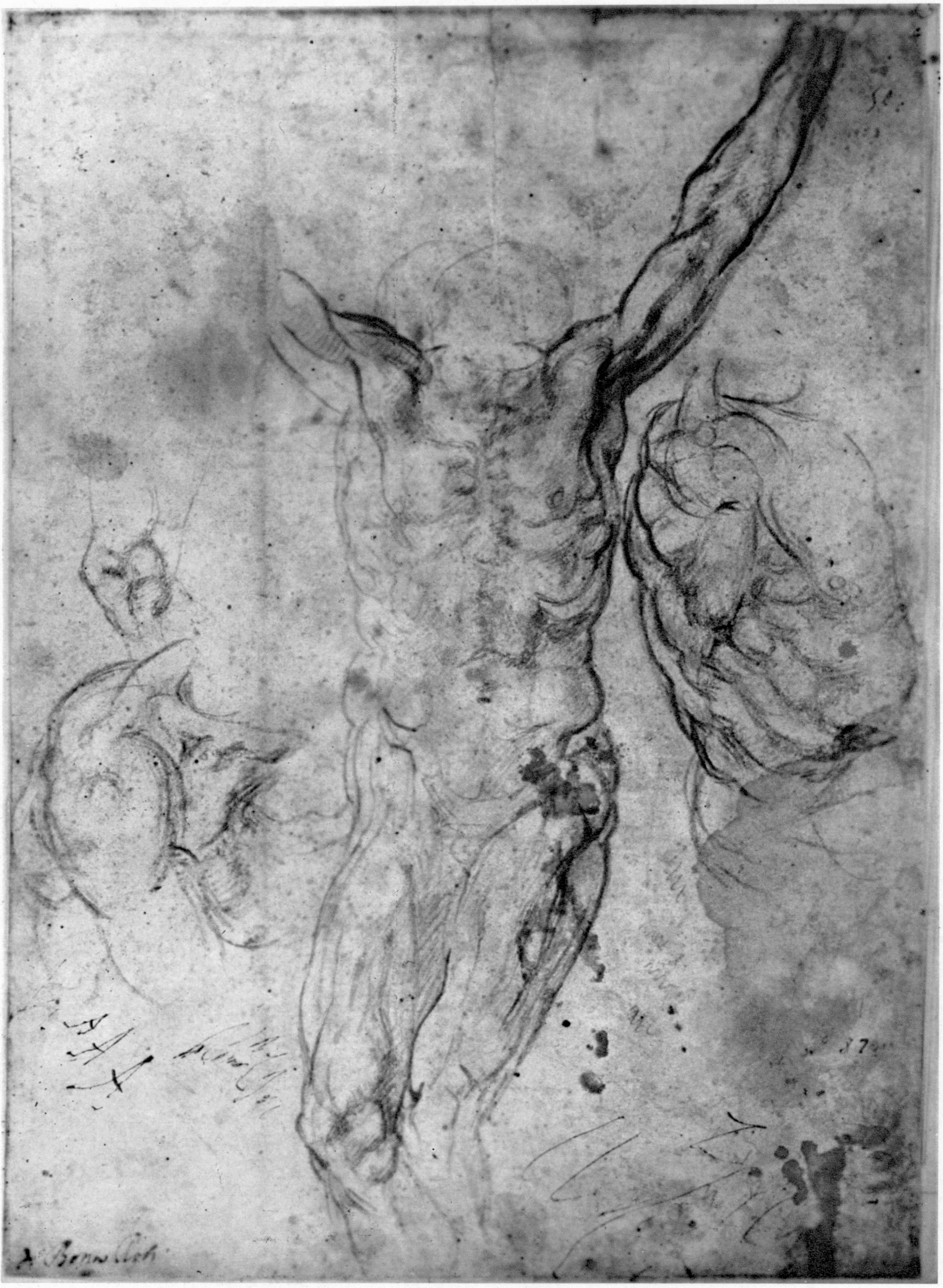

106. *Studies for a Christ on the Cross*. About 1538. Haarlem

107. *Christ on the Cross*. (Presentation drawing for Vittoria Colonna.) 1539–41. British Museum

108. *Pietà*. (Presentation drawing for Vittoria Colonna.) 1542. Boston, Isabella Stewart Gardner Museum

109. *The Holy Family* ('Madonna del Silenzio'). About 1538–42. London, The Duke of Portland

*110–111. *The Virgin and St John at the foot of the Cross*. About 1542–45. Louvre

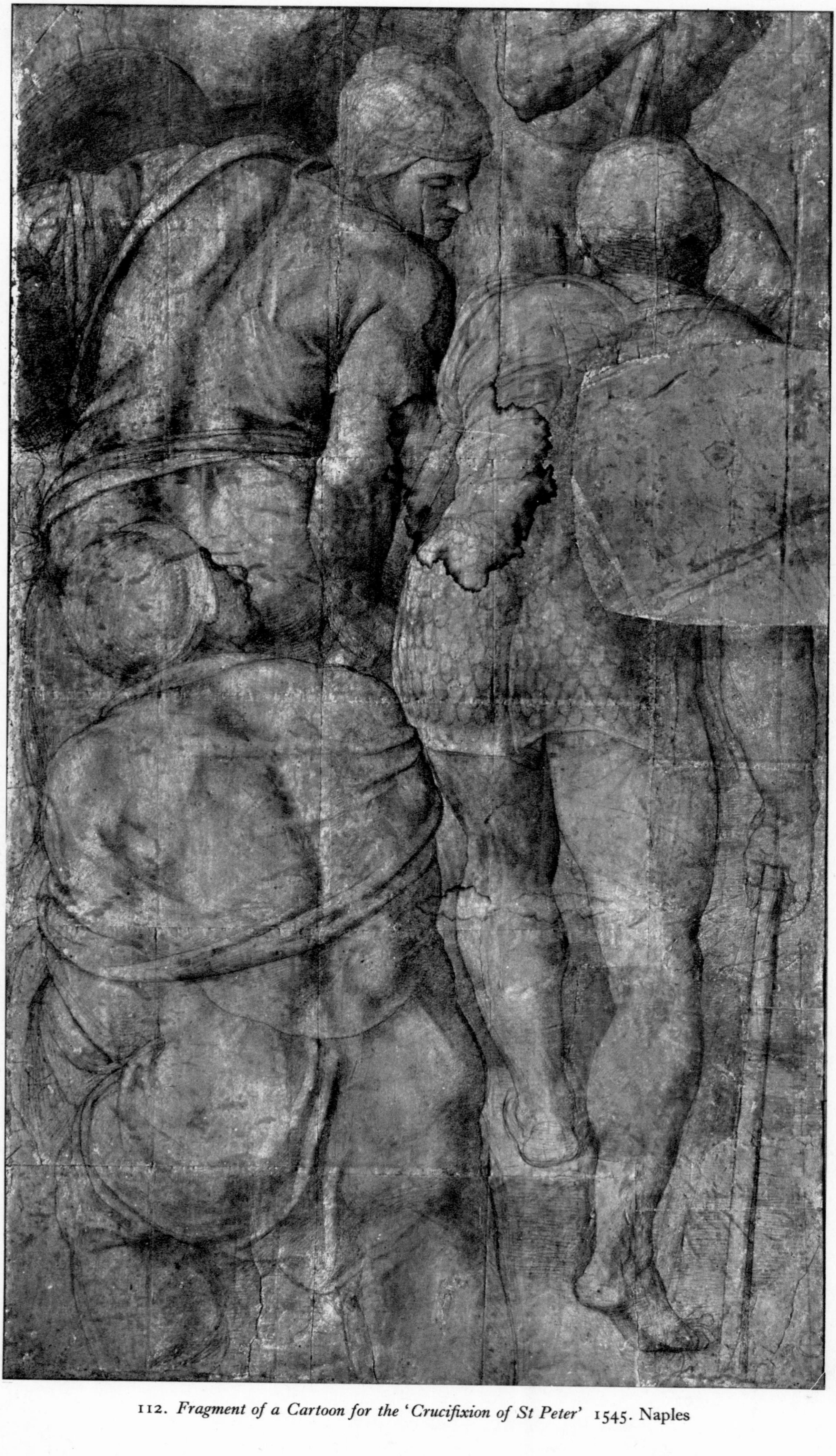

112. *Fragment of a Cartoon for the 'Crucifixion of St Peter'* 1545. Naples

113. *The Virgin of the Annunciation*. About 1547. British Museum

114. *The Annunciation*. About 1547. British Museum

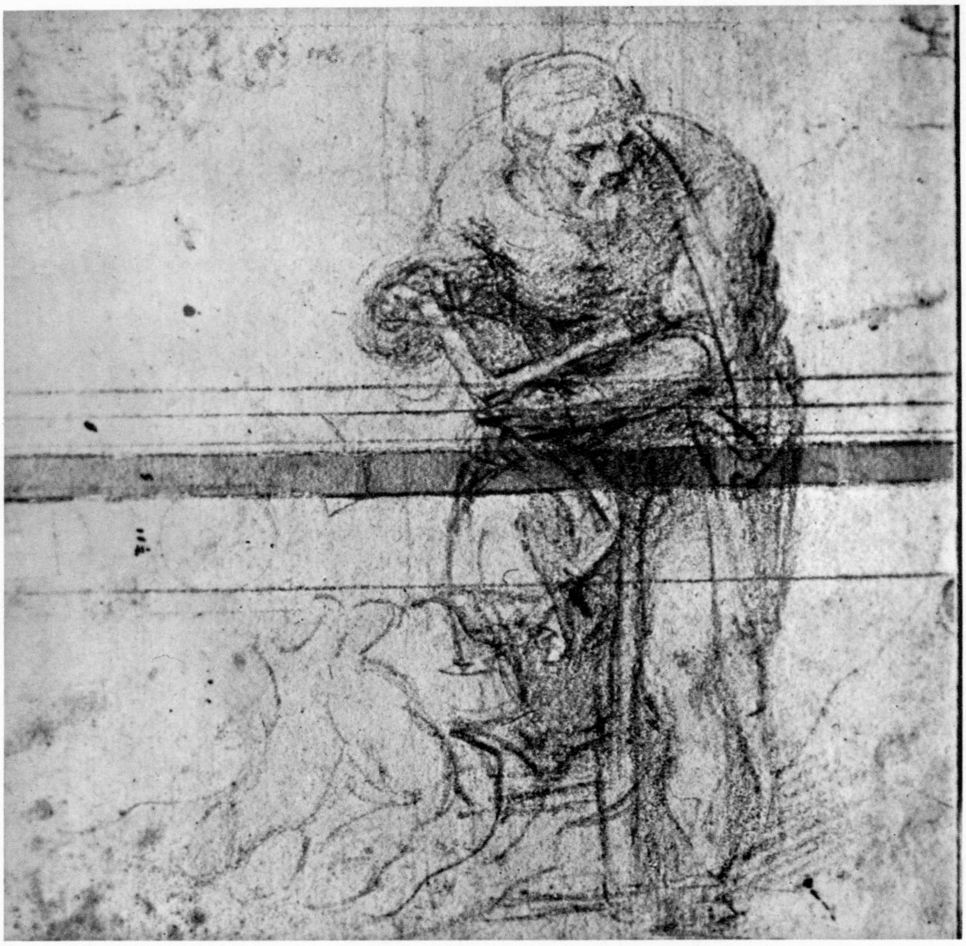

115. *Prophet* (*or Apostle*) *holding a Book*. About 1548–50. Haarlem

116. *Aeneas and Dido*. About 1548–50. Haarlem

117. *Cartoon for a 'Holy Family'* ('Epifania'). About 1550. British Museum

118. *Studies for a Battle Scene* (*and Studies for* '*Christ expelling the Money-changers*'). About 1550. Oxford

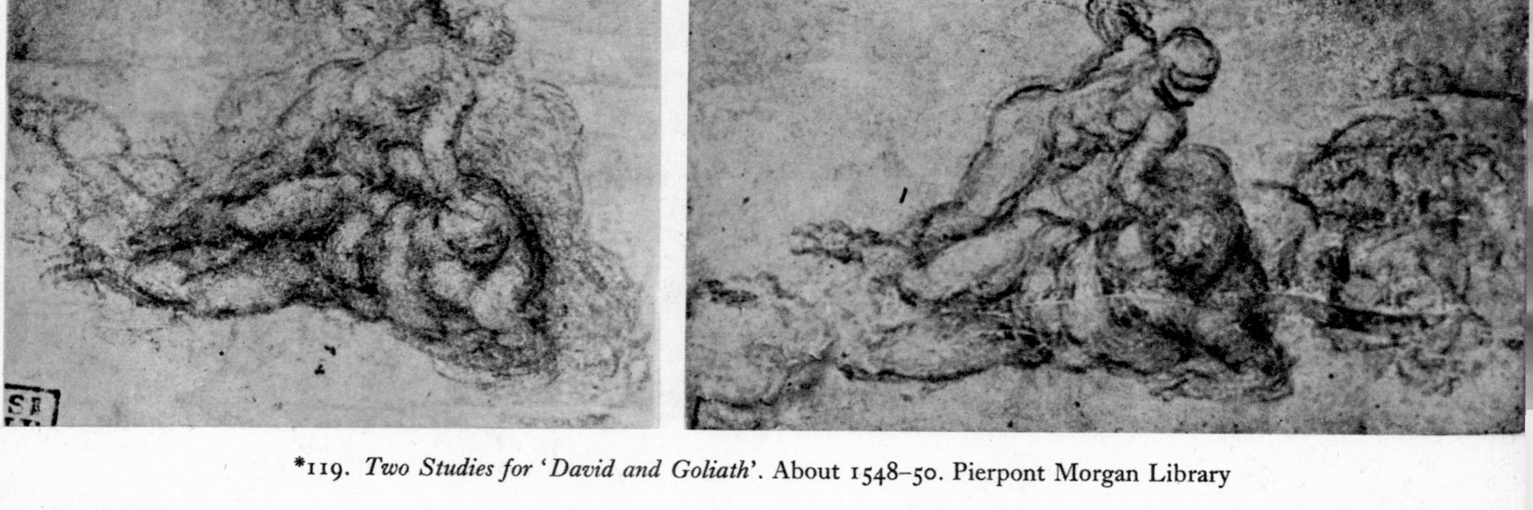

*119. *Two Studies for* '*David and Goliath*'. About 1548–50. Pierpont Morgan Library

120. *Christ driving the Money-changers from the Temple*. About 1550–53. British Museum

121. *Christ driving the Money-changers from the Temple*. About 1550–53. British Museum

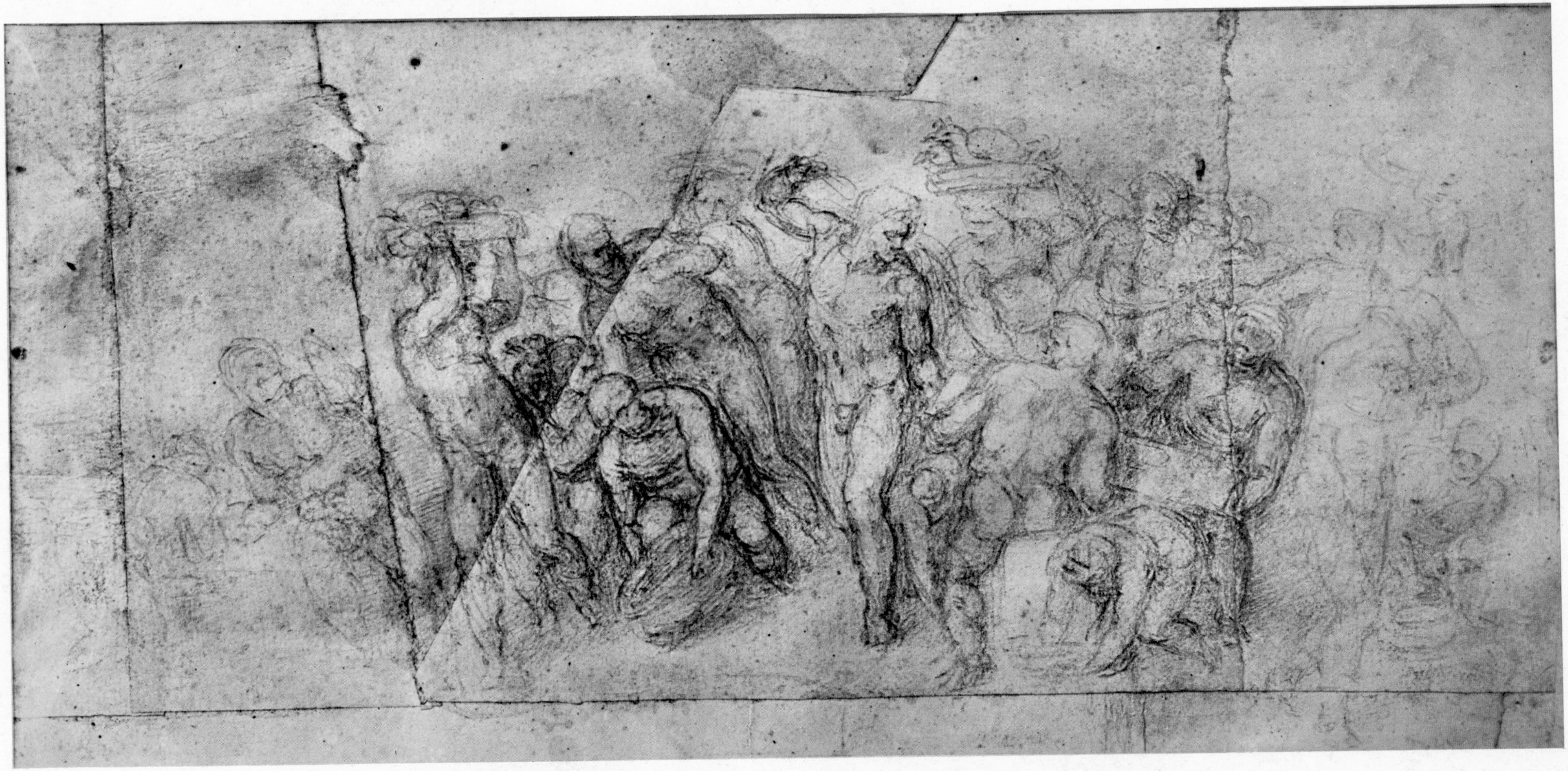

122. *Christ driving the Money-changers from the Temple*. About 1550–53. British Museum

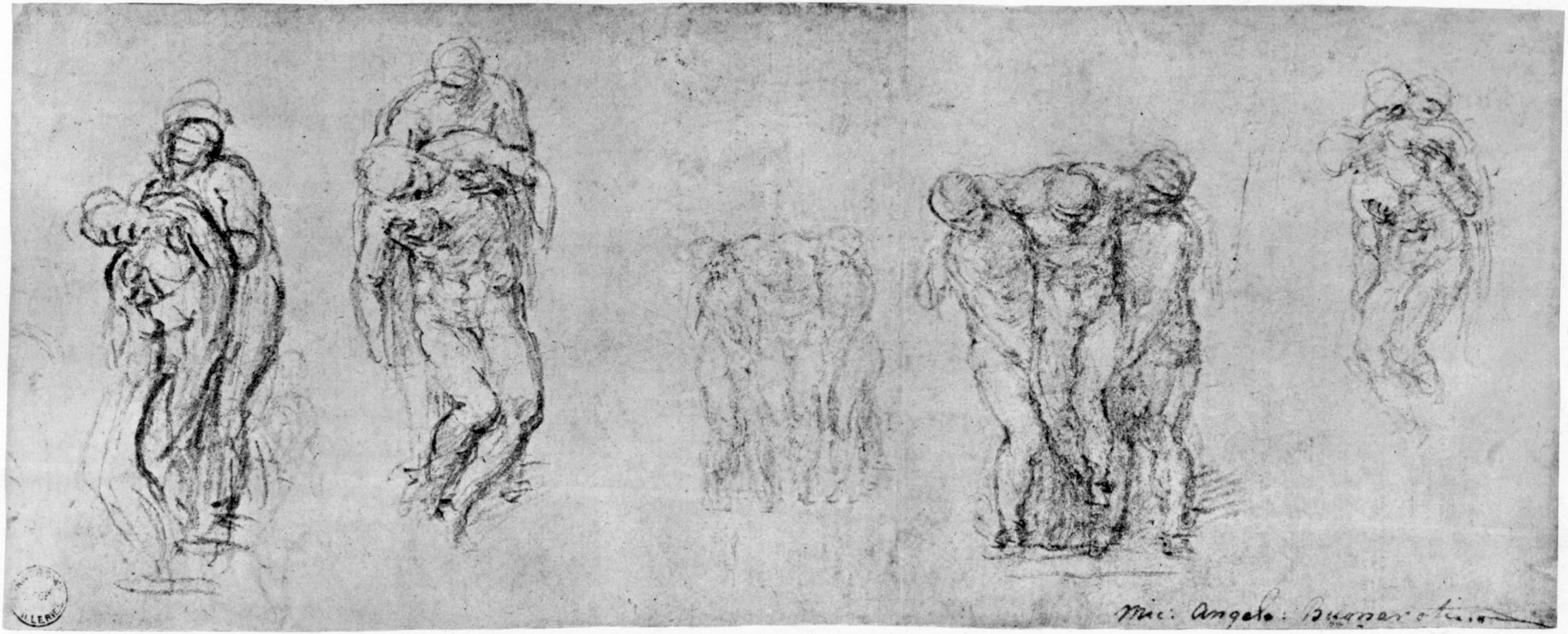

*123. *Studies for a Pietà and an Entombment*. About 1553–56. Oxford

124. *Christ on the Cross*. About 1553–56. Oxford

*125. *The Annunciation*. Between 1556 and 1560. Oxford

126. *Christ on the Cross*. About 1558–60. Windsor

127. *Christ on the Cross*. About 1558–60. British Museum

*128. *Madonna and Child*. After 1560. British Museum

APPENDIX OF PLATES

Jonson: So thou canst distinguish the false from the true?
Lister: I can, or I think I can, which is nearly the same thing.

GEORGE MOORE

a

b

PLATE I.—(a) Copy of Michelangelo's '*Battle Cartoon*', by Aristotile da Sangallo, 1542. Holkham Hall, Earl of Leicester.
(b) Attributed to Michelangelo: Sketch for the '*Battle Cartoon*', 1504. Florence, Uffizi.

PLATE II.—*Sixteenth century reproductions of Michelangelo's presentation sheets for Vittoria Colonna.*—(a) *Christ on the Cross*, engraving after Michelangelo's drawing of c. 1540.—(b) *Christ on the Cross*, painting by Marcello Venusti, after Michelangelo's design. Uffizi.

(c) *Pietà*, engraving by Bonasone, 1546, after Michelangelo's drawing of c. 1542.—(d) *Christ and the Woman of Samaria*, engraving by Beatrizet, after Michelangelo's drawing of c. 1542.

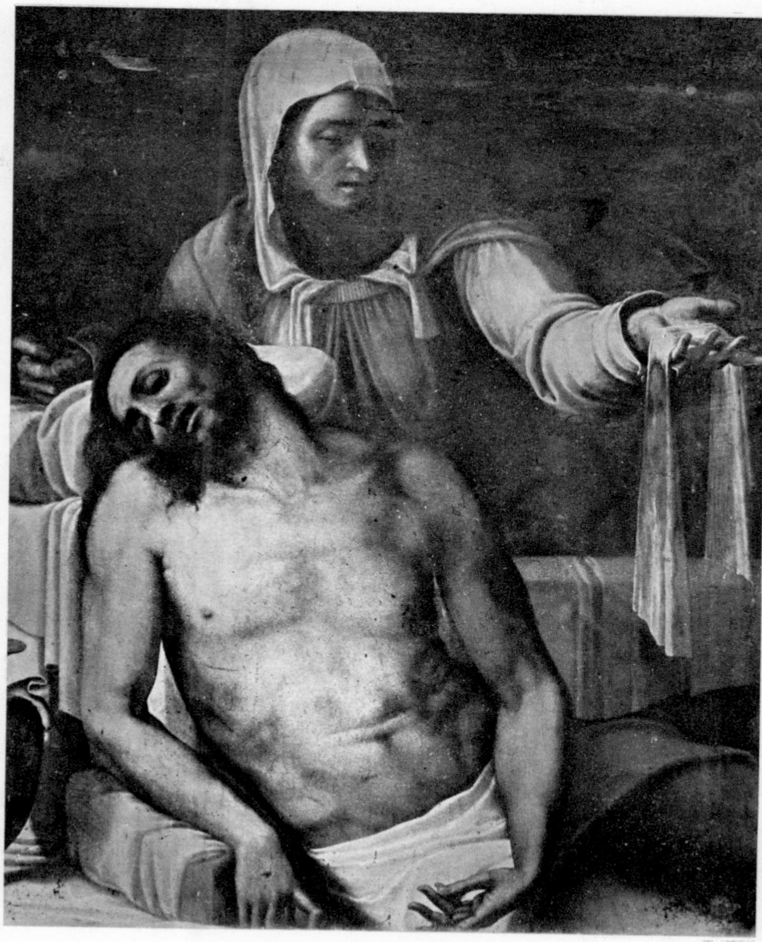

b

c

PLATE III.—*Three religious compositions, after cartoons by Michelangelo.*—(a) '*Noli me tangere*', painting by Battista Franco. Casa Buonarroti.—(b) *Pietà*, painting by Sebastiano del Piombo, 1537–39. Ubeda, San Salvador.—(c) *Annunciation*, engraving by Beatrizet.

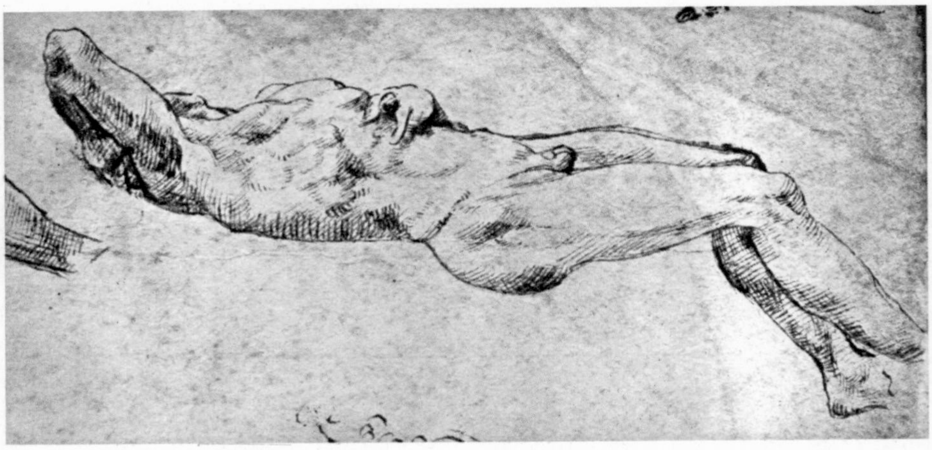

a

b

c

d

e

f

g

PLATE IV.—Michelangelo as a Humanist.—(a–b) Dying Niobid, antique marble statue, before 1540 in the Casa Maffei, Rome: details of a drawing attributed to Perino del Vaga. Private collection, London. —(c) The same statue, now in the Munich Glyptothek.

(d) Michelangelo: 'The dying Slave'. Louvre.—(e) Verrocchio: Medusa, detail of a terracotta bust, c. 1478. National Gallery, Washington.— (f) Raphael: Medusa, detail of a drawing, 1511. Oxford.—(g) Michelangelo: 'Damned Soul', detail of a drawing (Plate 50).

a

b

PLATE V.—The Bed of Polycletus.—(a) Designed by Niccolò Tribolo. Mosaic floor in the Biblioteca Laurenziana, c. 1534.—(b) Early Renaissance copy of an ancient relief, once in the collection of Lorenzo Ghiberti and his family. Rome, Palazzo Mattei.

a

b

c

d

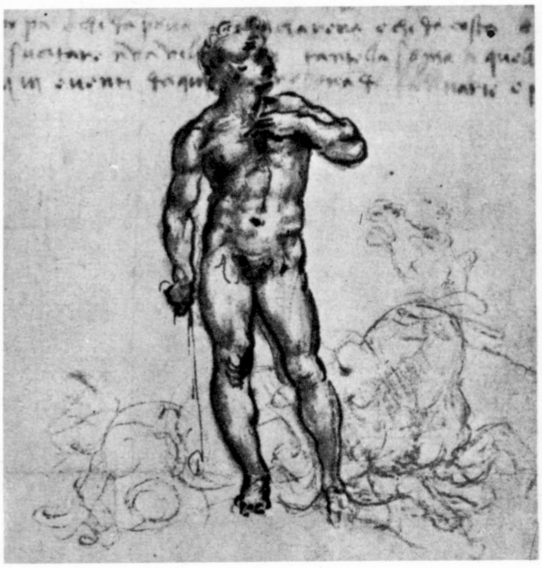

e

f

PLATE VI.—Michelangelo and Leonardo.—(a) Leonardo: Neptune, drawing, c. 1504. Windsor.—(b) Figino (after Michelangelo?): Neptune, detail of a drawing, c. 1580. Windsor.—(c) Detail of Plate VI-a. —(d) Michelangelo: Detail of a drawing, 1532. British Museum. (e) Leonardo: Copy of Michelangelo's 'David', detail of a drawing, 1504. Windsor.—(f) Leonardo: Copy of Michelangelo's 'Moses'. Fodor Museum, Amsterdam.

a

b

c

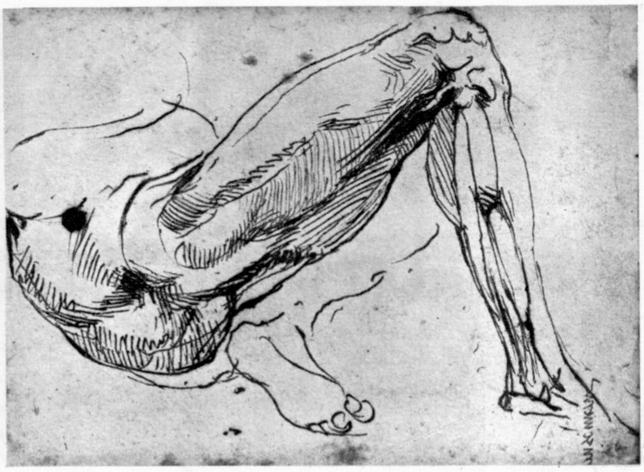

d

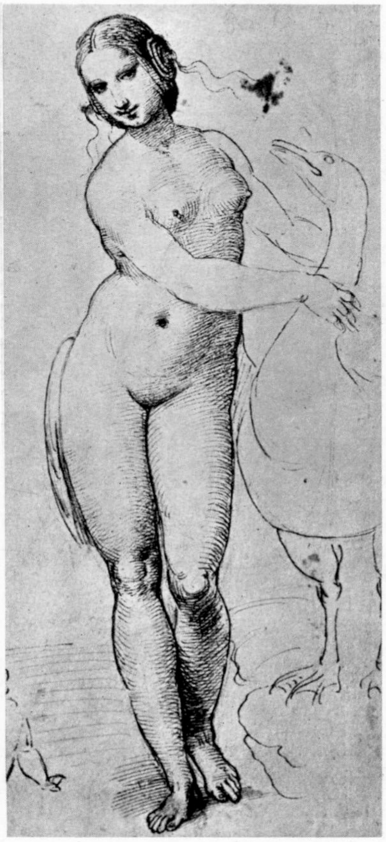

e

f

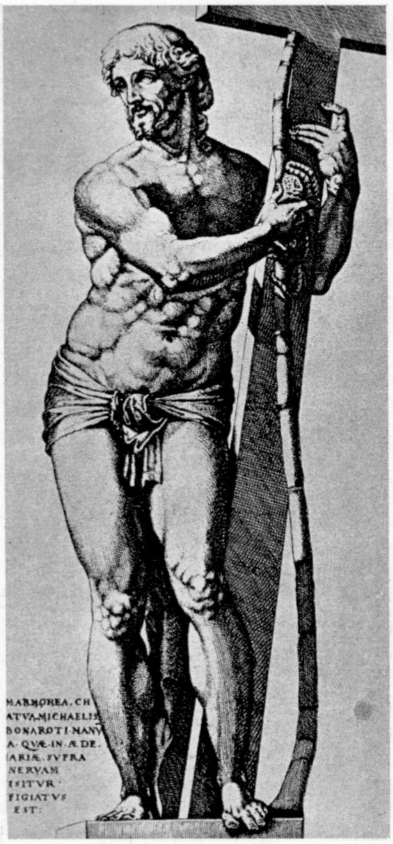

g

PLATE VII.—*Michelangelo and Raphael.*—(a) Detail of an engraving by Marcantonio Raimondi, 'The Judgement of Paris', after Raphael, c. 1512.—(b) Venus and Cupid, copy, attributed to Pontormo, after Michelangelo's cartoon of 1532. Uffizi.—(c) Raphael: Detail from the Farnesina fresco 'The Council of the Gods', c. 1518. (d) Michelangelo: Sketch for a 'River God', c. 1530. (Reversed.) Casa Buonarroti.—(e) Raphael: Copy of Leonardo's drawing 'Leda and the Swan' (detail), c. 1506. Windsor.—(f) Raphael: Detail of a drawing for the 'Disputa', c. 1511. Lille.—(g) Michelangelo's 'Christ' in S. Maria sopra Minerva, 1520. Detail of an engraving by Beatrizet.

a

b

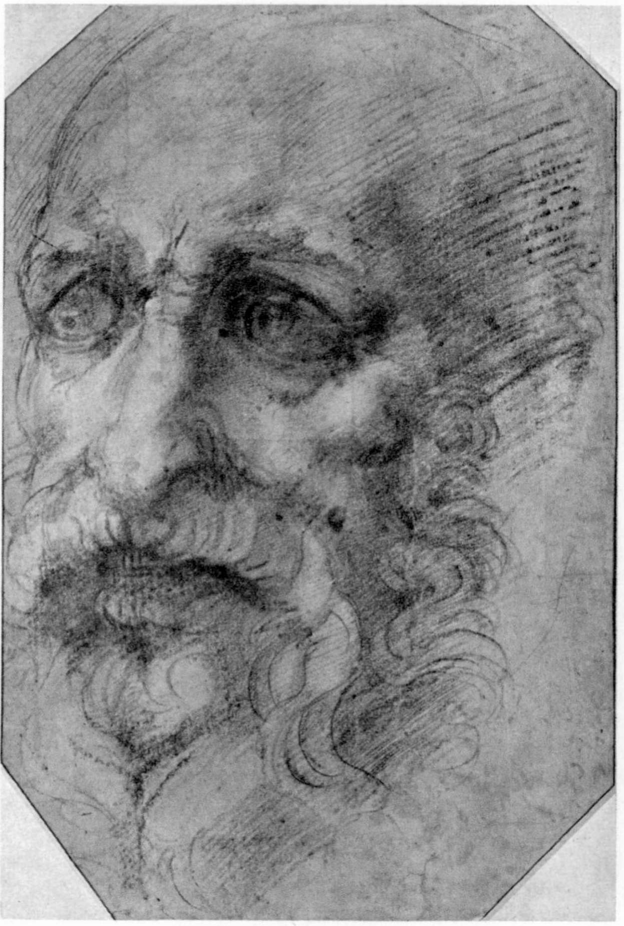

c

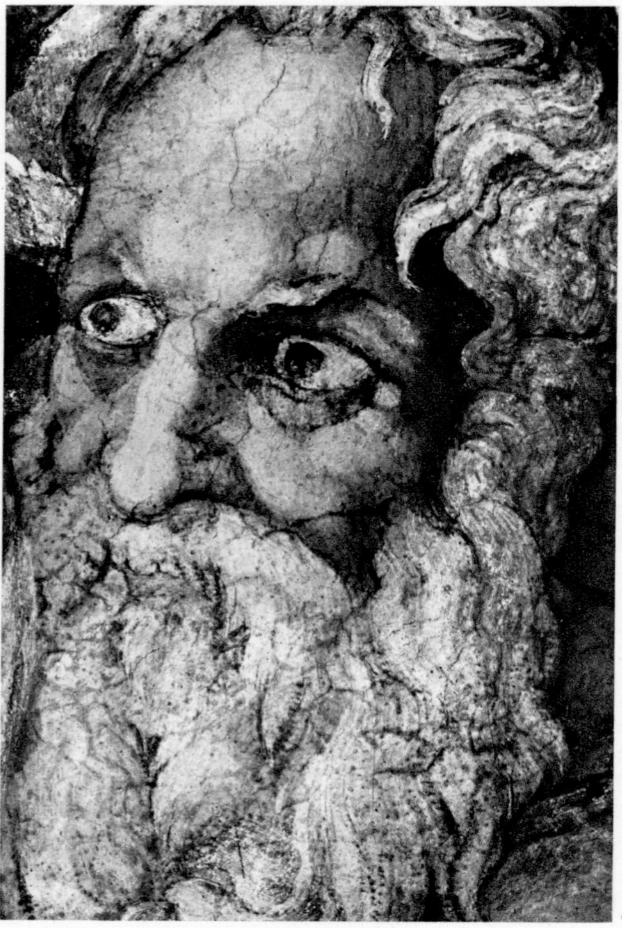

d

PLATE VIII.—(a) Raphael: *St Joseph*, fragment of a cartoon for a 'Holy Family', c. 1518. Bayonne, Musée Bonnat (Cat. No. 143).—(b) Michelangelo: *St Joseph*, detail of Plate 117, c. 1550.

(c) Michelangelo: Study for the head of '*Adam*', c. 1534. British Museum (Cat. No. 57).—(d) Michelangelo: '*Adam*', detail from 'The Last Judgement', 1536–41. Sistine Chapel.

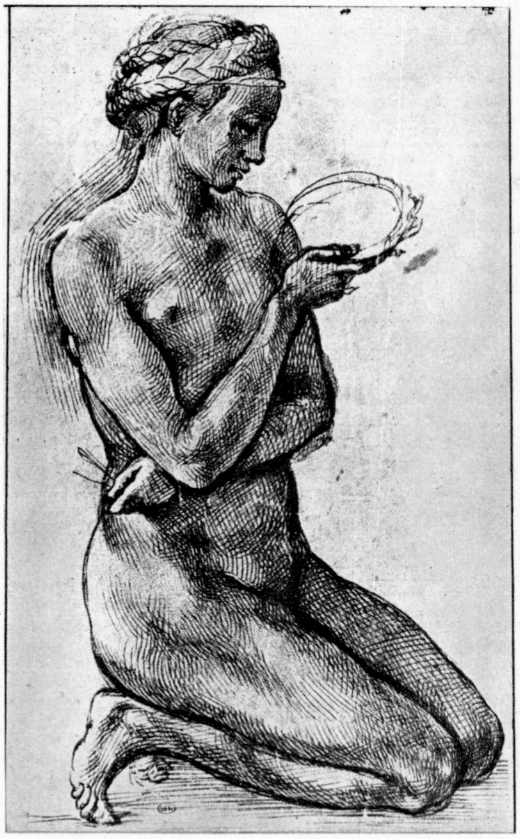
a

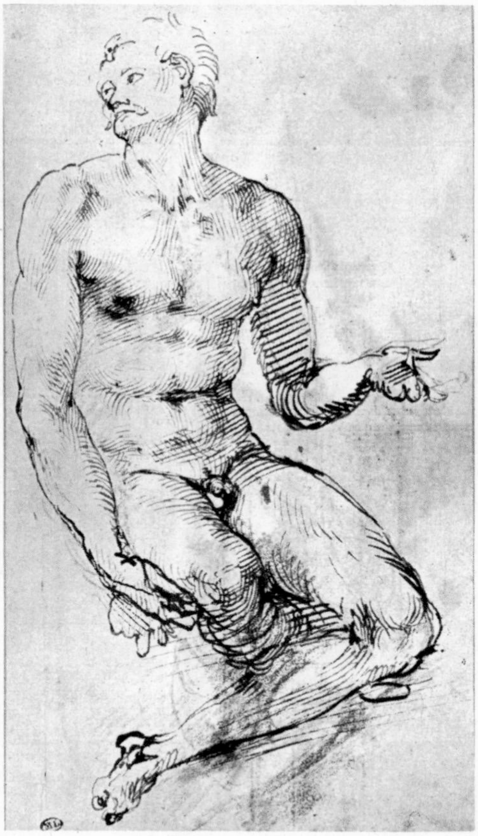
b

c

d

PLATE IX.—*The Master of the 'Manchester Madonna'*.—(a) Study for a figure of the 'Entombment' (National Gallery, London) Louvre.—(b) Sitting male Nude. Louvre.—(c) Studies for a Madonna and Child. Berlin, Print Room.—(d) Madonna and Child, cartoon in black and red chalk, 54×40 cm. Casa Buonarroti.

a

b

c

d

e

f

g

h

PLATE X.—*Battista Franco.* (a) Head of a Faun, c. 1530. Louvre.—(b) Head with Phrygian Cap. Ashmolean Museum.—(c) Shouting Man with Phrygian Cap. Ashmolean Museum.—(d) Two draped Figures, c. 1537. Haarlem.—(e) Three Men in Conversation, 1537. Oxford.—(f) Victory Group. Casa Buonarroti.—(g) Group of three Figures. Haarlem.—(h) Leonardo Cungi: Two draped Figures. Uffizi.

a

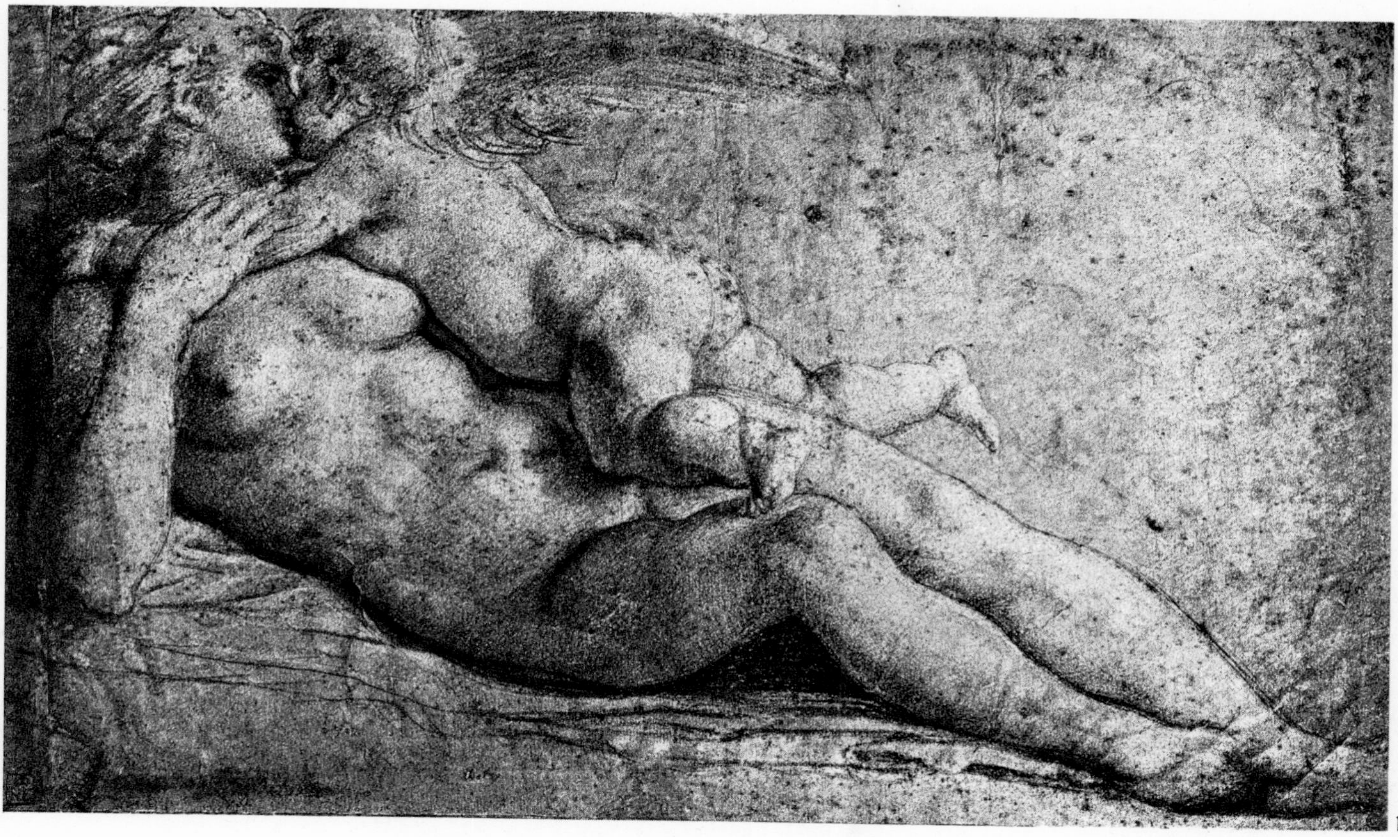

b

PLATE XI.—(a) *Rosso Fiorentino:* Michelangelo's cartoon 'Leda and the Swan', copy. Royal Academy, London.
(b) *Daniele da Volterra:* Venus and Cupid, c. 1538. Budapest.

a

PLATE XII.—(a) *Niccolò Tribolo:* Eight draped Figures. Signed and dated 1530. Louvre.—(b) *Niccolò Tribolo:* Two nude Figures. Casa Buonarroti.

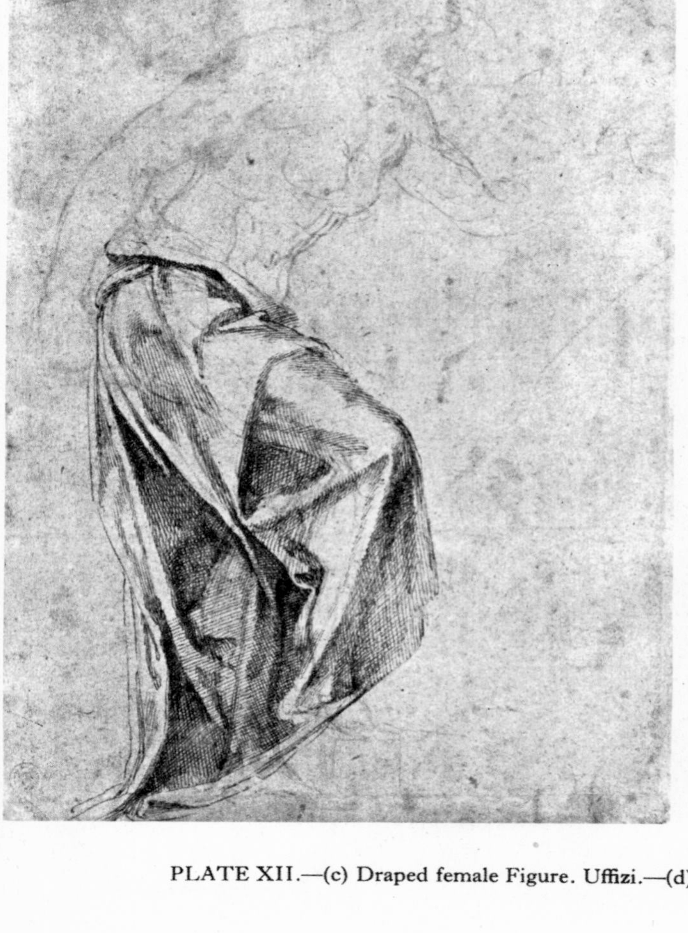

c

d

PLATE XII.—(c) Draped female Figure. Uffizi.—(d) Daniele da Volterra (?): Draped female Figure. Windsor.

b

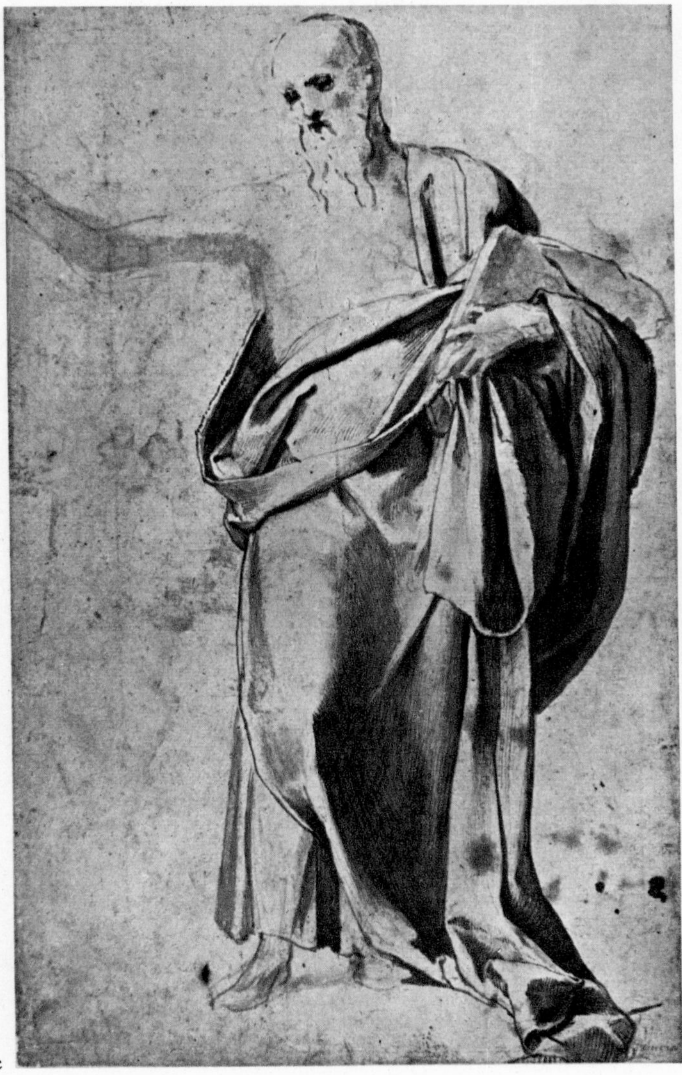

c

d

PLATE XIII.—*Taddeo Zuccaro*.—(a) Cartoon for the fresco 'St Paul healing the Cripple'. Oxford.—(b) Detail from the fresco 'St Paul healing the Cripple', c. 1560. Rome, S. Marcello al Corso.

(c) St Paul. Drawing for a figure in the same fresco. Windsor.—(d) Drapery study for a seated Figure, imitating Michelangelo's 'Erythrean Sibyl'. British Museum.

a

b

c

d

PLATE XIV.—*Ornaments designed by Michelangelo.*—(a–b) Details from Plate 27, about 1504.—(c) Detail from the original frame of the 'Doni Madonna', c. 1504. Uffizi.—(d) Ornament on a desk in the Biblioteca Laurenziana, c. 1534.

a

b

c

PLATE XV.—*Designs for equestrian monuments.*—(a) Michelangelo: Sketch for the monument to King Henry II, 1560. Amsterdam.

(b) Pupil of Michelangelo: Design for an equestrian monument, 1564. —(c) Cigoli: Design for the equestrian monument to Henry IV, about 1604. Ashmolean Museum.

a

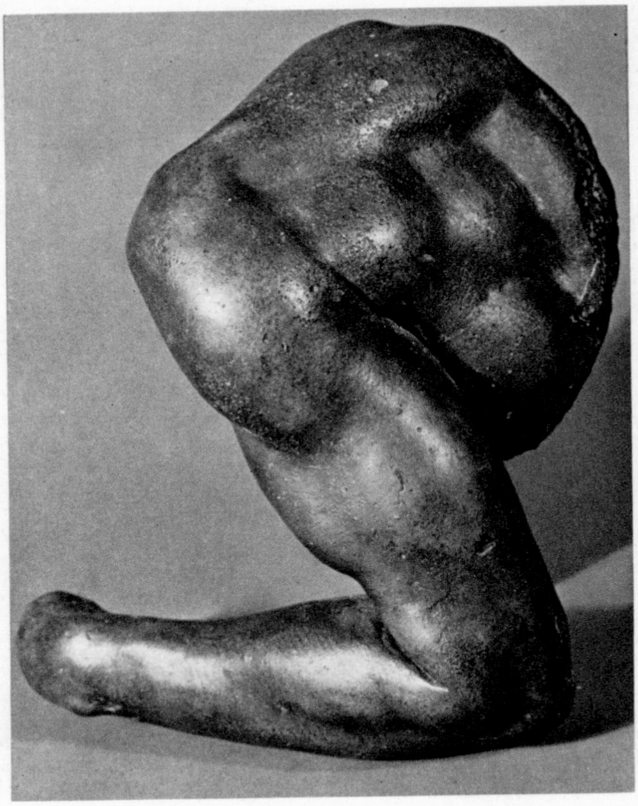

b

c

PLATE XVI.—(a) Michelangelo: Study for the left arm of the 'Night' in the Medici Chapel, c. 1526–30. British Museum.—(b) Terracotta model for the left arm of the 'Night', 1526–30. Attributed here to Michelangelo. Le Brooy Collection.—(c) Wax model of a horse. Attributed here to Michelangelo. c. 1520. Formerly in the Volpi Collection, Florence.

NOTES ON THE PLATES IN THE TEXT

NOTES ON THE APPENDIX OF PLATES

LIST OF COLLECTIONS

NOTES ON THE PLATES IN THE TEXT

Plate A: frontispiece.—*See Cat. No.* 129.

Plate B: opposite p. 14.—*Portrait of Michelangelo.* Pen and ink drawing (badly preserved). 36·5 × 25 cm. Paris, Louvre (No. 2715).
Ernst Steinmann, *Die Portraitdarstellungen des Michelangelo*, Leipzig 1913, p. 17 f.—D. 682.
Berenson (1598 D) regarded this drawing as a self-portrait of Michelangelo. Steinmann—but no other critic—accepted Berenson's opinion and suggested that Michelangelo made the drawing 'to help his friend Bugiardini'. A painted portrait, based on this drawing and attributed to Bugiardini, is in the Louvre (No. 1649; from the Collection of Louis XIV). According to the inscription on the painting, it represents Michelangelo at the age of 47. The picture was attributed to Bugiardini by Steinmann, Thode, Frizzoni, Borenius, Hautecoeur, and others. Berenson thinks, however, that Michelangelo is portrayed here at an age of 27 or less, not of 47, and he attributes the painting in the Louvre to Daniele da Volterra.
Cf. Daniele da Volterra's portrait drawing of Michelangelo in Haarlem, Teyler Museum (Inv. No. 21; ill. Steinmann, *Portraitdarstellungen*, pl. 47). See also a copy of Bugiardini's drawing at Oxford (Ashmolean Museum, Cat. No. 90); and Bugiardini's portrait of Michelangelo in the Casa Buonarroti, Florence.

Plate C: opposite p. 17.—*Design for the second project of the Tomb of Pope Julius II*, 1513.—Copy by Jacomo Rocchetti of a ruined Michelangelo drawing. Pen, ink and wash. 55·5 × 34·5 cm. Berlin, Printroom (No. 15305–b).
This is a copy, and an old inscription on the sheet states the name of the copyist. The almost disintegrated original is also in the Berlin Printroom (BB. 1623; To. 123; reprod. Tolnay IV, pl. 95; D. 374). On the *verso* are eight studies of legs—a badly preserved drawing, the outlines partly retraced (To. 135; reprod. Tolnay, IV pl. 118).

Plate D: opposite p. 36.
For (a), (b), and (c), see note to Plate 31.
(a) The head of the Prophet Jonah, about 1511, detail of a fresco in the Sistine chapel.—(b) Detail of Plate 31.—(c) The head of the 'Doni Madonna', about 1504. Florence, Uffizi.
For (d), (e) and (f) see note to Plate 36.
(d) The head of the Prophet Zechariah, about 1509, detail of a fresco in the Sistine chapel.—(e) Detail of Plate 36.—(f) The head of Moses, 1513–16. Rome, S. Pietro in Vincoli.
(g) Cornice with masks in the courtyard of the Palazzo Farnese, Rome, *c.* 1550. (See note on Plate 70.)

Plate E: opposite p. 39—*See note to Plate 70.*
(a) *Mask* on a capital in the Medici chapel, about 1524.—(b) *Mask* on the archivolt keystone of the Porta Pia, Rome, about 1562.—(c) *Mask* on the back-plate of Giuliano's cuirass. Medici chapel, about 1533–34.

Plate F: opposite p. 54.—*See note to Plate 75.*
(a) Roman stucco relief, *Ganymede and the Eagle*, on the vaulting of the 'Terme pubbliche', Pompeii.—(b) *Ganymede*, detail from a drawing by Michelangelo, about 1504 (BB. 1399 *verso*).—(c) *Ganymede*, copy by Giulio Clovio of Michelangelo's (lost) presentation drawing for Tommaso de' Cavalieri, 1532. Windsor Castle, Royal Library (Cat. No. 457).

Plate G: opposite p. 57.—*See note to Plate 68.*
Martyrdom of St Catherine, painted by Giuliano Bugiardini (with the help of Michelangelo?). Florence, S. Maria Novella, Cappella Rucellai.

APPENDIX OF PLATES

PLATE I.—(a) Aristotile da Sangallo (1542): Copy of Michelangelo's (lost) cartoon for the intended wall-painting '*The Battle of Cascina*' (also called 'The Bathers'). Holkham Hall, Earl of Leicester.
Photographed after the recent cleaning.
See notes to Plates 21–25, and 27.
(b) Michelangelo's first sketch (?) for the '*Battle Cartoon*'. Metal-point and black chalk (23·5 × 35·6 cm.) Florence, Uffizi (613E; Cat. No. 4; BB. 1397C; D. 499).
This is a doubtful drawing. It has been accepted as an autograph by Thode, Brinckmann, Barocchi (1962) and Berenson (1938 and 1961). Wilde, who in 1931 rejected it, accepted it in 1953. Berenson thought that the style of the drawing is similar to that of Allori; Tolnay (I, pp. 215–216) regards it as an imitation and dates it 'not before the middle of the (XVIth) century'; according to him, the style of the drawing is similar to that of Daniele da Volterra.—Dussler (1959) rejected the drawing emphatically and suggested a date of about 1530.—The drawing on the *verso*, representing a male figure flying upwards, has been described as a sketch for 'Ganymede'; by other critics as a sketch for a figure of the 'Last Judgement'; or else as a sketch for a variant of the beckoning man in our Plate 18.—Two small sketches for 'Ganymede' are on the *recto*, as Wilde has observed.
It is an important sheet, because it reflects to a certain extent the lost composition of the 'Battle Cartoon'; but I agree with Tolnay and Dussler that none of the sketches on this sheet are by Michelangelo's own hand.

PLATE II.—*Sixteenth-century reproductions of Michelangelo's presentation sheets for Vittoria Colonna.*—See Cat. Nos. 107, and 108.—(a) *Christ on the Cross.* Engraving after Michelangelo's drawing of c. 1540.—(b) *Christ on the Cross.* Painting by Marcello Venusti, after Michelangelo's design. (See Plates 110, 111.)—(c) *Pietà.* Engraving by Bonasone, signed and dated 1546, after Michelangelo's drawing of c. 1542.—(d) *Christ and the Woman of Samaria.* Engraving by Beatrizet, after Michelangelo's lost drawing of c. 1542.

PLATE III.—*Three religious compositions, after lost cartoons and drawings by Michelangelo.*—(a) *'Noli me tangere'.* Painting. Florence, Casa Buonarroti.—This painting was attributed by turns to Pontormo, to Battista Franco, and (Longhi's suggestion) to Bronzino. (See footnote 68, p. 50). —(b) *Pietà.* Painting by Sebastiano del Piombo, 1537–39, with Michelangelo's help (cf. Plate 103; and BB. 1586). Ubeda, Spain, San Salvador.—(c) *Annunciation.* Engraving by Beatrizet, after a cartoon by Michelangelo. (See note to Plate 113.)—The engraving is here reproduced reversed from left to right, to make it correspond with the painting in San Giovanni in Laterano, and with the cartoon. (Uffizi Catalogue of drawings No. 197; BB. 1644; D. 486.) There is no consensus among the scholars whether this cartoon is preserved in the original or only in a version by Venusti. Prof. Wilde stated in 1953 (*Catal. of Italian drawings in . . . the British Museum : Michelangelo and his studio*, p. 112, footnote) that the small cartoon of the Annunciation in the Uffizi (Cat. No. 197) was either 'Venusti's own cartoon', or else a copy by a later hand of Venusti's cartoon. Berenson (1938) had described it as an 'elaborate but lifeless study' and attributed it to Venusti. The attribution of the cartonetto to Michelangelo was first suggested by Friedrich von Portheim in 1889. Delacre, too, called it a work of Michelangelo's. This attribution of the Uffizi drawing (Cat. No. 197) to Michelangelo was taken up again in 1959 by Wilde (Burl. Mag., November, p. 374) who renounced his notes in the British Museum catalogue of 1953. He put his case very well but found no followers. Tolnay (V, 1960, p. 206) does not quote Wilde's important article of 1959 and speaks simply of 'Marcello Venusti's cartoon'. Paola Barocchi, in her catalogue of the Michelangelo drawings in Florence, 1962, pp. 245–247, knows Wilde's article but is nevertheless in agreement with Tolnay and Berenson.

PLATE IV.—*Michelangelo as a Humanist.*—(a–b) *Niobid*, antique marble statue. Details of a drawing, attributed to Perino del Vaga. Private collection, London.—(c) The same statue, now in the Munich Glyptothek.—Until 1540 the statue was in the Casa Maffei in Rome, and after that in the Palazzo Bevilacqua in Verona. A drawing made after the statue is to be found in the 'Wolfegger Skizzenbuch' (Fol. 33 v., attributed to Amico Aspertini; Fürstlich Waldburgsche Bibliothek); another, smaller reproduction is in Marten van Heemskerck's sketchbook (Fol. 3 *verso*, about 1535; Berlin, Print Room); a third, by Figino, is at Windsor Castle (Cat. No. 326–23 *recto*). The sculpture itself is now in the Glyptothek at Munich. There is another version in the Uffizi.—(d) Michelangelo: *Captive*, marble statue, c. 1514–1516. Paris, Louvre.—(e–g: *Head of a shouting man.*) —(e) Verrocchio: *Medusa*, detail of a terracotta bust, c. 1478. National Gallery, Washington (Mellon Collection).—(f) Raphael: *Medusa*, 1511. Detail of a drawing for the 'School of Athens'. Oxford, Ashmolean Museum.—(g) Michelangelo: 'Damned Soul'. Detail of a drawing (Plate 50), c. 1522. Florence, Uffizi.

PLATE V.—(a) *The Bed of Polycletus.* Designed by Niccolò Tribolo, c. 1534. Mosaic floor of the Biblioteca Laurenziana, Florence.—(b) *The Bed of Polycletus.* Early Renaissance copy of a ancient Roman relief once in the collection of Lorenzo Ghiberti and his descendants. Rome, Palazzo Mattei. (Cf. Plate III–b.) Plates IV and V demonstrate in which ways antique sculpture was used by Michelangelo in his own compositions. The statue Plate IV–c was not directly repeated, but reversed from left to right. The ancient 'Dying Niobid' is lying prostrate on the ground—Michelangelo's so-called 'Dying Slave' expresses a similar dolorous feeling, but is standing upright.
The Roman relief 'Bed of Polycletus', the 'Torso of the Belvedere', the 'Horse Breakers', the 'Lacoön', the 'Apollo of Belvedere' inspired Michelangelo's own work, but he never copied them without adapting them to his own style and spirit.

PLATE VI.—*Michelangelo and Leonardo da Vinci.*—(a) Leonardo da Vinci: *Neptune.* Drawing, c. 1504. Windsor Castle, Royal Library.—(b) Giovanni Ambrogio Figino (after Michelangelo ?): *Neptune.* Detail of a drawing, c. 1580, Windsor Castle, Royal Library.—(c) Detail of Plate VI–a.—(d) Michelangelo: Christ. Detail of a drawing (BB. 1507A), 1532, London British Museum.—(e) Leonardo da Vinci: Copy of Michelangelo's 'David'. Detail of a drawing, 1504. Windsor Castle, Royal Library.—(f) Leonardo da Vinci: Copy of Michelangelo's 'Moses' (?). Drawing, c. 1515. Amsterdam, Fodor Museum.
Michelangelo's relationship to Leonardo is far more transparent than his relationship to Raphael. It is generally agreed that his 'St Anne with the Virgin and Child' (Plate 8) is a free copy after Leonardo's cartoon of 1501. Conversely, on two occasions Leonardo copied Michelangelo (Plate VI–e and –f), namely the 'David' (1504) and the 'Moses' (1515).—Leonardo's drawing 'Neptune' is of about the same date as his copy of 'David'. At the top left of the Neptune drawing is a note in Leonardo's handwriting *a bassa i chavalli* (to lower the horses). This was done by Leonardo in the copy of 'David' (Plate VI–e) where the sea-horses appear under the feet of the full-length figure.—The movement motif of Leonardo's cartoon is found again in the Zeus of Michelangelo's 'Phaethon' (Plate 95) and of his 'Risen Christ' (Plate VI–d).—From an old report we learn that a similar Neptune composition by Michelangelo in red chalk also existed. (See Thode, V, p. 375. Giovanni Gaetano Bottari, *Raccolta di Lettere sulla Pittura*, VI, 1768, p. 247.)—Giovanni Carrara, who in 1768 was the owner of the Neptune drawing attributed to Michelangelo, thought that it was a design for a fountain. E. Moeller (1926) declared that Leonardo's copy of the 'David' was likewise a design for a fountain. An inscription on this drawing stated that it first belonged to Giovanni Paolo Lomazzo and later (1578) to Giovanni Ambrogio Figino. This drawing, however, cannot be identified with the Leonardo drawing at Windsor Castle (Plate VI–a), since the latter is not in red, but in black chalk, and does not

contain the above-mentioned inscription. On the other hand, it is evident that Figino really owned this red-chalk drawing by Michelangelo, for he repeatedly copied it (e.g. in Plate VI–b). The Neptune in Figino's copy is akin to several other figures of Michelangelo's, to the Christ in the 'Last Judgement' and the Christ in the 'Expulsion from the Temple'. As, however, Michelangelo's Neptune drawing has disappeared and the date of its creation is unknown, the only facts we can establish are that Leonardo, on the basis of Michelangelo's David, designed a Neptune (Plate VI–e); that Michelangelo himself, at the same time or later, designed a 'Neptune driving his Sea-horses', and that Leonardo did likewise. At all events the relationship between Leonardo and Michelangelo must here have been very close, for Leonardo's starting-point—a very curious one for a Neptune composition—was Michelangelo's statue of David (Plate VI–e).

Just as Leonardo's Neptune was used as model for bronzes (Vienna, Museum, and London, Beit Collection), so Michelangelo's Neptune would seem to have been given plastic form, for in his drawings Figino shows Neptune and his horses seen from various angles.

PLATE VII.—*Michelangelo and Raphael.*—(a) Detail of an engraving by Marcantonio Raimondi, 'The Judgement of Paris' (B. 245), after a lost drawing by Raphael of c. 1512.—(b) Venus and Cupid. Copy, attributed to Pontormo, after Michelangelo's lost cartoon of 1532. Florence, Uffizi. (Cf. note to Plate 72, and Fig. 16.)—(c) Raphael: Detail from the fresco 'The Council of the Gods', c. 1518. Rome, Farnesina.—(d) Michelangelo: Sketch for a 'River-God', c. 1530. (Reproduced here in reverse, cf. Plate 60.) Florence, Casa Buonarroti.—(e) Raphael: Copy of a drawing by Leonardo da Vinci 'Leda and the Swan' (detail), c. 1506. Windsor Castle, Royal Library.—(f) Raphael: Detail of a drawing for the 'Disputa', c. 1511, Lille, Musée Wicar.—(g) Michelangelo's statue of the 'Risen Christ' in Santa Maria sopra Minerva, Rome, 1520. Detail of an engraving by Beatrizet.

It has been repeatedly asserted that the inspiration for Michelangelo's drawing 'Damned Soul' (Plate 50) came from a screaming head in Leonardo's Battle Cartoon. But this head of Leonardo's can be traced back to Verrocchio, and is found again in the form of a shouting soldier in the Resurrection relief from the Villa Careggi, and also as a Medusa on a terracotta bust of Giuliano de' Medici (Plate IV–e). It appears once again as a Medusa in a drawing by Raphael (Plate IV–f). The first link in this chain was undoubtedly an ancient Medusa mask which was presumably in the collection of antiques at the Casino Mediceo; but it remains uncertain whether Michelangelo drew the inspiration for his drawing (Plate IV–g) directly from this antique Medusa, or whether it came to him indirectly through Leonardo or Raphael.

A second instance likewise leads us to the domain of Raphael. The drawing Plate VII–d is held to be an independent sketch for one of the River-gods in the Medici chapel. If, however, we compare this sketch (Plate VII–d) with the nymph in the Raphael engraving (Plate VII–a) of the 'Judgement of Paris'—the characteristic common to both is the way in which one leg is tucked in and drawn up—we begin to doubt the independence of Michelangelo's sketch and to ask ourselves whether the inspiration came from Raphael or whether both artists used an antique sculpture as model. The latter supposition is strengthened if we examine the river god in the Raphael engraving (Plate VII–a), the movement of which corresponds with the Venus in Michelangelo's composition of 1532 (Plate VII–b, and the sketch reproduced as Fig. 16, p. 48). In this case a drawing made from the antique model has been preserved—the drawing of a Hercules torso in the Ambrosiana, attributed to Sebastiano del Piombo. (Palluchini, *Sebastian Viniziano*, 1944, Plate 90–b; O. Fischel, in *Old Master Drawings* 1939–40: 'A new approach to Sebastiano del Piombo', figs. 17–18; cf. also Delacre (8, 1938, fig. 292).

Michelangelo's Christ in Santa Maria sopra Minerva (Plate VI–g) likewise seems to owe something to Raphael. The characteristic feature of the movement (namely, the arm thrown diagonally across the breast and the head turned towards the other side) was borrowed by Raphael himself from Leonardo (Plates VI–e and f).

PLATE VIII.—(a) Raphael: St Joseph. Fragment of a cartoon for a 'Holy Family', c. 1518. Bayonne, Musée Bonnat (Cat. No. 143).—(b) Michelangelo: St Joseph, Detail of Plate 117.—(c) Michelangelo: Study for the Head of 'Adam'. Black chalk, c. 1534. London, British Museum (Cat. No. 57 *recto*).—(d) Michelangelo: 'Adam'. Detail from the fresco 'The Last Judgement', 1536–41. Rome, Sistine Chapel.

PLATE IX.—*The 'Master of the Manchester Madonna'.*—(a) Drawing for a figure of the 'Entombment' (painting in the National Gallery, London). Paris, Louvre (BB. 1742).—(b) Sitting male Nude. Paris, Louvre (BB. 1596).—(c) Studies for a Madonna and Child. Berlin, Print Room (BB. 1396).—(d) Madonna and Child. Black and red chalk, Florence, Casa Buonarroti (Cat. No. 121).—This colourful drawing has been variously dated: c. 1506 by Thode and Brinckmann, who ascribed it to Michelangelo; c. 1520–25 by Knapp and Wilde, who also accept it. Berenson called it 'Bugiardini'. Tolnay (No. 142) is doubtful ('the black outlines of the Virgin are hesitant; the forms of her hands are weak . . . The modelling of the Child seems to be made by a later hand'). He groups it with the 'early drawings anticipating motifs of late works', c. 1505–06. Paola Barocchi, who regards the drawing as authentic, dates it after 1520; Dussler (No. 447), who rejects it with decision, dates it 1522–24.

PLATE X.—*Battista Franco*, c. 1498–1561.—(a) Head of a Faun. Drawn in ink by Battista Franco (?) over a female profile by Antonio Mini (?), c. 1530. Paris, Louvre (BB. 1728).—(b) Head wearing a Phrygian Cap. Pen and ink, c. 1530. Attributed here to Battista Franco. Oxford, Ashmolean Museum (Cat. No. 327 *recto*).—(c) Head of a shouting Man wearing a Phrygian Cap. Red chalk, c. 1530. Attributed here to Battista Franco. Oxford, Ashmolean Museum (Cat. No. 322).—(d) Two draped figures. Pen and ink drawing, c. 1537. Attributed here to Battista Franco. Haarlem, Teyler Museum (BB. 1474 *verso*).—(e) Study for Battista Franco's 'Battle of Montemurlo', 1537 (now at the Palazzo Pitti). Pen and ink drawing, between 1526 and 1537. Oxford, Ashmolean Museum (Cat. No. 326 *recto*).—

(f) Pen and ink drawing of a 'Victory Group'. Florence, Casa Buonarroti (Cat. No. 200 *recto*).—Tolnay (IV, 1954, p. 148, No. 45A) dates the drawing, which represents a Winged Victor, c. 1513. Wilde, Dussler and Barocchi attributed the sheet correctly to Battista Franco. The drawing may have some connexion with the victory of Montemurlo, and it is certainly not earlier than Plate VI–e. It is derived from Michelangelo's marble group in the Palazzo Vecchio at Florence (*Ph. M.*, Plate 209), datable c. 1525–30.—In Greek vase-painting such a winged genius would mean a representation of Eros.—(g) Group of two Men and a Woman. Pen and ink drawing, attributed here to Battista Franco. Haarlem, Teyler Museum (*recto* of Plate X–d).—(h) Man holding a book, another draped figure next to him; Sketch of 'Ganymede'. Pen and ink drawing. Florence, Uffizi (Cat. No. 211).—The lower part of this large sheet is not reproduced here; it contains the coat-of-arms of the 'Casa Bembo', and another sketch of 'Ganymede'. On the *recto* of the sheet are some sketches by the same hand, probably after Michelangelo, c. 1541–46.—This drawing, which—as far as the composition is concerned—is akin to Plate X, d–g, has been rightly attributed to Leonardo Cungi by Jacobsen (1905) and Barocchi (1962).

PLATE XI.—(a) Rosso Fiorentino (1495–1540): *Copy of Michelangelo's lost Leda cartoon.* London, Royal Academy (No. 156).—From 1504 onward Leonardo da Vinci, and at the same time Michelangelo, were concerned with the theme of 'Leda and the Swan'. Leonardo finished his painting in c. 1506, Michelangelo in the autumn of 1530. Both paintings were taken to France, sold to the king and kept at Fontainebleau, but 'on ground of indecency' burnt about 1640. In the French editions of the 'Poliphili Hynerotomachia' (published in Paris 1561 and 1600, when Michelangelo's 'Leda and the Swan' was still at Fontainebleau) one woodcut among 'the four triumphal cars', is a free adaptation of Michelangelo's painting (see illustration).

Woodcut, from 'Hypnerotomachia, ou Discours du songe de Poliphile'. (Paris 1561.)

One may suspect that the 'four triumphal cars' of Poliphili Hypnerotomachia, representing the amorous adventures of Jupiter with Europa, Leda, Danaë, and Semele, were really exposed to view in a masquerade procession at Fontainebleau, probably under Henry II.

If so, it would have only been a revival of an antique performance: According to Prudentius (*'peri stephanon'*, X, VI, 221), the story of Leda was demonstrated *ad oculos* in the theatre.

PLATE XI.—(b) Daniele da Volterra (1509–1566): *Venus and Cupid.* Drawing, black chalk, 26 × 43·5 cm. Budapest, Museum of Fine Arts.—Datable c. 1538. Compare Plate VII–b; Plate 72; and Fig. 16.

PLATE XII.—*Two pen and ink drawings by Niccolò Tribolo* (1485–1550).—(a) Eight draped figures. Signed and dated 1530. Paris, Louvre.—(b) Two nude Figures. Florence, Casa Buonarroti (Cat. No. 202).

PLATE XII.—(c) Draped female Figure. Black chalk and pen. Florence, Casa Buonarroti (Cat. No. 234; in May 1965 transferred to the Uffizi).—Thode, Delacre, and Wilde attribute this weak drawing to Michelangelo himself; Dussler (No. 430) believes it to be by some later mannerist. Barocchi denies that this drawing has any technical relationship with our Plate XIII–d, and attributes it to an unknown pupil of Michelangelo (*'un artista che studia su Michelangelo'*).—(d) Daniele da Volterra (?): Draped female Figure. Black chalk drawing. Windsor Castle, Royal Library (Cat. No. 263).—The attribution to Daniele is due to J. Wilde (1949); Simon H. Levie (*Der Maler Daniele da Volterra*, Cologne 1962, p. 167) regards the drawing as a copy. A better version of this figure is in the Louvre.—Illustrations Plate XII–c and d (and XIII–c and d) illustrate the problem of the attribution of such drapery studies.

PLATE XIII.—*Taddeo Zuccaro* (1529–66).—(a) Cartoon for the Lame Man in Taddeo Zuccaro's fresco in the church of San Marcello al Corso, Rome, 'St Paul Healing the Cripple'. Oxford, Ashmolean Museum (Cat. No. 761).—In 1949, when I studied this cartoon in the presence of the keeper and remarked that it was certainly a work by Taddeo Zuccaro, I was informed that this has already been observed by Dr Vitale Bloch.—(b) Detail of Taddeo Zuccaro's fresco 'The Healing of the Cripple', c. 1560. Rome, San Marcello al Corso.—(c) Taddeo Zuccaro: St Paul. Drawing for a Figure in the fresco 'The Healing of the Cripple'. Windsor Castle, Royal Library (Cat. No. 1069).—(d) Drapery Study. Attributed here to Taddeo Zuccaro. London, British Museum (Cat. No. 10 *recto*).—Attributed by Thode (No. 337); Wilde (1953), and Berenson (1961) to Michelangelo; but not by Tolnay (No. 38) and by Dussler (No. 566).

PLATE XIV.—*Ornaments designed by Michelangelo.*—(a) and (b) Details from Plate 27. (See note to Plate 27, and Footnote 15.)—(c) A detail from the original frame of the 'Doni Madonna', c. 1504. Florence, Uffizi. (Compare (a) with (c), and (b) with (d).)—(d) Ornament on a desk in the Reading Room of the Biblioteca Laurenziana, Florence.—The ornaments on the desks were carved in wood (1534) by Battista del Cinque and Ciappino, after Michelangelo's designs.

PLATE XV.—*Designs for equestrian monuments*.—(a) Michelangelo: Design for the monument to Henry II, king of France. Black chalk, 1560. (Reproduced in original size.) Amsterdam, Rijksmuseum (D. 244; Wilde, in Burl. Mag., November 1959, fig. 15; Tolnay, No. 256). From the collections of Baron von der Heidt; Ferruccio Asta, Venice (1939); and Leo Franklyn, London.—Mr Franklyn, who bought this sheet at the Asta sale, showed it to me in 1950, as by Leonardo da Vinci, and presented me with a photograph. I informed him in a letter that this was a late Michelangelo drawing. Wilde and Regteren Altena (*Vereeniging Rembrandt*, 1952–53) connected the drawing with the monument to Henry II, who died in 1559. His widow, Catherine de Medici, wrote to Michelangelo (in July 1559, and 14 November 1960) and offered him a contract for a bronze equestrian monument to her deceased husband. Michelangelo excused himself because of his old age and suggested Daniele da Volterra, whom he would help. (Thode V, p. 299 f.) In 1565 Daniele's bronze horse was cast, a year later the artist died. In 1586 King Henry III gave the bronze horse to Orazio Rucellai. Nicolaus van Aelst made an engraving of the whole monument as it was intended (Tolnay V, fig. 255), including the highly original pediment, which was never executed. This pediment shows three fields, and two lateral niches with standing figures.—In 1639 Daniele's bronze horse was used for a monument to Louis XIII, which was destroyed during the French revolution (Vasari-Milanesi VII, p. 68, footnote; Tolnay V, p. 229).—(b) Design for an equestrian monument, 1564, on the *verso* of a sketch for Michelangelo's Catafalque at the obsequies in San Lorenzo, Florence. Pen and ink drawing, Munich, Staatliche Graphische Sammlung.—The pedestal in this composition is an echo of Michelangelo's design of the monument for Henry II (Plate XV–a); there are the same three fields and the two lateral niches with standing figures; the four hermae are as in Nicolaus van Aelst's engraving (ill. Tolnay V, fig. 255) and the movement of horse and rider are also repeated.—(c) Lodovico Cigoli: Design for an equestrian monument to Henry IV, king of France. Pen and ink drawing, about 1604. Oxford, Ashmolean Museum (Cat. No. 198). See K. T. Parker, *Catalogue of the Collections of Drawings in the Ashmolean Museum*, Vol. II: *Italian Schools*, 1956, pp. 93–94.

PLATE XVI.—(a) Michelangelo: Study in black chalk and ink for the left arm of the 'Night', about 1526–30. London, British Museum (Cat. No. 49).—(b) Michelangelo: Terracotta model for the left arm of the 'Night', about 1526–30 (Thode, No. 561–a). Vancouver, B.C., LeBrooy collection.—(c) Wax model of a standing horse. Attributed here to Michelangelo. Formerly Volpi collection, Florence. (Cf. Plates 43, 44. Reprod. by W. Suida, *Leonardo und sein Kreis*, 1929, figs. 74–75, and attributed by him to Leonardo da Vinci.)

ERRATA

p. 31, right-hand column, No. 18, line 4 from bottom –
Study for the Brazen Serpent, Plate 88 (not 90).

p. 35, note 23 –
Plate 43 (not 45).

p. 40, left-hand column, No. 47, line 3 –
Kristeller (not: Kristller).

p. 48, right-hand column –
Goethe (not Goeth).

p. 63, note 105 –
St John the Evangelist (not Baptist).

p. 70, Bibliography, No. 65, add –
Vol. II, Italian Schools, pp. 132–197.

p. 45, Figs. 14 and 15 –
Fig. 15 (not 14) is reproduced in reverse.

Caption to Plate 47: About 1520 (not 1520–22).

p. 205, note on Plate F –
read: BB. 1399J (not 1399 verso).

p. 206, note on Plate V –
read: an ancient Roman relief.

THE COLLECTIONS

INDEX TO THE CATALOGUE AND THE PLATES

BAYONNE, Musée Bonnat
Study for the 'Last Judgement', 99

BOSTON, Isabella Stewart Gardner Museum
Pietà, 108

CAMBRIDGE (U.S.A.), Fogg Art Museum
Design for bronze Lamps, etc., 69

CHANTILLY, Musée Condé
Studies from antique Statues, etc., 13

FLORENCE, Casa Buonarroti
Studies for the 'Battle Cartoon', 21, 22
Head Study (for the 'Doni Madonna') 31
Studies for 'Ignudi', 37, 38
Studies for Statues in the Medici chapel, 60, 61, 62
Head study for the 'Leda', 65
Figures in violent movement, 68
Three Studies for the 'Resurrection of Christ', 77, 78, 79
Study for the 'Risen Christ', 84
Cleopatra, 96
Study for the 'Last Judgement', 100
Study of a Torso, 103
Sacrifice of Isaac, 104

FLORENCE, Uffizi
Head study for Zechariah, 36
'Damned Soul', 50
Three female Profiles, 51
Venus, Mars, and Cupid, 52

HAARLEM, Teyler Museum
Abduction of a Woman, 67
Descent from the Cross, 86
Study for the 'Last Judgement', 101
Study for 'Christ on the Cross', 106
Apostle with Book, 115
Aeneas and Dido, 116

LONDON, British Museum
'Philosopher', 14
Head of Satyr, 15
Running Youth, 16
Studies of a naked little Boy, 17
Studies for the 'Bruges Madonna' and for the 'Battle Cartoon', 18
Studies of a Putto, etc. 19

LONDON, British Museum (contd.)
Nude Man, 25
Cavalry Battle; Apostle, 26
Ornament Sketches, 27
Head study, 32
Studies for the Sistine Ceiling frescoes, 33, 34
Study for the 'Raising of Lazarus', 42
Girl with Distaff, 53
Sibylline Figure, 54
Madonna and Child, 55
Two crucified Men, 57
Sketches for a 'River-God', 59
Study for the 'Leda', 64
Four Masks, and 'Hercules and Antaeus', 66
Design for a Salt-cellar, 71
Resurrection of Christ, 82
The Risen Christ, 83
Study for a 'Holy Family', 85
The Three Crosses, 87
Phaëthon, 91
Studies for the 'Last Judgement', 98, 102
Mourning Women at the foot of the Cross, 105
Christ on the Cross, 107
Annunciation, 113, 114
Cartoon for a 'Holy Family', 117
The Purification of the Temple, 120, 121, 122
Christ on the Cross, 127, 129 (Frontispiece)
Madonna and Child, 128

LONDON, Brinsley Ford, Esq.
Study for a Statue of Christ, 41

LONDON, The Duke of Portland
'Madonna del Silenzio', 109

LONDON, Count Antoine Seilern
The Dream, 97

MUNICH, Staatl., Graphische Sammlung
Drawing after Masaccio, 4

NAPLES, Pinacoteca Reggia di Capodimonte
Cartoon for 'Crucifixion of St. Peter', 112

NEW YORK, Metropolitan Museum
Study for the Libyan Sibyl, 39

NEW YORK, Pierpont Morgan Library
David and Goliath, 119

OXFORD, Ashmolean Museum
Torso, and five Heads, 7
St. Anne, the Virgin and Christ, 8
Triton, 11
Studies from the Nude, 12
Studies for the 'Battle Cartoon', 23
Study for the Boy behind the Libyan Sibyl, 40
Sketches of Shackled Captives, 40
Studies of Horses, 43–45
Cavalry Battle, 46
Dragon, 48
Profile with oriental Head-dress, 49
Study for the 'Giorno', 63
Samson and Delilah, 72
The Brazen Serpent, 88
Battle scenes, 118
Study for the 'Purification of the Temple', 118
Studies for a Pietà and an Entombment, 123
Christ on the Cross, 124
Annunciation, 125

PARIS, Louvre
Drawing after Giotto, 1
Studies from antique Statues, 5, 6
Man digging, etc., 9
Studies for the marble David, and for the bronze David, 10
Nude Youth and other Studies, 20
Salome (or Judith?), 28

PARIS, Louvre (contd.)
St Anne, the Virgin and Christ, 29
Captive, Putto, etc. 30
Studies for the Sistine Ceiling frescoes, 35
Madonna and Child, 58
Resurrection of Christ, 80
The Virgin beneath the Cross, 110
St John beneath the Cross, 111

SETTIGNANO, Villa Michelangelo
Triton, 47

VENICE, Accademia
Phaëthon, 92, 94

VIENNA, Albertina
Drawings after Masaccio, 2, 3
Study for the 'Battle Cartoon', 24
Madonna and Child, 56

WINDSOR CASTLE, Royal Library
Decorative Mask, 70
Three Labours of Hercules, 73
Archers shooting at a Herm, 74
Tityus, 75
Studies for the 'Resurrection of Christ', 76, 81
Bacchanal of Children, 89
Head study, 90
Phaëthon, 93, 95
Christ on the Cross, 126